THE TIMELESS MIND

By

Kathleen Fraser

www.thetimelessmind.co.uk

This book is dedicated to my daughters and sons, without whom these events would not be described.

Kathleen Fraser

© Kathleen Fraser 2007

All rights reserved. No part of this publication may be reproduced, introduced or stored on a retrieval system or transmitted in any form or by any means (electronic, mechanical, photocopying, recording or otherwise), without the prior written permission of both the copyright holder and publisher of this book.

A CIP catalogue record for this book is available from the British Library

Published by Frameworks4u
67 Longley Lane
Almondbury
Huddersfield
HD4 6PR

Printed in the UK by Think Ink Ltd

ISBN 978-0-9555907-0-2

THE TIMELESS MIND

Chapter 1 – The Small Beginnings 4
Chapter 2 – Growing Pains 14
Chapter 3 – Living The Impossible 20
Chapter 4 – Youthful Learnings 25
Chapter 5 – Salad Days Ended 31
Chapter 6 – Verification 45
Chapter 7 – Evading Christians 52
Chapter 8 – Escape To Reality 61
Chapter 9 – Why? 75
Chapter 10 – Collapse 88
Chapter 11 – A Little Hope 99
Chapter 12 – 'Eureka: Greek – it is found.' 111
Chapter 13 – Risk Takings 122
Chapter 14 – Avalanches 131
Chapter 15 – Answers to a Multitude of Questions 141
Chapter 16 – Struggles 149
Chapter 17 – Moved to Reality 158
Chapter 18 – Involvement 168
Chapter 19 – Dispensing 175
Chapter 20 – Trying to Solve an Enormous Jigsaw 183
Chapter 21 – Attempting Explanations 190
Chapter 22 – Healing 204
Chapter 23 – Attempts to Clarify 213
Chapter 24 – The Impossible Made Valid 220
Chapter 25 – What Lives, What Dies? 224
Chapter 26 – More Amazements 231
Chapter 28 – A Conclusion Shaped 238
Chapter 29 – Losing Conventions 248
Chapter 30 – Looking Back 259
Chapter 31 – Reprisals 265
Chapter 32 – Challenge 271
Chapter 33 – The Supernatural is the Natural State 276
A Kind of Summary 291

Chapter 1 – The Small Beginnings

At the age of four years I saw my first ghost. Of course, I didn't know she was a ghost for at such a young age one does not know anything of ghostly beliefs, or disbeliefs, or conjectures. No one had ever instructed me on the subject of ghosts and in retrospect I suppose it was because no one ever supposed I would see one at that age. But there was something about the experience which was different from what appeared to be normality. It was out of context; very odd; although even by then I found adults to be very odd, quite unfathomable, behaving in strange ways which I could not understand. So although I was used to oddities, this which was happening seemed to be more odd than usual, but also in some inexplicable way very natural too. Certainly it was interesting, equally certainly it wasn't in the least frightening, so I simply watched.

I was lying in the big soft bed and thinking how lovely was this silvery white wallpaper festooned with tiny pink roses and delicate green leaves. Really, it was so peaceful I seemed to be floating in it, for the only sound was from the gas mantle and I thought that was the softest reassuring noise, like fairies whispering to each other. I was safe and utterly content. My Father was sitting on my bed without making the smallest rustle. I knew he wasn't asleep because one of my hands was buried inside one of his big brown dry hands and I knew he must be going to go out later because he had his navy suit on, the one he wore on weekday evenings. He wasn't in any hurry though, so it didn't matter. Nothing mattered. He was there, huge and nothing could happen to me for he wouldn't even let Auntie have her own way, no one had their own way when my father was there. My other hand was tracing the hills and valleys in the white Alhambra quilt.

When I saw the little woman come out of the wall it didn't seem too strange at first because she was so ordinary. Across our room there was a huge beam and as soon as she came out completely I could see she was dressed for work because she was wearing a mob cap, a blue working frock and a linsey apron. She didn't waste a minute of time and with the blue and white checked duster she was holding, began to polish the beam. It was very odd for I knew with absolute certainty that she didn't live with us, so what was she doing coming into our house and polishing our beam? I thought: If my Daddy sees her he'll order her out. I wonder if I should tell him about her? He'll get mad if he knows, even if she's doing some work for us. I wonder who she is? She doesn't live anywhere round here, that's for sure. She looks like a lot of old ladies do for they're always cleaning something even if it isn't dirty, but she's rubbing away as if this house belonged to her and it doesn't. Had I better tell my Daddy? Then I thought: No it doesn't matter; I don't need to say anything because he'll know. If anything goes on round here he knows and if it's all right he won't mind.

Having reached these conclusions I watched the small, plump little biddy polish our beam from end to end and although from where I was lying I could only see one half of the room, I could still effortlessly see her polishing the beam behind my head. Indeed, she worked her way the whole length of the room, then plied her duster the whole way back again. When she reached the wall in front of me she simply melted into it and was gone. It never occurred to me that in order for such a small person to reach the beam there would have had to be a stepladder to climb upon. She operated in mid air. But that is one of the natures of ghosts; they don't require physical objects in order to perform physical tasks.

Before proceeding I would make it clear that what is to follow is not an inventory of 'ghosts I have known' for I have actually seen very few. Rather it is that I was to live experiences which exist beneath the identical umbrella: the Supernatural.

At the age of eight years, to my amazement I had another sister, a tiny sickly mite whose continued existence appeared to be in grave doubt. Throughout my family and its extensions in the form of sundry aunts and cousins the consensus of opinion was that almost no hope could be entertained. Very naturally, my parents' attention was concentrated solely on the care of the tiny one and I became a nuisance, so I made myself as scarce as possible as often as possible.

There entered a weird factor in this situation for I knew that she would not die. Admixed with this knowledge was the utter conviction that it was no use my voicing this knowledge as no-one would believe me and consequently this caused me great discomfort. I wanted to reassure my mother whilst knowing that she would not believe a word I said on the subject. After all this was an adult world; there were plenty of experienced relatives and doctors thronging the scene, so who in their right mind was going to listen to a child of eight? But my sister did not die.

Shortly after my sister was born I became aware that there was another world, another dimension and it began as I was sitting on a stone wall talking to my friend Elaine who was rather more than a year older than me and self-willed to boot. For as long as I could remember stone had held an absorbing interest for me and there was an abundance of subject matter for the town was built almost entirely of stone. I can still feel the smooth yet raspy irregularities of that wall. What preceded the conversation I do not know but I said:

'Those are not my parents, you know and that isn't my home.'

Elaine said robustly, 'Don't be so daft. I've known you for oh, ages and ages and you've always lived there. It's your house and it's your mum and dad who're in it. I know they're your mum and dad and you live there. You haven't got anywhere else to live. You go to your auntie's a lot, but you don't live there and if you'd got another mum and dad I'd have heard. Everybody round here knows us and somebody would've said if you'd come from somewhere else.'

I said that I didn't belong again, knowing as I spoke that Elaine's summary was true. Except in a way I couldn't explain it wasn't true. Yes, I lived with my parents, loved them but somehow I didn't belong to them nor did I feel as if they belonged to me. It was ludicrous. It was inexplicable. But all the time we argued I could see beside me a kind of tunnel of such an immense distance it was totally beyond my powers to describe. Yet the end of the tunnel was glowing with colour, rich like the end of my glass kaleidoscope when I looked through it on sunny days. Even the impossible distance of this tunnel didn't preclude the fact that somehow I knew it was more familiar to me than the solid stone houses surrounding us; so although I could not say 'that's my home' it seemed familiar, more natural, more absolutely right than the home I actually lived in. Yet I could not involve Elaine for somehow I knew conclusively that she couldn't see this tunnel, so on the face of it she won the argument. But I did not know just how facile such faces were.

It was a strange period when I was very young, because although there was love between us at some unplumbed depth, I felt isolated from my parents. It was as if some cleavage had occurred even though on the surface nothing appeared to have changed. There was a residue of isolation and thereafter for the rest of our lives it was as if an independent observer watched and listened. Certainly a perception had been born and one that flared quickly into, for me, a conflagration.

The subject at issue was, in worldly terms, too mediocre for mention: to me it was the destruction of part of my tiny world. I quickly learned tolerance for losers. Victorian values still permeated all aspects of the social and ethical climate and consequently we were brought up by strong disciplinarians but for me there had been a crowning pinnacle; I loved going to school because there I was spoiled, whereas at home I certainly was not. Loving learning and having inherited a small amount of my father's prodigious memory, I was the unspeakable 'teacher's pet', recipient of all minute badges of office that were available. Of course, the axe fell …

Dispassionately, gazing above all heads, our teacher announced:

'Most of you lot are lazy and you don't know the work involved in being a monitor and a leader. They have to see to all the equipment being stored and there is going to be a change; you are all going to have these tasks in turn and we begin now.'

So it was done. Neatly, impersonally and I was the victim, the target. At no time did she even glance in my direction but I knew as surely as the sun would rise each day that the whole exercise was simply to demote me and I burned. Who had I offended? What awesome remote power had struck me down? What could I have done to be so humiliated? Questions raged in my burning head and weirdly I could recognize the kindness which had prompted my teacher to effect the change by changing the system for all; nor was it the wish or will of my teachers in general, it was some powerful outside source that had issued this decree. Why? Why?

Temporarily discarding chronology, I will give the sequel to this small incident, for I learned the truth forty two years later. My mother and I had been discussing the frenzied attack on Profumo, with all its attendant media slime.

I said 'I feel sorry for the man. I know what it's like to be at the top of the tree and to have the tree felled beneath you. I had it done to me as a child and all the wolves that are attacking him won't lead blameless lives. Yes, he's been a fool, but I still feel sorry for him.'

My mother said serenely 'Oh yes, I knew you'd recognize the symptom. I cut you down to size when you were at school. You were bossy and cheeky at home, too big for your boots, so I went to see the headmistress and told her that you'd to be treated like everybody else. I told them I'd only go once and if they didn't do as I said I'd go to the Director of Education and have their jobs.'

Much time was to pass before I realized that I could see thoughts inside heads. I had not known the implacable force of my mother, I couldn't believe that she would seek to destroy me so. Now of course, I see clearly; I was trouble with a capital T and she wanted no distractions from a troublesome daughter, for all her attentions were centred upon my small sister. So as I said, I learned from the episode, I learned tolerance.

1937 was the year of appeasement: it might be supposed that a British Prime Minister would have learned the simple fact that it was impossible to appease bullies. Or perhaps he did know and it was a time-buying exercise. Whatever the motives I knew there would be a war. My mother took me to see a film and this was a great treat as she would only sit in the best seats and I usually sat in the cheap ones. Before the major film was shown there was a documentary film delineating masses of German troops and armour, a crashing crescendo of vast iron power motivated by a gesticulating madman. Inside my body there was a congealing iron terror. This was war. It could not be, would not be averted and the subsequent placatory statements washed over me like so much floss. I began to feel a strange unease as the adult world about me appeared to absorb the soothing syrupy statements for I knew in my cells they were untrue. Be silent. Who would believe you? You're not old enough to have an opinion.

I was not happy with the stiff regimentation at the minor grammar school on a hill at the opposite side of the town. I was competing now with equals and the curriculum was tightly scheduled, enforced by dispassionate discipline in almost all cases. The school was a breeding ground for secretaries and as my mother had wished to be one herself so she determined that I would be one too. In truth, it was the last career I would have chosen although it must be said that I did not know what I wanted to be or do. I was not a lonely child, there were family and friends a-plenty, but within me was a core of darkness which did not seem to be attached to anyone or anything. It seemed as if true living was there so that although all about me was busy, interesting and filled with noise, colour and movement the true reality lay somewhere inside myself. What it could be I did not know. There were no means of identifying it, yet it always remained.

Some months earlier I had had a great shock and tried not to think about it, although I told no-one of it. It began as I was lying in bed one evening when the sky was still light. There had been a light rain and through my window I could see a long pale shiny roof, a few shades lighter than the sky above. A scene of pale soft greys. Then I was outside of the universe. Flying in empty space through eons of time, seeking, convulsed by consuming terror in a strange darkness, knowing utterly what NOTHING really meant, for this was Nothingness. Not a spark, not a being, a face, an identity of any kind. I began to pray, begging incoherently for the sight of a star, a daisy, anything whatsoever which would show me that I was not alone, but this was Nothingness, the true meaning of utter isolation. Mad with terror I seemed to move at immense speed, seeking, but not finding, for there was nothing to find. This was Nothing...

Then I was gazing once more at the silvery roof, grateful beyond measure to be back, promising wildly that I would be good in future, would not argue or be bad-tempered. I would even love slugs and worms if only I didn't have to go back to Nothingness for the inchoate terror of being there was insupportable. I remembered it for many months and always pushed away the memory as fast as possible. The implications were hidden. I was too young for thinking; this was a time of experiencing. Then I had the first experience of knowing a small section of my own future. I was eleven years old.

It was customary to walk into the town from school as by doing so I could save a half penny. My mother scrupulously gave me my fares for the whole journey, so anything that could be saved by walking one half of the journey added to my pocket money. On this particular day I was alone, which was rather unusual. To reach the stop which would allow me to catch the bus for the final two miles to my home entailed taking one of three choices. As I had always liked it immensely I chose to take the route through the Pack Horse Yard. This was a town of stone and cloth, for the best in the world was produced of the latter and this ancient yard had been for centuries the heart of the town. Here the pack ponies were gathered and loaded for their journey over the Pennines to Liverpool with cloth to be sent all over the world.

Entrance to the Yard was by way of an ancient arched tunnel, the ground flagged by uneven lovely stone setts, so that I moved from comparative darkness into light. At the far end of the Yard an identical tunnel gave access to a major road so that the Yard itself was a haphazard arrangement of buildings of various heights and usages, all erected without benefit of stereotyped planning. Roughly rectangular, this caused the light to fall on the Yard in irregular triangular patterns of shadow and on this particular day in spring the light was strong and clear. Above the roofs the sky was of an intense clear blue, ocean-like, as if it went on forever and it was dusted by bouncing clumps of cloud like fine cotton wool. As it was late afternoon, the right hand side of the Yard was illuminated sharply and the old stones gleamed golden where the soft sandstone had worn concave.

As I emerged from the tunnel the world before me changed and I saw the Yard illuminated in silvery light as if I were seeing through a prism which reflected rainbow colours. Halted by the unbelievable beauty I paused at this gauzy transformation scene. To my right, illuminated by the brilliant clear sunshine and the silvery light, a dray stood in the Yard, for men were loading bales of wool from a warehouse. Drawing the dray was an immense Shire horse which was pawing a white ruffled hoof in impatience at the delay. Its great mane was flaring into white silken splendour and its harness brasses glittered. As the bales were lowered the flashing links of chains spun a rhythmic delightful clinking accompaniment to the great shod hoof's sparking of the setts. Lost in awe I stood before this incredible beauty, this miraculous fairyland of wonder.

Then I 'saw'.

It was as if I were standing at the end of a giant telescope and the view at the end was an impossible distance from my position; but I could see myself there as I would be and, of course, to my eleven year old eyes I seemed to be ancient, incredibly old, but functioning, for I was painting pictures of the Yard. As I gazed I spoke to the Yard in my mind:

'I will come and paint pictures of you, I promise. It won't be yet, not for ages, but I will, I will come back and paint you. I can't do it yet; I don't know enough, but I will one day. I promise.'

And I did. But there was much living to do before that could occur.

My mother's disillusion with me finally reached its peak when I refused to take the secretarial course, for the only purpose in the expenditure of sending me to that school was so that I would be what she had wanted to be, which was a secretary. At the age of eleven I had maneuvered her into agreeing that I could give up attending church and as she was a devout Christian this had been accomplished with reluctance.

She said 'It obviously isn't doing you any good, so yes, you might as well stop going.'

This latest rebellion was the final straw where she was concerned, so although she loved me (for she was incapable of not loving me) she disliked me thereafter and I must tell that the feelings were mutual. Her beliefs, her attitudes, her social acceptances were all in conformity with the general ethical climate. I could offer no challenges to dispute these ethics and so a rather uncomfortable vacuum was created. So it was that when the following episode occurred I was neither surprised nor resentful nor alarmed at the outcome.

Having left school much discussion had taken place as to what I should do and although I had the opportunity to take several jobs, I had elected to go for the one which paid the best wage. For a number of years I had pitied my mother and intended to give her all the financial support possible. That my young sister was her ewe lamb was of no consequence. One may as well have argued against the sun rising, so although I was capable of resentment in other quarters there was no resentment concerning this situation.

To my surprise a letter arrived inviting my mother and I to an interview at the Art Department of the local Technical College. Without my knowledge my old art mistress had submitted some of my work and I was offered a college scholarship. My mother and I stood outside the building and with crystalline clarity I watched the scene, which would take place as she talked to my father.

She would be scrupulously fair in presenting her argument against this proposal by saying:

'We have three daughters and it isn't fair that the other two should suffer in favour of one. We couldn't afford to send the eldest and Kathleen's had her chance and wouldn't take it. In any case, how can you make a living in the art world? Artists always struggle to sell their work. I think we have to treat them all alike, don't you? After all, if they're any good they can make their own way sooner or later.'

And my father would concur, 'Yes, I'm afraid we'll have to tell her she can't go. D'you think she'll be very upset?'

'No' said my mother, 'I think she'll see it reasonably. When I've talked to her about it she'll see that it's fair.'

So as my mother and I stood outside the building and she said uncertainly:

'You know I'll have to talk to your father about this offer, I can't say here and now that you can take it up. After all, the grants they're offering aren't much, you spend more than that in paints already and it will be years before you qualify ... Yes, we'll have to see what your Daddy says.'

It was all I could do not to start laughing for I could see the scene which was to occur, knew exactly what would be said and the conclusions which would be drawn. But there were consolations a-plenty: we had a library and it was full of books, all for free. Always there had been books in our home and we had been encouraged to read – subject to strict monitoring from my mother for she would not permit anything of an even faintly salacious nature in the house. 'Eric' or 'Little by Little' was fairly standard matter, although we always read the Bindle books, because my father liked Bindle. A naughty rogue who made his own rules. Very akin to my father. Now I could really read and I read my way around the world. A book a day was the average, some relatives once twitted me as to why I always had a book in hand.

The reply became standard, 'I want to know what makes people tick.'

Overall, there was no disappointment at being denied my 'big chance' for it was quite agreeable to have had it offered, but I knew that it was but an adjunct in my life. There was something else, but I had not the most remote inkling as to what it would be, but there was something else; a darkness as yet. Meanwhile I began to notice that I could often see thoughts inside heads and this was disconcerting, for the thoughts inside some heads were the absolute opposite from the words which were being spoken to my face. It was uncanny and I wondered if this happened to everyone, but never dared to ask.

In retrospect, all that I thus described was simply the preliminary moves. My true life was to begin when I was seventeen years old. So what did those curious little episodes actually indicate? I hadn't the faintest notion, only that they seemed to own some unusual kind of identity in spite of the fact that they all differed widely from each other. Why did I remember them so clearly for in a wider sense they were of no significance to anyone and I well knew by then that many people experienced strange little oddities in their lives, some of which were of great significance.

My own small precognitive encounters were of no significance to anyone, so I told no one of them. They owned a curious indestructibility so that they remained like tiny pinnacles, which reared out of my unimportant existence and could be neither understood nor forgotten; but I had not the smallest notion as to why they intruded with such persistence. Overall my precognitive experiences could be neither understood nor forgotten, so I thought of them, when I thought at all, as being part of the fabric of life. But yet not quite … There was a difference …

Chapter 2 – Growing Pains

My tastes in reading may best be described as 'Catholic' in the sense of being prepared to read anything and everything which took my fancy. Certain titles simply invited reading and in such a manner I had read what was then thought of as a classic: Dunne's 'Experiment with Time'. It had been prompted by the author's having experienced a major dream in which he witnessed a huge natural disaster involving the deaths of many people. Within a few days he saw the newspaper reports of such a disaster and was thus moved to conduct some research of his own which culminated in his discovering that people did, in fact, dream of very tiny trivial events in their own futures.

As I had dreamed in what I had thought of as 'Technicolour' for most of my life, I decided to do some small research of my own and discovered that there was some foundation to this theory, although what I discovered was extremely banal, but it established in my mind something of the nature of dreaming. There the matter ended. It has been written to establish clearly the difference between ordinary commonplace dreaming and what was to follow. I make the distinction to emphasize that the next events bore no resemblance to dreaming.

Without warning or with any sense of being transported anywhere, I found I was standing in a large room and a room I did not recognize and had never entered in my life. But this awareness had been preceded by consciousness of my person for I was dressed in my best grey flannel suit; makeup on and my hair as tamed as it could ever hope to be. In all, dressed for best, but the knowledge was almost instantaneous for I was riveted to a very small area. The room was very clean, at least what I could see of it. A small area of flooring just before me was beautifully kept wooden planking, immaculate in construction and maintenance. Indeed, I could see everything in minute detail, for the room was full of brilliant sunlight and although I could not see the windows to my left, I well knew them to be there. As the room was rectangular I knew (but could not actually see) that a door was at the far end. There was not the smallest hope that I could get to it and leave this room, although I would have sold all I owned to escape.

There was no escape.

The rest of that room rose to a height of perhaps fourteen feet, but halfway up the walls was a monstrous sea of insects and writhing creatures. Swamp Green. Billious Green. A sea of heaving wriggling slime, all alive, and the purpose of each nameless monstrosity was to slide from the pulsating morass and engulf me. I saw an enormous slug-like thing squirm itself from its fellows, its tiny unseeing bead-like eyes unresponsive. It managed to rear itself for perhaps a couple of feet, only to fall back to be obscenely sucked down into the morass which was trying to envelope its target. I was the target.

Less than a yard from my right a monstrous travesty of a spider, black as soot, was struggling to detach all its legs so as to clamber over me. In microscopic detail I could see its angled legs scrabbling upon the polished boards, see the minute hairs upon its monstrous limbs, each as thick as cigars.

Petrified with terror I dared not move an inch. In this tiny space I was safe, but only so long as I made no move in any direction. It seemed as if my breathing was suspended, for I knew that if one of these malignancies even brushed me I would die.

Instantly I was awake, knowing it was the middle of the night, knowing that I still dared not move, dared not sleep, for my worst nightmare was of being in any situation where I was locked in by creepy crawlies. As a tiny girl my elder sister had once held her hands out to me saying:

'Choose which hand you want, I've brought you a present.'

I, thinking she was going to give me a sweet, took her present. She put a daddy-long-legs in my palm and the obscenity of those legs struggling in my palm had engendered a pathological horror of insects, which never abated. And now I had been in a situation where those terrors had been realized.

This was no dream. I had been there in that horrendous room. I was rigid, totally immobile, as if my limbs were congealed in solid ice. It was fear which had locked me, not the inability to move. I slept no more that night.

I will now describe Agnes and the rather poignant relationship which existed between us, for in a strictly familial sense the relationship was quite slight, yet in many other senses she felt more near to me than my sisters. My great grandfather (distaff side) had been left a widower with seven children and he married a much younger woman who also bore him seven children. My mother's father was one of the first seven children and Agnes's mother, the lady my sisters and I called 'auntie' was one of the second set of children. As a girl my mother had liked her step-aunt and although she spent her childhood in another town she visited great grandmother's house for holidays, accompanying auntie both before and after the latter's marriage. At the age of twelve, my mother was orphaned completely and it was arranged that she should live with my aunt and uncle. In consequence, she always referred to them as 'mother' and 'father' and she and Agnes thought of themselves as sisters. Our two families always lived very near to each other and behaved, on the whole, as one family.

On the evening following the insect experience my mother, Agnes and I were sitting together as we often did. It was July and the weather was glorious. Not knowing why I was suddenly urged to tell them of my dreadful experience and I related it with much hyperbole. To my chagrin it evoked little response, I rather wished I had kept my own counsel. There was a tiny moment when I thought that a swift flicker of understanding passed between them, but it was so sudden and slight that I couldn't be sure.

My mother said smoothly, 'I think it's time we all had some tea.'

And they began at once to talk of other topics.

On Monday morning I awakened with a headache, which felt slightly unnatural as I was not headache-prone. It didn't improve and by lunchtime I felt rather worse; as the day progressed the ache also progressed. There wasn't much use in complaining for my mother had famous headaches of her own, which imposed silence on the house. Tuesday morning began not with an identical headache, but something much worse and as the day wore on I felt as if I had a scold's bridle on my head. That evening I made my complaint, which annoyed my mother into irritability,

'For goodness' sake child, can't you take a couple of aspirin like everybody else does?'

So I did but the headache worsened. Wednesday and Thursday were infinitely worse, by Friday morning the lights had begun, intense rainbows of colour, searing and piercing. In my left eye the vision had gone and my mother said crossly

'I don't know why you can't take aspirin like everybody else does. Heaven knows I've only kept going on aspirin lots of times. I suppose' she ended reluctantly, 'I'll have to take you to the doctor's this afternoon. You'd better get yourself ready.'

All I really wanted to do was die and end the agony, but we duly presented ourselves, whereupon our doctor ordered me to the hospital. Blow by blow accounts of illness bore me, so I will only add that a perceptive sister realized I had glaucoma. Later I learned that it was unheard of for a person of my age to contract this illness. My family was horrified. I wished I'd known earlier for I could have spared them worry: none of the insects had actually touched me. My eyesight was damaged, of course, but I've managed without too much trouble.

Came the evening when my mother, Agnes and I were sitting together talking.

Agnes said 'We knew there would be illness when you told us about your dream. You've inherited this and it goes back in the family for generations.'

My mother said 'Yes, d'you remember how great grandma used to go round to all the family warning mothers to watch the children extra carefully?'

'Yes, she did,' said Agnes 'and it always happened that one of the kids fell ill. With her it was lice in the hair, she was paranoid about lice. There's always one, isn't there, Alice, one in every generation,'

Turning to me she added, 'it's you love, you've got it now. I'm glad it isn't me' she ended with a shudder, 'I'd rather not know in advance.'

As a theory it all sounded feasible except for one discrepancy: the lady I had known as great grandmother, whom I remembered well for she lived to a great age, was actually no blood relative of mine. My mother's father was the son of a lady long dead, the first wife, not the second.

During the hiatus period in which I convalesced there seemed to be a curious atmosphere about me of suspension, of marking time in some weird unfathomable manner. Too tenuous for identification, yet a kind of breathing space. It couldn't be said that I thought it; rather it was that I felt it. It gave me no discomfort or fear and was best described as suspended animation. Certainly, it did not interfere with my normal functions and even with one eye padded over I still read Trollope and laughed my head off at his characters.

By now I was convinced of one thing, I had a Sixth Sense and I strongly suspected my father had one too. I neither knew any better name for it, nor understood how some people had it in abundance, whilst others had not. I had not the smallest notion as to how a Sixth

Sense was acquired, or if it could be acquired at all. Perhaps it was inherited. It cannot be said that I thought too deeply about the subject.. It was there and I was very glad it was there for I couldn't imagine how it was possible to function without this extra sense. Indeed, I felt very sorry for people who did not own this extra sense and wondered quite seriously how they managed to cope.

More strongly than any other of the vague fog-like assumptions there emerged one, which could be recognized as definite language; it seemed to swirl and form itself in words: This is not an end, this is a beginning. You are old enough now, so pay attention. You know what could have happened, you could be blind, but you're functioning well enough, so grow up and pay attention. There's more to come.

It could have been a threat, but it was not. It could have been alarming, yet I was not alarmed. Rather it felt as if whatever was to happen I would be supported through it, but what the support would be I did not even think to enquire.

None of this was told, of course; it was all too tenuous for speech. I felt it. Something of major importance was looming. I knew it. My generation was fighting a war and there was no possibility that I would help too, it had been forbidden and I felt guilt. One image emerged with immense clarity: Your war is yet to come.

Acceptance of and recognition of the fact of a Sixth Sense did not worry me or cause any discomfort, but neither did it make me feel different from my fellows in any respect. On the whole I was pleased it existed for it never felt to be unnatural in spite of the fact that I had experienced prior warning of that serious illness in a symbolic form.

Without actually analyzing the situation it was fully evident that it operated only in future time and this, of course, was where the heart of the problem lay; not in the fact that I knew what the future was going to be, but in the fact that all the social ethics and conventions of the time forbade the possession of a Sixth Sense for there were many who owned this mysterious faculty and socially they were the object of much derision.

To my mother and Agnes I could speak with a certain amount of freedom, but in my small social world I was circumspect.

Nor was this sense operative in major issues only, but in many small, mundane and quite banal situations to the extent that my mother, whose decisions were laws-to-be-obeyed began to ask me what the outcome of some developing situations were likely to be. And that was very odd indeed.

This Sixth Sense seemed to be an integral part of my fabric, similar to the hair on my head. So although I could not understand it in any manner one fact emerged which was beyond dispute, this was True, irrespective of whether the answers appeared to defy logic, were unfashionable or detectable by formal means, the approaching truth was unquestioned. If it alarmed me, made me uneasy, that truth was not an issue. Nothing I could do or say would circumvent it. Nor, to be candid, did it ever occur to me to try. I might as well have tried to halt moonrise.

When I was no longer ill I did as young girls do, laughed and danced and sang and flirted with young men; all of which is unnatural only if you do not.

Chapter 3 – Living The Impossible

Ostensibly, I was sleeping in bed. The scene before me was familiar enough but eerily different. Everything was the same; I knew this area like the back of my own hand, but I couldn't understand how or why it was different. Yet I was there, of that there was no doubt, but I was very, very puzzled. Why had I come? I couldn't find an answer for there seemed to be a strange swift blurring between where I had come from – my own home – to this place. There was no apparent reason and I ceased trying to find one but simply looked about me, struck as always by the sheer unusual feeling of isolation this area always produced. I thought:

'When I was four and came here to school I knew then there was something odd about it. It hasn't changed one bit, it's still odd. But why have I come to School Street for heaven's sake?'

I was standing in School Street, two or three feet from the pavement. To my left the land sloped upwards towards Oakes Road and Plover Road. Behind me was the school playground which extended upwards to Oakes Road. There was a terrace of stone built houses along Oakes Road and its end house had a large semi circular garden before the road branched into Plover Road. At the corner of Plover Road and School Street was a weaving shed which had huge double doors that opened directly into the top of School Street. Beyond the weaving shed, at the start of Plover Road, was a wall bordering a field, and to the right was a tree lined private estate.

'There used to be a well in that top wall', I thought 'and I've drunk from it lots of times when I was a kid.'

I suddenly shuddered as I remembered the cold clear sweet water, seeing myself as an infant pottering about this area as safe and unhindered as a curious puppy. Me in navy interlock knickers and with a packet of Sunmaid raisins because I couldn't eat breakfasts.

'My childhood here', I thought. 'I always liked those houses on Oakes Road. Oh, it's chilly.'

Involuntarily I looked up the hill; the trees were bare of leaves and the sky above them a palest soft grey. I thought: 'It's winter now and it all looks just as it did when I was a kid.'

I had been standing there musing when I was struck again by the strange isolation of the scene; it seemed to belong to another time, another place, part of the area, yet weirdly detached. Apart from the times when the children came and left the school, likewise the people who worked at the mill, hardly anyone walked the area for the main roads were far to the left and right and there was no reason for anyone to come this way. With sudden shock I thought: 'What on earth have I come for? There's no-one here, I think I'd better go.'

With even greater shock, like a chilly douche, I realized that there was someone there after all and I could not imagine how I'd not noticed earlier for I'd looked at the top of Union Street before looking at the weaving shed doors and I'd have been bound to notice if there'd been anyone there then. I must have stood reminiscing for ages.

Three people were standing on the pavement to the right of the doors. None moved but somehow I felt they knew I was there and as they were facing me they were bound to have seen me, yet there was no word or greeting. There was a woman with a figure on each side. They looked as if they were just waiting and I wondered for a split second if they were lost.

As country people always greet each other: 'How do?' I decided to cross and have a word. My left eye was now impaired and to see clearly I had to move. I did move and rather rudely stood before the small group, none of whom gave the smallest indication that they knew I was there.

Now I looked at the woman's face and my world exploded into shreds of stabbing light … It was impossible … Unbelievable … It couldn't happen … A denial of reality … A conversion of reality … It could not be … Shock immobilized me and my person seemed to split apart, each cell screaming at this dissolution of reality.

This face was my face. This woman was me. I was looking at myself.

How long it took before I settled I cannot say. It was as if the vast explosion had to be allowed to return the shreds into position before I gazed again, thought again, but eventually some measure of calm descended and I looked at her carefully. Throughout she remained immobile, I inspected her, me, in minute detail. Her hair, my hair, had been tamed. Still thick, brown, springing, it surged over her, my head, in bouncy curls. She was, I was, wearing a long coat halfway down her calves, my calves, it was slimly cut, heaven's above, this was a closely shorn curly fur with an unusual collar, it seemed to flare like a half halo around the back of her, my head. My goodness, I thought, fashions are to change a lot for my hair hung down my back like a mane and all our clothes were knee length.

Her face, my face, older now, early middle age, but still my face. White, so frozen white, not that I had ever had any colour to speak of, but this whiteness was bone chilling. Her eyes, my eyes, still blue, but no laughter here, these were eyes of Arctic blue, withdrawn, as if they were seeing some unimaginable Arctic region. Her nose, my nose, prominent; the kind said 'Roman-like' and the unkind said simply 'Big'. Her mouth, my mouth, compressed now, drawn in, a line, a line of what? Oh, God, oh my God I knew now, knew what had compressed this mouth, drawn laughter from this face I would own, oh God...

Grief! Grief such as my seventeen-year-old mind could not grasp, could not visualize as being. All that lay behind that frozen mask, which was her face, my face, came roaring in like a choking torrent. She, I, knew this grief. Her grief was the grief I would live. So much, all instantaneously, too much to grasp; I was drowning in the knowledge of what I would be, would live. I had been on a journey, oh God, of all places I had just returned from the Wesleyan Churchyard at the end of the village. Someone had died. Someone I knew. Someone infinitely dear and precious.

And I spoke to the woman I would be.

'Oh God' I said 'you poor thing. I am so sorry.'

Somehow, without being conscious of doing so I moved again and gazed at her, me and my companions. They were here, my children, the children I, we, would have. The smaller reached about halfway up her, my, upper arm and the other to shoulder height. Peer as I might I could not see their faces for their heads were obscured by some material finer, yet more densely opaque than the darkest smoke. How I was so sure I didn't know, but I felt they were girl children.

Again I moved without conscious intention or volition to resume my original position in School Street. Without intention I looked to my right and saw, to my amazement, a large shining sphere of light, silvery white yet reflecting rainbow-like colours. Inside, curled up in sleep, was my own seventeen-year-old person.

Instantly, I was fully awake. No more sleep. Who could possibly sleep following this? That which I had just lived was more real, more vivid than the physical reality of my surroundings. This was going to happen. However mind bending, however impossible, this was to be a part of my future. The experience of being ill had only been a preparatory incident, yet I had lived the truth of that and this was identical in all respects. I had known that the earlier experience was not an end, but I could not have supposed in my wildest dreams that anything like this was to happen. It was going to be a hard future, a hard life; I knew it as surely as I knew the sun would rise. Whether or not it was in accordance with accepted physical laws didn't matter. This was truth, there was no gainsaying, a weird, implacable:

'This will be.'

As I lay there thinking I decided:

'It looks as if I'll be widowed early and have to bring the children up on my own.'

Children, oh my goodness yes. I'd planned never to have any, but it looks as if I will. In that private soliloquy there were two wrong assumptions made solely from the viewpoint of a young girl. Excusable, perhaps. One was very minor and of no great account; the other was major, of very great account. I did not know myself. Each was drawn from the obvious and that is facile truth. Dangerously so.

Agnes and I were alone so I told her the whole story. She said almost nothing, but gazed at me with her huge loving brown eyes – like pansy hearts. Indeed, what could be said? But she believed me.

Life went on. I was usually in some minor trouble or other, although by comparison with real troubles my minor peccadilloes were very mediocre, stemming usually from my inability to accept the rigid Victorian conventions which were so stultifying. A universal cry of the young.

Futile to write that I was shattered, for my brain was reeling with shock. How was it possible to be in two places at one and the same time? Within that exquisite circle of light I had seen my person lying, asleep, yet I had stood in School Street, fully aware of seeing all about myself. How was it possible to see oneself as the woman I was going to be? It was as if I had been in an earthquake and none of the rules we took for granted and which governed the world had been set aside … How was any of it possible?

It was as if my very mind had sundered, flying, screaming into inchoate shreds … Was I going mad? No, weirdly, this was not madness, of that I was certain. Yet the me-to-be was wearing a hairstyle which had not even been invented and the coat was a funeral coat to be worn at the Wesleyan Churchyard, but I had extricated myself from the Christian religion years ago, so why there, of all places?

And the children? Girls. How did I know they were girls? I could not see their faces so how did I know with this implacable certainty that I would have two daughters? But I did know ...

Knew also the lacerating grief, which lay beyond the frozen ice of that face, my face, the face I would have in years to come. How would I live through such unimaginable grief? All the griefs I had ever known were seen now as infantile irrelevances, the clamouring idiocies of a child who wanted a certain dress or pair of shoes; nonsensical, demeaning, futile in the face of true agony.

My mind, my brain howled: this could not be true; it was a dream, a defiance of every known natural law. But they were the protestations of a child, for superseding all of the infantile protestations was that which cannot be circumvented, cannot be denied no matter what conventional theory was defied.

This you will live, this is truth. And Agnes knew it too, but I did not tell my mother. It was going to be a hard life, but somehow I would get through it.

Eventually I came – not to terms, for there is no arguing with a truth one knows to be absolute – but to some kind of acceptance. Surfacely I lived the life of any young girl, sometimes frivolous, sometimes frothy, but always the truth by time. As compensation there were books, my refuge and my drug, for in reading Trollope I could laugh again; books were my only palliative.

Chapter 4 – Youthful Learnings

On the night the war ended I wept inconsolably, unable to tell the young soldier with whom I was walking why I wept. The reason was not that I was as relieved as the rest of Britain that it was ended, for I was unutterably relieved that young men of my generation would not now have to die. It was the death of the world I had known for which I wept. I saw and I wept. I saw that the civilization in which I had grown was gone forever. In the world's history this end was abrupt, cruelly so. It was as if I gazed at a huge panorama of life which had died, not piecemeal, not in the slow expectable decay of all living beings, or social attitudes; it was conclusive, a complete reversal of all I had known and loved. And I did not know until I watched this rapid dissolution just how much I had loved it.

Later that year, on my way to work, I called on the newspaper vendor by my bus stop. It was a lovely morning, hazy as yet, but with the promise of a lovely day to follow. As was customary I opened the paper at once for it never seemed at all strange to be reading and walking at the same time, I'd done it for years. But the bold black headlines stopped me in my tracks:

'Atom Bomb on Hiroshima.'

'Oh my God' I muttered to myself 'they've done it.'

Much later it occurred to me to ask myself how I'd known they were even trying to split the atom. Instantaneously, I knew that nothing would ever be the same again. As I had watched the dissolution of the world I had known a vacuum had formed and this was what was filling it.

Entirely without volition I flew upwards into a vortex of coloured clouds, swirling masses of enormous dimensions, indeed I could not estimate the dimension for this vortex was beyond measure or explanation. Writhing helplessly in the vast bands of colour were civil service figures, the black coat and striped trousers brigade, all flailing, their powers futile in the enormity of this immensity.

Then I was standing once more holding the newspaper, thinking over and over again:

'Pandora's out of the box. Pandora's out of the box.'

At work I questioned everyone I knew and to my amazement no one seemed to think there was anything extraordinary about this momentous news. Slightly aggrieved I held my tongue, deciding to wait until I got home. They'd be talking about it for sure. To my utter amazement my family evinced no surprise at all. A bomb was a bomb was a bomb. Goodness knows, the British had grown accustomed to bombs these last years, what was so surprising about them? I wanted to shout and tear my hair but I had been too well disciplined for that, so I shut up, feeling that they'd know the awfulness of this malignancy sooner or later. I instinctively knew that no matter what spurious whitewash emerged from Whitehall, this power was uncontrollable.

During this period of my life two convictions emerged, formed and became impossible to ignore; they were impelling. Someone will come to me and say:

'Come with me' and when that happens I shall go with that person.

Knowing myself as I was then, this was a most peculiar admission; for the truth was that I declined involvement with any club, organization, creed or ideology. It was as if an impassable barrier (not of my own making) lay between any large or small formal group and me. To none could I commit myself, nor was it because I despised or disliked groups of people for I liked people very much and was never too particular as to whom I spoke or associated with. As with books my tastes were Catholic, frequently rather too Catholic for my mother's approval, but as I kept many of them out of her jurisdiction it didn't matter. But to admit to myself that I would follow a complete stranger to some unknown destination seemed as alien a concept as it was possible to swallow. Yet I would do it at some time in my life. I didn't know how, or when; all circumstances were blank as to details, but go I would. Very odd.

The second conviction was of an entirely different nature and quality:

'I must live alone with as much space about me as I can gather.'

On this topic I expounded a lot, fleshing out the details from a purely imaginative viewpoint. On the moor would be best I thought and it didn't need to be any more than a simple single cottage, a bare flagged floor would do and I could make a rag rug for the hearth. A bed which would do for a sofa, a small table and a couple of chairs. Luxuries didn't matter; it was isolation and space that I wanted. 'Why?'

I hadn't the remotest notion. Why would a well reared young woman wish to leave all comforts, family and friends to isolate herself on a wild moor and our moors were wild indeed? What would I do if I got there? I'd no idea. Why did I want this in the first place? Unanswerable. Gradually, this conviction hardened. It was not a wish; it was a thirst which developed into need. Over the years and flouting chronology, I say now the need was so great it became hot, generating further heat until a slow fire began to burn inside me. Isolation. Space. Nothing else mattered. Why? I did not know.

On the face of it I lived a comfortable safe existence; a reliable family background, plenty of friends and interests, rather a butterfly existence if the truth be told.

My mother said with exasperation: 'You, madam, will turn your nose up at shoes 'till boots won't have you.'

For indeed, it didn't take much to put me off a man then there was usually another boyfriend close behind. Quickly I had cottoned onto the games young men played so casually and light heartedly and resolved I too would play this game, whilst ludicrously hoping one would love me for my mind, not my body. Green as grass I was. My father had spoiled me where men were concerned for I had supposed that men in general thought as he did and nothing could have been more contrary. Repeatedly we were subjected to the maxim:

'Try everything once. If you don't like it you don't have to have it again, or do it again, or go again, but try everything once.'

It was a most uncommon thesis for the time and it did not end there for he believed that brains were universal, organs to be used; therefore if a woman chose to learn a man's job then he would willingly teach it if he knew it. There was no distinction between the genders; the people who refused to use their brains were the ones he despised. Knowing so little of men when I was very young and impressionable and having been taught only by women, together with living in a female society, I had much to learn. My general impressions were not favourable; men lied too easily.

Boarding the train at King's Cross I noticed with pleasure that it was but sparsely filled and obtained a corner seat with my back to the engine. Bags on rack, book at the ready, I looked forward to a pleasant journey. There were only three other people in the compartment, each of us in a corner seat. Engrossed in my book I did not notice the first station at which the train halted, but a number must have been waiting for two entered and the last one was a young pale curate. Only the centre seat to my left was vacant and as I looked up I met his gaze and read the mind instantly. A female dangerous creature, wearing makeup, smartly dressed and a snare to the pure. Ostentatiously he pulled down the arm rest and I thought 'Fear not, you lanky length, you put me in mind of a damp flannel and I wouldn't touch you with a bargepole, nor allow you to touch me, for that matter.' With equal ostentation I snuggled into my corner as far away as possible.

In the total British silence so prevalent at the time the journey proceeded. Again the train was halting and I looked up from my book. The platform we were drawing into was a solid mass of people, hundreds, thousands and the nearest were dangerously close to the platform edge. Idiotically, I supposed there were waiting for another train, they were not, they were waiting for this train and it barely halted before the stampede began. It appeared like the hordes of Genghis Khan; the first to enter was a large black Scottie dog, which made a beeline for me, put its rear end up to the carriage wall and laid itself across my feet. Arm rests flew up and people must have forced themselves into seats for in seconds I was jammed against the curate from shoulder to knee.

I thought: 'if my mother could see me now she'd be delighted to find me so near the church. P'raps I ought to break out a verse of Nearer my God to Thee.'

The animal's owner had followed it, but fetched up glued to the window. He was a big hairy chap, a bit of a bruiser, but he'd made a bad move for now he was pinned immovably by the window – as we all were pinned.

As the journey continued the atmosphere thickened. I could not read for a large bottom was suspended but inches above my lap. From the dog across my feet there arose a radiant heat, which was rapidly becoming unbearable. Then a most curious phenomenon evolved: I could see inside the curate. Weird beyond measure. Desperately I tried not to begin laughing, for he was in turmoil. The old Adam was rearing its ugly head and he was trying to suppress lust with prayer, but not succeeding. Rather cynically I thought: 'It serves you right you sanctimonious fool. How can you get up in a pulpit and preach to others unless you know about life yourself? And you can only know by living it.'

Then I got so physically over-heated from the dog that I left the fascinating battle inside the curate. What to do to rid myself of the animal? Impossible to move my feet forwards for not a spare inch existed. Then I remembered: in the old carriages a small space existed on the floor behind the seat, so I drew my right foot back as far as possible and shoved the dog. An anguished cry arose. The curate howled at the dog's owner in a swaying pulpit cadence:

'Your dog has bitten my ankle' and he couldn't even get down to rub it.

Weirdly, the owner said 'Oh my God and I only had it at the vet's last week.'

Total silence descended on the carriage. There was silence previously, but this thundered. What did he mean? Did he think the curate's ankle would poison the dog or vice versa? Did it bite curates on a regular basis? No one knew, for the man spoke no other word.

At the next station they all got off the train so we original travelers spread ourselves. Callously I thought of the curate. 'It serves you right' but I was a little sorry also, for I had never dreamed that the irascible animal would actually bite. A thin well dressed individual in the opposite corner said quietly:

'There were twenty-two people in the carriage, I counted them as they left.'

It had only been built to hold eight people.

A couple of years later I was offered a small stone cottage to let and told my mother with delight.

She said levelly 'You will leave this house to be married and for no other reason. No daughter of mine is going to live in sin.'

Judge, jury and executioner. There was no appeal, no discussion, no other court and no explanation, only a decree. We were reared to obedience. I was twenty-four years old. A year later I was married. Six weeks after my wedding day I said to my new husband:

'By the way, I forgot to tell you; I have a Sixth Sense.'

To my utter amazement he said coldly:

'Never speak to me again of this. I don't believe such rubbish and I will never believe it until someone proves it to be true. Don't forget, Kathleen, you are never to speak to me of this again.'

And I realized I had exchanged one loving tyranny for another.

So ended my salad days. From now on it would be life-is-real-life-is-earnest. On the flat surface face of it my encounter with the curate was amusing and frivolous and when I regaled the story to my family they all fell about laughing, but it was actually not at all hilarious. What I did not tell was too strange for words and I did not understand the experience. In truth, a part of me entered into the body of that curate yet still retained its individuality. A dispassionate observer, I could see and feel his thoughts and emotions without being distorted by them. It was as if some part of me, the thinking part, had physically invaded him, yet he was totally unaware of this involuntary invasion. He was praying passionately to be relieved of carnal lust and he wasn't getting his prayers answered. Indeed, I felt rather sorry for him as I looked through his body, but his beliefs had blinded him to the world about him, isolated him from Nature that it was as if by the denial of Nature he had hoped to emasculate himself, but it hadn't worked. It was all very sad and I watched his futile struggles with some pity, but I still thought him a fool.

More pertinently, although I did not notice this at the time, how was it possible to enter the body of another person without apparent intention or violation? It did not seem strange at the time for it all happened without the smallest convulsion or discernable hiatus. In one fraction of time I was gazing physically out of my own body then with no perceptible transference I was gazing out of his.

Apart from the experience being very weird, in retrospect it is odd that I never questioned the strangeness at the time, for it all seemed so smooth and natural. Not out of the ordinary at all, almost as if I was used to doing it.

Chapter 5 – Salad Days Ended

Within two years of marriage I had a small daughter and had shed many illusions. In many instances my Sixth Sense was thwarted and in consequence I was to realize just how much I had comfortably rested upon it. This produced a kind of illness for which there was no name or cure, a disjointed sense as if my cells were out of kilter. It was as if I operated now with an essential part of me bound and fettered. He, my husband, had been reared in a strict conventional mould: the man makes the decisions and the woman obeys. Discussion on important topics was negated. Yet he was a good man and the only difference between him and my mother was that she accepted the fact of a Sixth Sense and he did not.

Almost three years passed and I discovered I was pregnant again. I said to my husband:

'I will not have another child in this awful cottage. We will have to find something better.'

He did not commit himself in words, but I could see he saw the justice of my argument. There the matter lay. But days later my elder sister and her husband called in the evening and I had a shock. Harry said kindly:

'I've come to tell you about a house that's going to be sold and it's just right for you, I think. I go to work with the chap who lives there and he told me that their landlord is putting them in the Gate House. It isn't general knowledge yet because this chap and his wife don't want hordes of people looking round, but if you want to have a look at it I think I can make arrangements for you to see it.'

Betty said 'It's a lovely house with a big garden. It'll be marvellous for children and you'll be near us all again.'

'Where is this house?' I asked.

Harry said 'It's the one at the top of Plover Road, you know, the one with the big side garden at the beginning of Oakes Road.'

Instantly, I saw down the years to the time when I stood in School Street seeing the self I would be. In the same swift instant I felt a choking horror: it would be true, I was going to have to live that experience in reality. How could I have ever supposed it would not be true? This knowledge had a feel about it, an absolute which no other experience could match or obviate. In all surface-shifting changes, this was the one, which neither shifted nor changed. During the intervening years it had lain there pristine, untouched by time:

'This is what will be.' And I was trapped in it.

My destiny. It could no more be avoided than Canute could halt the sea. The others were talking and did not notice my silence. Pros and cons, it was all so much surface fluff: we would live in that house and the mountainous obstacles would all be circumvented. How, I didn't know. Only that it would be so.

After Betty and Harry left my husband said:

'I've made arrangements with Harry for you to go and see that house.'

In due course I went to view, feeling rather robot-like, as if I were being driven by a force I could neither see nor identify. In turn I asked if my husband could also view the property, for the decision would be his, he would allow me no say in whatever property we occupied. That was the man's prerogative.

On his return from his own viewing expedition he came in with a look of bright ambition, saying:

'I like it and we're going to go for it.'

I was sent upon the tiresome round of arranging mortgages, etc; and I shall not write of the mountainous obstacles which had to be negotiated, except for one detail. At the very end I 'saw'.

The house was to be auctioned and as we were green our kindly solicitor said he would bid for us. On the rostrum the auctioneer and his clerk were ready to begin when I 'saw' the exact progression of the bids and the figure at which the bidding would halt. It would not halt at our solicitor's last bid and I whispered:

'If you bid another twenty-five pounds that's the figure it'll stop at.'

That is exactly what occurred. There was a sixth factor in these proceedings. Over the years Norman, my solicitor and I became friends. I felt he knew what was going on and although he was a downy old bird he was very good to me and I miss him.

In that house on a hot day in late spring my second daughter was born. After the disastrous experience of giving birth in a hospital I resolved to have no more repeat performances and thus I met the District Nurses and Cherry (that is not her name, but I do not have permission to use her real name).

There followed a few years, which were lit by a number of curious oddities, strange experiences that, although completely different from each other, all combined to illustrate that another sense, another force was active in my life. One, moreover, of which I had no control, could not summon at will, was impossible of manipulation and in the final analysis could only be described by the tired worn cliché: the Sixth Sense.

By flat surface transpositional methods it would be possible and probable that I would expose the inference that I was a dim, malleable female, easily cowed and maneuvered. Most surely I was not, at least in the physical sense. I had been reared by two tough strong minded parents with whom I argued and who precluded the helpless feminine role, although my mother – as a last resort to get her own way – would dissolve into tears and then I was undone. Overall, I was lucky to have had them as parents, for they were both resourceful, intelligent and skilful, all of which I needed for I had to learn to 'turn my hand to anything'. A jack-of-all-trades and thought ruefully: master-of-none.

Beyond the surface trivia there was the other force, the other sense and that was the real director, the ultimate truth. There was no estimate as to when it would emerge, no knowledge of what events would ensue if it did emerge; when I 'saw' it was always a staggering truth, which I could have learned in no other manner.

One Sunday morning as I was peeling vegetables for lunch, I was suddenly aware of the chicken sizzling in the oven and hearing the small familiar sounds made by my family in the sitting room. Then I left the known world.

Before me lay a huge area, a vast unbroken plain of what appeared to be pure white marble. At the end of this plain I could see regal buildings made of the identical marble, columned, carved with exquisite capitals surmounted with carved frescoes and I thought instantly of the Parthenon (which I had never seen). Yet those superb artists could never have laid such flooring for this was laid all of a piece, with not a joint to be seen, the acme of artistry, beyond the capability of men to try.

Grouped loosely before me were a number of people, men and women. I could see their faces, but all were dressed identically in some black filmy material so fine as to make gossamer appear rope-like. Instantly, I knew them and began to grope for names in greeting. Stupidly, I could name no one and they all knew this and beamed at me, but the beam was a force of stupendous power. It was love and I was saturated with it. Yet they were all dead people, these ones I had known at some time in my life, except they lived now as a concentration of power which is impossible to convey in words. Brilliant, blazing, Life.

At the centre of the group was a small lady and she moved toward me lifting her palm as she did so. It was an exquisite gesture, not in any respect a hail or a prelude to handshake, rather it was as if she were showing me something, but I couldn't see what – if anything – lay on her palm. Again I wanted to greet her properly by name because I knew her, knew her name, yet search as I might I could find no name for her. Yet the gesture was in the nature of giving, but they were already giving for I was suffused with pure love.

A dissolving now, a rising, I was being taken upwards into faintly but beautifully coloured masses, cloud-like except these swirling masses had no substance but one and it was a Force: Love. Stupendous Love, of a nature unequalled, unparalleled, impossible of description. Purist, yet titanic in nature …

Then I was gazing stupidly at the red handled peeler and the grubby water and I wanted to die in despair at having been removed from that titanic Love. For months I mourned, sodden with frustration, why did I have to return? I thought I knew love, for I loved my girls and others, yet I realized how puny, how pale and insubstantial this love is by comparison with the true nature of Love.

Obliged to stay, I had to make the best I could of it. Some months later there was a sequel.

I was at the sink again. I seemed to spend the greater part of my existence beside that dreadful piece of furniture and it will feature again I fear.

Agnes said 'Well, come on then and say 'hello'.'

She had a naughty little grin and she grinned now:

'I've brought you a present.'

'Why?' I asked, 'It isn't my birthday.'

She said 'Does it have to be a birthday to give anyone a present? Here, this is for you' and she lifted her hand, palm upwards, on which lay a tiny white box wrapped in white tissue paper.

I hesitated 'What is it?'

She replied impatiently 'Well, if you take it you'll know, won't you. God, you are difficult. You can't even take a present without wanting to know all the ins and outs of it. See, stop messing about. It's to you from me.'

I dried my hands, opened my present and tipped from the box a heavy ring of red (rose) gold, then looked at her in utter amazement:

'You can't give this to me' I whispered.

Agnes was very small and apparently docile, but not many suspected the core of steel which lay inside. It emerged now.

She said 'This belongs to me and I'm giving it to you because I want you to have it.'

I said firmly 'You should give this to Betty because she was their favourite. Oh, I know your mum and dad treated us all alike, they were scrupulously fair about it, but I've known for years that Betty was their favourite and I never said anything to anyone except now. It's true, though, isn't it?'

Agnes said 'I might have known you'd twig, yes it's true.'

I replied 'Then do the right thing and give it to Betty.'

Mulishly she answered 'It's mine now and if you won't take it I can tell you now that nobody else will get it. It's yours. Try it on.'

It slipped on my finger as if it had been custom built, simple but beautiful. Inside my head it was as if a knocking was taking place, a drawing of attention but I ignored it. My actual personal possessions were meagre but I should have refused the ring and established exactly which of the rings had belonged to my auntie and uncle. I knew they had each worn rings and owned more than one each, but I should have asked and I did not. Why? It was greed. Plain unvarnished greed. The ring was beautiful; it fitted me perfectly and sat on my hand as if we belonged together.

I gave one last try 'Are you sure about this, love?'

Agnes replied, 'I couldn't be more sure.'

So I said 'very well, I'll keep it and thank you.'

Nothing I owned compared with this ring so I showed it with pride to friends and family, wearing it daily. After a few days had passed, I noticed as I was paring vegetables that I felt a curious malaise although there was no valid reason why I should feel so, there were no outstanding troubles or even minor disasters to cope with and I told myself not to be silly. But I couldn't shake it off. Indeed, it got worse and descended into real and active melancholia. Day by day the melancholia grew into a state beyond tears (although I was not particularly weepy in any case) beyond isolation, foundationless, it bore no resemblance to any physical source, but simply a groundless misery.

There came a day a fortnight later at the sink when I saw I would have to leave, cross the upper road and lower myself into the dam above. No other action was feasible. No thought of distress to my family or friends. Only the water. Then I 'saw'. Over my head and so near I felt that if I lifted a hand I could touch it, was a darkness of such opaque malignancy that it was terrible to behold. Involuntarily I looked down and saw the gleam of gold. Then I knew. Ripping it off my finger I rushed to my bedroom and replaced the ring in its original wrappings, then looked through the window and the world was lovely again. Now I knew to whom that ring had belonged and how it had come to be charged with its dreadful history. I would wait. Agnes would come.

A few days later I turned to find her standing in the kitchen. At once, not even stopping to greet her, I fetched the ring and laid the box in her hand.

'How could you?' I asked 'How could you do it to me? You knew, didn't you?' Immediately the tears spilled from the great brown eyes and she wept heart-brokenly:

'Oh my God love. It's done it to you too.'

'Yes,' I answered 'I was just going over the road to the dam.'

'Where were you going?' sniffled Agnes

'I was actually going up the street to Sykes' dam when I came to' I said.

Agnes's voice trembled 'Oh, this is terrible. I wouldn't hurt a hair of your head, love and I thought that of all people in the world you could cure it.'

Somberly I said 'Well, it didn't get its own way, did it; something comes to stop it. It was Auntie's wedding ring, wasn't it?'

'Yes' Agnes said despairingly 'It was the ring my damned brother tried to get your mother to take off her hand three weeks before she died. He wanted it for Caroline, he said she'd always wanted it and when your mother wouldn't do it he cursed it and it's still cursed.'

I said 'Yes, I remember. My mother was so furious she couldn't contain herself. She raged around the house.'

'Kathleen, what are we going to do with it?' asked Agnes.

I replied slowly 'Would you agree to selling it and we'll give the money to the Church? They're always on the beg and they're begging like mad at the moment. Would you agree to that?'

Agnes said fervently 'That's the best solution of all.'

Thus the affair ended and I began to think. The tiny person who had moved toward me on the concourse had been my auntie and the gesture she had used was the gesture her daughter Agnes had used when giving me the ring. But there were wider implications also for now I realized that apparently inanimate objects could and most surely did, absorb human passions. For a number of years I had suspected this fact to be so for a certain area, a valley, hidden in a fold of huge moorland had always held something inimical for me. Each time I went there I suffered some accident or other and it had happened too often to be dismissed as coincidental. One may stretch coincidence to a limit and when a number began to coalesce some other factor must be conjectured. Now I was sure that something in that lovely valley was not only inimical, but also positively hostile. I thought of Belsen, where, it is said 'No birds sing'. I thought again of the Dean Head valley and the last time we ever visited it, the terror which made me decide never to set foot there again.

It was glorious summer weather, the moors lay glistening, smoothly heaped and boundless. In these spaces it was possible to be at one with the earth and believe that the filth of cities was but a mirage. Long sloping lines of the earth itself like the outlines of great somnolent animals furred by heather and tough fine grasses. Yet within this valley fold were pastures, soft greens, quite adult trees for they were protected here from the racing winds above. A splendid stream began in the upper 'V' of the fold to form a curving pool, which was perfect for children. My husband had not known of the valley's existence until I persuaded him there, whereupon it delighted him.

We picnicked leisurely, the girls played and my husband slept. There was born in me a growing, nameless unease, which jittered along my nerve endings. We ought to go, there was something wrong, something impending, it seemed to bleed from my skin without lessening in the slightest. I began to gather up the detritus, for it was a self-imposed rule that we never left any scrap to mark our passing.

At last I roused him 'Let's be going, love. It's a long way to the top and you know what they get like when they're too tired.'

He said 'You are the most fidgety woman I've ever known. We could stay another couple of hours yet and even then it won't be dark.

Can't you rest anywhere?'

'Neil, please let's go. It'll take an hour to get to the top and then we'll have to walk to the bus stop. If we miss it there'll be a four mile hike and they are getting tired.'

Eventually, crossly, he got to his feet and we began to cross the fields, always upwards, to the lane which would take us to the moor top. People had once lived in this valley, for the fields were divided by ancient dry walls, now only sparsely evident. Not cut stones, these were boulders of irregular shapes that had stood for centuries, the gaps between the stones filtered the winds. Slowly we made our way diagonally across the fields coming at last to the ones which bordered the lane. The field we were crossing had lost its wall in the centre, or perhaps it had been demolished for there was now no sign of a wall having been there. At the end of the field we were crossing was a deep ditch impenetrably sealed from the lane by a dense thorn thicket, but here the wall remained and it was huge, possibly six feet in height and it extended into the ditch itself allowing no possible access to the lane.

My elder daughter was a child who liked to do her own investigating and she continued forward as the rest of us crossed above through the space.

My husband called to our daughter:

'Come this way, you can't get out that way.'

By now my antennae were bristling and my husband realized I was going to fetch her. He said angrily:

'Don't be such a fool. You're not going back, she'll have to come back herself. Stop pampering her, come on.'

It was then I paused, irresolute and 'saw' them for the first time: tall glorious figures composed of radiant white light. There was no sound, rather it was that what they were telling me arrived through the fabric of my body: Go, go now. So I ran down the hill, hearing my husband calling in deep anger, telling me I was a fool, a fool, but I paid him no heed whatsoever, call me what he would. Turning the corner I saw my daughter lay a small hand upon one of the great stones and somehow I managed to leap and grasp the other hand to hurl her bodily out of the way. For the small pressure of that small hand must have disturbed the fulcrum which had held the wall. Its toppling sounded as if an earthquake had begun and tons of stone fell where my child would have been.

Then I shook like a woman in the last stages of ague. My husband ran toward us, babbling now that he couldn't have reached us, could only stand in terror watching, not knowing what he would find when he did reach us. So many meaningless words to which I paid no heed, but held my daughter, abject with remorse for disobedience, not caring, not listening, she was safe, thinking only:

'He says there is no such thing as Sixth Sense, but it is by that that he still has a daughter.'

But I said nothing, only to my little girl:

'It's all right, darling, you're safe, that's all that matters.'

During this period of my early and middle thirties I had managed to interest my husband in ancient buildings, artifacts and houses together with pictures and insofar as finances would permit we hauled the children along to visit and learn how people had lived centuries ago and admire the beautiful craftsmanship. Bradford's Bolling Hall became an often-visited venue with its haunted room in which I felt nothing. The rest of the house was a very different story.

Passing through some upper rooms of Bolling Hall we turned sharply to the left and mounted over one of the old fireplaces was a large oil painting. A man in medieval dress and instantly I knew him. No names. But I could feel the blood coursing through his body, his thoughts were my thoughts, his nerve ends tingled with my identical awareness. As I breathed I could feel his chest rise and fall; knew his loves and dislikes; it was as if I had stepped into the portrait and entered his painted body.

Beyond a shadow of doubt I had lived an earlier life. This was a man I had once been. And I never saw the portrait again and was told, on enquiry – that it had probably been loaned for a period. On a parallel course I turned from one room to another in Bolling Hall and my husband was in front of me. Across the room and to our left was a tiny picture, perhaps seven inches by ten. A black and white drawing and from where I was standing I could see no more with my indifferent eyesight but that it was a woman. I needed no more information for acid slivers were emitted from this picture and I cried out involuntarily:

'Oh my God, it's a witch.'

My husband gave me a hostile piercing glance, then strode across the room. His eyesight was excellent, but he could not read the caption below this picture from where he stood; it was very simple and in black and white copperplate handwriting 'A Witch'. Young and beautiful when I could finally see her, but the inner woman was pure evil.

In my mid thirties I had a strange visitor. It was a very chilly autumn day and for some reason I had gone into the side garden. Why, I do not know. Memory begins with the intense indelibility with which these experiences occurred. Even yet occur, come to that. In spite of the chill I looked about me, thinking – as I had thought countless times – how strangely desolate this area was. From this garden I could see the length of Plover Road, its division, which continued above the garage at the rear, see Oakes Road and the entrance to Union Street. Not a soul in sight, nor even a slinking cat or swooping bird. The only place hidden was behind the wall above the garden, but only a young child could have passed there without being seen. I shuddered. There was something eerie about the whole area. Go back to the fire; I chided myself, what are you standing out here for?

So I crossed the lawn, mounted the couple of steps to the back garden and made my way to the back door. Even then I paused and looked at the upper road and the lane. The gate was closed, purposely fitted so that it was hell to open, but it ensured that the girls couldn't run out easily. Then I went in the tiny entrance, opened the door to my left, took the five strides to the sink when I heard knocking on the back door. For a second I froze: it was impossible. No one could be there. But there was someone there and I could see her. When I opened the door I already knew who stood there.

There was a woman of medium height, slender, wearing a faded cotton dress, which might have once been green but now was a shadow of its former colour. Over it she wore no more than a thin cotton-like cardigan, again perfectly clean but so indeterminate as to defy description. No stockings and on her beautifully shaped feet a pair of thonged sandals. Involuntarily, I shivered for her. The poor thing must be nearly frozen for I had not yet thawed from my stint in the garden and I was wrapped in a thick woolly jacket.

But it was her head which riveted me, for it was remotely, classically beautiful. Ageless, sculptured, composed and crowned with plaited bands of hair, which was neither copper nor brown, nor golden. A perfect oval face, devoid of makeup, straight brows reflecting the colour of her hair and eyes of a colour which seemed to be an amalgamation of all natural woodland colours and which gazed at me levelly. Indeed, under my rude scrutiny she stood motionless, her arms hanging by her sides and a pair of twigs in one hand. She was the epitome of Nature, coalesced into fleeting colour, fleeting shape and when I had absorbed this regal creature she spoke:

'I am a Romany.'

And I thought: ' if you had said you were the Queen of the Romanies I would have believed you.'

'Will you give me a cup of tea?' she asked

'Yes' I replied, 'Come in.'

Before lunch I had banked the open coal fire and now it was a clear glowing mass of heat. Moving the big fireguard I seated her before it and plied her with tea and cake before returning to the sink to begin the endless task of paring vegetables. During this small interval I do not know what conversation we had, or indeed, if any conversation ensued. Possibly not, for she was totally composed, not with the arrogant composure bestowed by great wealth or worldly position, but rather as one who lives entirely within a body and is at one with the body.

There commenced on my part a most curious interlude for I was watching a scene being enacted by several people who seemed to be discussing something with great intensity and all the colours in the scene were brilliant, jewel-like colours. What they were discussing I couldn't follow, only that it seemed of great moment to them, nor could I estimate the importance of the discussion, only that it seemed to be of a really staggering import. Then abruptly it was gone and I turned my head to the right, returned completely now to the scene in my kitchen and it was as if time slowed, slowly dilated, so that I was gazing now in microscopic detail, knowing from the outset what my visitor would do and realizing I had known what she would do from the moment I noticed the twigs in her hand.

With no surprise I saw her lift her hand and toss the twigs onto the clear blazing fire. Amazingly, I saw them leap back onto the hearth, to lie intact and glowing. Instantly, I knew the significance of this: I had a choice. Now time whirred at impossible speed, I could barely breathe, but I had to choose and the choices were triple:

I could avert my head and ignore the episode

or

I could pick up the twigs and throw them onto the fire myself

or

I could pull away the hearth tidy and brush them beneath the fire to join the other ashes.

How long I was irresolute I cannot say, but it cannot have been for more than an instant or two. The twigs, which were near, but separate from each other, lay glowing but intact and for a fraction I could see beyond them, the reality beyond them, for these were symbols. Then, like a sleepwalker, with no conscious decision in my mind, I walked to the hearth, knelt, pulled away the tidy Betty with the tongs and took up the small hearth brush and shovel to put the ashes of the twigs beneath the fire to join the other ashes. Then I looked up at my visitor.

With utter composure she said:

'You will have two children only, remember what I say, remember my words, you will have two children only.'

Words rose in my throat and I could not speak them. I wanted to say: 'I know that, I've got two already', but it was impossible to voice the words.

The entire ambience changed. Before my eyes she changed from a queen into a slight worn figure; drank her tea, ate some cake and my younger daughter, who had been playing behind the sofa in silence emerged. They talked and the woman, bereft now of magic, talked a doll from my daughter, as is the way of gypsies. But as she left she turned to me and said:

'Remember my words, you will have two children only.'

She had been taken over by another mind, just as I had been. I was as skeptical and suspicious of charlatans as my husband, believing truly only what I myself lived. Having no taste for absorbing the pronouncements confidently bestowed upon the gullible I therefore embarked upon an enquiry at a number of houses in the area:

'Have the gypsies been round?' and the same reply from everyone 'No, we'd have warned you if they had.'

For periodically a group of swarthy brash women brandishing baskets of violently garish objects they insisted were 'flowers' used to threaten housewives who refused to buy their unspeakable goods and many women feared them and locked their doors. So who had my visitor been?

Feeling now a sense of impending doom, I had committed myself, or been committed to some tribulation which I dreaded. Cowardice consumed me. Not an agreeable sensation nor an attractive one.

Shamefully, I adopted an ostrich-like attitude: if I did not give credence to what I innately knew, it would not happen. This must not be put into words which my conscious mind could recognize as actual thoughts, for if I did so the thoughts would then have to be examined, giving them validation. Bury it all. Keep it all below ground, self deception is a very human characteristic, but for all my flat surface pretensions the truth would not and did not, could not be obliterated. I knew...

Two years later I became pregnant and went berserk. Ludicrous plans had formed in my mind: my girls were growing up now and in a few years time they would take off to live their own lives. After that I too would leave and hopefully find that cottage and space. Why I needed it so badly I did not know, only that I needed it as a thirsty desert traveller needs water. What I would do there I did not know, nor what might happen there; but the need was so great it seemed as if a slow fire was consuming me from the very centre of my person, given air it would have developed into a conflagration. At fifty-six I would die, but if I had to bring up another family there would be no time left and I would die as the most disappointed woman on earth. Luxuries had no value in this, just a roof, four walls and space; it seemed little enough to ask, but even that was going to be denied.

Eventually I calmed. Inevitably I settled down. Committed, I had to live with this and the subterranean knowledge surfaced. Faith in truth I had, but not enough; I had allowed the facile flat surface appearances to deceive me.

How could I have ever supposed that the seventeen year old self's experience would not, inevitably, come to fruition? During the intervening years the memory should have faded like an ancient photograph; it was as indelibly diamond-clear as if it had happened the previous night.

Together with the admission of truth I began to be enveloped in a strange, immensely benign, soft darkness, so filmy that smoke would have seemed coarse beside it and it was invisible to everyone but myself; so that in some strange manner I could not see it with my eyes, yet I could see it quite clearly. I knew also that the child to come would be a boy who would die and be buried in the Wesleyan graveyard.

I remembered something, which had occurred six weeks after our marriage. For no apparent reason, I had suddenly turned to my husband and said:

'You will never have sons from me.'

Even I, who had lived with this other sense all my life was startled, for it was as if I had opened my mouth in order to allow another person to use my voice and that which issued forth so positively belonged to another person. We had never discussed the possibility of children and we had been talking of another topic when the statement came forth. But when the statement appeared I knew it to be a truth, but not a truth which had originated in my brain, not a thought. Another truth had emerged on a very conscious level: I was not to be a widow: the infinitely dear person would be the child, not the man, for I knew now that I could love no man as I loved my children. How to cope with the grief? No choice now, it would have to be coped with somehow or other, but the insulating darkness helped.

Chapter 6 – Verification

Old friends arrived, laughing and ribald, I could hear the joking as my husband admitted them into our tiny front porch, but the first thing I noticed was Mary's coat. Black, rich looking, it swung from her shoulders shrieking 'Quality'.

I began 'By Jove, someone's come into money. Persian lamb, no less. Have you come to impress the poor and needy?'

Laughing, she shed the coat and laid it over my knees saying:

'It's partly why we've come, love. It isn't fur, it's fake. Roy can get it and we wondered if you'd like some. It's only a pound a yard, but it's a hell of a price in the shops.'

Instantly I rejected this proposal. I recognized this stuff for I had worn it twenty-one years earlier, before it had been invented.

I said 'Well it's kind of you to bother, but we've a lot of expense to face. There isn't a thing in the house for a baby and we'll have to start from scratch, pram, clothes, the lot. Anyway, I have a winter coat.'

Mary said 'And you've had it a long time. I know.'

Roy began 'For somebody who's starting all over again you deserve a present, doesn't she?' and he turned to my husband for agreement.

My husband was now in difficulty; to all others he was a generous man, but to me he was parsimonious. It was as if he dared not indulge me in any small luxury. It was as if he considered that I needed no luxury whatsoever, as if I were some kind of self-perpetuating mechanism, which only needed to be wound like a clock. If I made some small request his invariable answer was 'No' and he was in difficulty now for Roy cared little for money and Mary was quite indulged. Faced with the problem now of appearing mean he had to return something, so he muttered:

'She can have it if she wants it.'

I was determined not to have a coat of this stuff so I said:

'My old machine wouldn't sew this stuff.'

Serenely Mary said 'No problem, you can borrow my electric machine.'

I returned 'Look at me, love, I'm like a house end already. I couldn't even lean over to cut it out'

but Mary persisted 'I'll cut it out for you'

I insistently replied 'You're busy enough. I'm not having you cut out for me.'

But Roy said 'No problem, I can help cut it out. I'm not just a pretty face.'

Desperately I seized at straws 'I couldn't lean over to sew a coat, I'm too big already and I seem to get bigger by the day.'

Decisively Mary returned 'We'll make it for you, won't we Roy?' and he nodded.

I reiterated, 'I can't have that. We can't afford it, there's too much expense to face.' Lifting his eyebrows Roy turned to my husband 'Doesn't she argue? I don't know how you put up with it, lad.'

Mary said decisively 'We'll settle this once and for all. We'll buy the stuff and we'll make it for you. It'll be our present to you and you'll be able to wear it after the baby's born. O.K. Roy?'

I wanted to shout in despair: Don't you realize this baby is going to die? I've known for years this would happen. I saw the coat I'd wear for the funeral and it's this, this stuff. I don't want it. But I could not speak and finally, bowed to the inevitable yes, I would buy this cloth-that-looked-like-fur and make it myself.

Later I asked my mother if she would buy a suitable pattern, specifying no particular style and she brought a long, slimly cut style with a large face-framing collar. The hem was mid-calf, for the fashions had changed from the wartime cropped hems. I made the coat and as I mounted it on a hanger to put in my wardrobe I gazed at the finished article with choking despair. It would be. It would come.

However could I have supposed otherwise? This was truth, truth which was absolute. One may wriggle like a worm on a hook, may try to evade or gainsay, but no feeble maneuverings could alter what was to be. What my seventeen-year-old mind had supposed was fur was fake fur and what my seventeen-year-old mind had supposed was widowhood was also a fake illusion.

Bloated and ill I dragged myself through the summer months. Cherry had given me a list of home requirements one of which was a water repellent pad to cover our bed.

Inspecting my finished equipment she said, startled:

'What ever have you made it too thick for?'

Numbly I shook my head, unable to answer. It was as if I operated now on two levels. But the pad was needed, I had carried a cofferdam of water and Cherry, who had delivered Simon at the end of August said somberly:

'You needed that cover.'

The house exploded with visitors. 'A boy, a boy'. Wondering how they could all be so blind I lay, shattered. Only one of that excited throng knew the truth. Silent, without intrusion, he looked at me. My father knew. He said nothing, not then, not ever, but he knew. It was the following day before I was permitted to see Simon and he was blue. I knew what that meant. Heart trouble. Icy cold, the cold of death. That evening words emitted from my mouth which did not originate in my brain and certainly no medical knowledge existed there nor any previous information of a similar natural necessity. It was not I who spoke:

'Neil, if you want your son to live you have to hold him against your body, because only human body heat will warm him.'

Without demur he took his son inside his shirt and warmed him into life. This was for him the most precious being on earth, he loved his daughters and was a good father to them, but now he had a son, an extension of himself and for this child he would kill if need be. And it worked.

All medical staff involved with Simon expected him to die, but he did not, not then. It wasn't the right time. The right time would be in winter, no snow, no frost even, but it would be the northern chill where the winds blew from the sea, for there were no barriers for the Pennines.

Through the succeeding months Simon grew and survived. Friends came frequently, but one whom I'd known all my life, lovely Sybil, came almost daily. One day she said 'Won't he be a handsome man, Kathleen? He really is gorgeous. All your family are good looking, but you don't expect boys to be beautiful.'

I muttered something non-committal wondering if I had some physical defect. How could these people not know the truth? It seemed to flare in great black capitals throughout my days and I couldn't understand why they couldn't see them. Was I deformed in some respect? Was there some misalignment in my brain?

Christmas was just over and I had refused to feed the hordes we used to entertain, so we were quite quiet. One evening the girls had been invited somewhere or other and I had the evening to myself in the sitting room. My husband piled the kitchen table with his papers and set to work. Simon was asleep in his pram and it was quite late when I went into the kitchen to make tea. In horror, I walked into an icebox, for my husband had let the fire go out although a huge bucket of coal was ready to hand.

I said crossly 'Have you no sense? How could you let it go so cold, you know he mustn't be cold' and I lifted Simon, but it was too late, he was blue with cold. Immediately, the convulsions began. The beginning of the end. Late as it was our doctor came and as the convulsions had ceased I began to apologize.

Kindly, very seriously, he said this was no wild goose chase. I could have added that it was a futile chase, but I did not. Seven days passed during which Simon periodically suffered convulsive attacks. Drearily I thought that it didn't seem possible for a small baby to last for so long. Then I had another vision.

At once I knew this was Buxton and wondered helplessly what on earth I was doing in Buxton of all places? I had visited the place a few times in my life, but knew it very slightly. It was very lovely there and I looked about. This was quite a steep hill, but part of it had been made into a garden, terraced in stone, but the small holding walls were double sided and filled with multicoloured flowers, which spilled in profusion, so it seemed as if the whole hillside up to the forest, which lay along the perimeter, was a glorious tumbling cascade. Warm, too. Involuntarily I looked down and was astonished to see that I was wearing a frock of pale lavender silk with a wide flowing skirt. Having never owned such a frock I wondered how I had come by it for it wasn't a colour I'd ever have chosen to wear.

As I puzzled an appalling phenomenon began, for baby mice fell from beneath the hem to lie around me in a circle. Palest softest grey, with underbellies of almost white, each tiny paw rigid in the air.

Instantly I awakened. It would not be long now. Death was very near. And for three days there was no more sleep. The last night of Simon's life my husband chose to stay up, for someone stayed with him all the time. At four am he said brokenly:

'This has been the happiest night of my life.'

I thought: 'Oh, you poor creature.'

Words did not come easily to him and he choked on the little he was able to say:

'We, we've been together all night and he laughed sometimes' then could go no further.

I guessed, knew, the bond which had been exchanged. Essentially a lonely man, for his parents were dreadful people, he had sought all his life for such a bonding, for that curious alchemy which defies description yet which is possible between two human persons. It is as if a powerful invisible rod of steel magnetizes them into a whole. I bled for him that morning. Then he left.

Later I sponged Simon very lightly. His tiny hands could no longer grasp and the death rattle had begun, interspersed with dreadful convulsions. Then I did something I have never done earlier with babies, I propped him against a pillow. My mother arrived, took one look and cried in horror:

'Kathleen, you mustn't prop him up like that. He can't die like that, you must lie him down' then she softened and went on gently 'Look, love, let me do it for you. I can see it's something you can't do for yourself.'

I said abruptly, 'No, this is something I must do. Just give me a minute.'

I walked into the kitchen to gather myself together. Then I walked into the sitting room, lifted my son's downy head and laid him down. He gave a long shuddering gasp and was gone. He had only been on loan, so to speak and I had to voluntarily give him back.

Agitated now, my mother said 'I'll have to go and tell your father. There are arrangements which have to be made and he'll do all that's necessary, but it means leaving you on your own. Shall I fetch somebody, love? Shall I fetch one of your neighbours?'

'No, thank you' I answered 'if you'll go and do what has to be done you don't have to worry about me. I'll be all right here.'

She bustled off and when she was out of sight I walked to the big mantel mirror and saw the face I had not seen or noticed for days. But twenty-one years ago I had seen this face, ice cold, frozen in grief and the grief was here, now, splintering and lacerating as if tiny knives were slicing all my cells. Yet none of this showed in the white immobility, which stared back at its identical twin. More than grief here, there was a numbing inexplicable horror. A nameless unidentifiable dread.

On that pristine hearth there had been two twigs, two symbols and I knew now what the symbols had represented. This was not ended. There was more to come. That frozen mask must not splinter; my husband would need my strength.

Later that morning I saw Agnes walking up School Street, so by the time she arrived, I had the door opened for her. For a moment we stood in the tiny porch and from the fanlight above the door I could see the tears pouring down her face although it was obvious that she was oblivious to them.

She cried 'Oh, love, oh my love, I don't know what to say to you.'

I replied, 'It's all right, pet, you don't need to say anything.'

She went on 'I met your mother as I was coming from work and she told me. So I called at home first to bring you this. D'you remember my mother having that vault built when my dad died?'

Wonderingly I said 'Yes, now you come to mention it I do. It was brick lined wasn't it?'

'Yes,' said Agnes 'She had it done properly. She decided that we should all be buried together but I'll be damned if my brother's going there and I don't want to be buried there, I want to be cremated. But I couldn't bear the thought of you burning that beautiful little boy, Kathleen. Please don't have him burned, love, I, I couldn't bear it. See, I've brought you the grave papers, they're yours now.'

And poor Agnes broke down completely.

Later I thought with icy detachment: All the pieces are assembled now. I am the woman in the vision and the girls are just the right height. The funeral will be in the Wesleyan Churchyard and the coat is ready and waiting. Involuntarily I ran my fingers through my bouncy untamable hair and thought: there's only the funeral to make the vision complete.

On a chilly day in January under a sky of unbroken palest grey we buried our son and as I tore off a red rose to drop on the tiny coffin I tore my finger and my blood joined the rose. Somehow it seemed as appropriate as the words of Ernest Dowson which had haunted me at every turn throughout the whole pregnancy and which I had written upon the sheaf of roses:

'They are not long, the days of wine and roses
Out of a misty dream
Our path emerges for a while
Then closes within a dream'

But which was the true reality and which was the dream? No doubt as to the answer. That which I 'saw' was the reality. That was truth. This was the misty dream. There was a factor which I could not understand. When I had stood in School Street at the age of seventeen I had seen my person inside a large shining sphere. Immediately following Simon's death, there were many callers bringing condolences and I saw all, buildings included, outlined in this shimmering radiance. I found I could see inside people and when the surface idiosyncrasies were discarded, they were beautiful and the surface characteristics of no account.

Nothing need be said of the grief, it is already written; I lived with it on a daily basis from the time I knew of the pregnancy. I thought often of the words of the drunken Persian poet:

'The moving finger writes; and, having writ,
Moves on: nor all your Piety nor Wit
Shall lure it back to cancel half a Line,
Nor all your Tears wash out a Word of it.'

The Rubàyàt of Omar Khayyàm

Chapter 7 – Evading Christians

My mother had told her cronies of Simon's death and at the church she attended a new minister had been appointed. Filled with zeal he came to visit me and asked if I would like to kneel with him to pray. Immediately I decided that he must rid himself of the assumption that because my mother was one of his flock, ergo, I must be one also. I had no desire to injure him, or belittle his beliefs; nor had I any desire to inform of my beliefs, for to strangers that was a forbidden area. To my friends in general also, come to that. I had made no secret of the fact that Simon would die to a few, a very few of them and to one I had even disclosed where he would be buried. But to the world in general and to this young man in particular I was not about to declare:

'I have a Sixth Sense'.

To his credit he did not argue as I explained with all the politeness I could muster that I had my own beliefs; they were not his beliefs; that I would not attempt to disrupt his beliefs, but I would not accept his. He took it very well. It was succinct, but it left a vacuum and as it was obvious that he was Welsh I diverted the conversation immediately by saying that I loved the works of his native poet, Dylan Thomas. It worked very well and to my surprise we became good friends. The friendship surprised many who knew me and delighted my mother who supposed he'd talk me round eventually. I did not disillusion her.

Below the Christian ethic lay a Welshman and below the Welshness lay a Celt. And the Celt it was that knew … Subsequently, I shall write his name as 'Eli' plagiarizing the name of the distracted old person in 'Under Milk Wood'. Eli's wedding was imminent and he asked permission to bring his new bride after the honeymoon. She was a passionate believer and at first she assumed that after meeting her I would belt into church like a ferret down a rabbit hole.

Eli said warningly:

'Gwynnie, I told you before we came …'

'But she's one of us' cried this slender evangelist; unable to comprehend that we could be friends without automatically sharing the identical beliefs. Not one to abandon a battleground without a fight she pursued the matter until Eli decided he'd had enough and ministerially brought an end to the argument. I simply listened.

Their visit was short and crisp and I did not doubt that hot words were exchanged on their way home. In a way I felt rather sorry for her, for her beliefs and adherence were so plainly sincere, so why not tread their avenue? Cautiously I admitted to belief in 'something' without being any more specific. All the unspecified she provided from theology. It has to be said that I felt sorry for her also, for I had had years of fending off eloquent appeals to 'Come and join us' of many persuasions, could have advised her to 'box at your own weight, love' but I refrained. She was an innocent: who was I to damage her illusions?

Inevitably, matters came to the boil. They called one evening during the week and Gwynnie began:

'I know how you feel Kathleen and I won't go on. But a friend of ours is coming to preach on Sunday and I'm asking you now to come and hear him. He's getting famous for his preaching and he's just brilliant. If you'll only come on Sunday you can hear him and then come to supper afterwards and meet him. I promise you'll be amazed.'

Eli said sternly 'Gwynnie, don't start.'

She would not be gainsaid this time:

'If we don't bring Kathleen into our church we won't be doing our Christian duty. You know as well as I know that Phil has brought more converts into our religion than anyone for years. If she hears the word of God from him she'll come, I know she will.'

As this flowed I was standing with my hand on the back of the sofa and I then made the first declaration of my life concerning what I believed:

'Understand me well for I shall only say this once to you. I do not believe what parsons, ministers or priests say concerning God, especially those who talk of God as if they were holding one-to-one conversations. Something exists, yes, a mighty Force, but a person who issues directives as to what this Force thinks is to me, a blasphemy. It is my belief that simply to know that such a Force exists is a bonus for any human being, but I will not listen to anyone who claims to interpret, on behalf of a God they have never seen, what that God thinks. It is not only an insult but a blasphemous insult.'

As I spoke a vast benign atmosphere, dark, yet darkly brilliant formed in my room like a vapor without end. A huge smiling Benignity and I can summon no other words to describe it. But for all her passion, Gwynnie could not feel it, nor could Eli, but I think something passed and brushed him. Certainly it cured Gwynnie of her attempts to the Sunday luring, although we went out together frequently. I showed them something of Yorkshire and it surprised them to find it was not coated in 'dark satanic mills' from end to end.

One evening Eli and Gwynnie brought a visitor who was staying at the manse and when I learned she had just returned from Africa I plied the dark, rather saturnine faced woman with questions. For some time I had developed a passion for that riotous land and read all I could lay my hands on about it. Here was a feast indeed. But when she said:

'They used to come out of the bush with terrible ailments, but they had to accept our religion before we treated them. If they didn't we sent them back.'

Was she a true representative of the missionary fervour? Futile to speculate. I shall write no more on the topic.

Almost a couple of years since the death of Simon. Grief had wounded my husband. My grief stayed inside, sealed. Then I began to be quite ill and noises were made implying that I would have to have surgery. Within a couple of days I felt the baby move and I knew I was pregnant again. The following night I had another vision.

It wasn't a large room that I found myself in, but it was larger than a domestic sitting room and it was quite empty. Cream coloured throughout and functional, no more, but there was no clue whatsoever as to its function. Perfectly rectangular in shape and before me was the longer side of the rectangle. To my left, at the end of the facing wall was a door and somehow I supposed that another door lay at the far end of the same wall. There being nothing else to see I looked at the door and decided that as doors went it was a poor affair. Plain narrow architraves, so it was a modern door. It struck me that the whole building was modern, no stone here, this was a newish construction and to one who had always lived in stone built houses with solid wooden doors and architraves I rather snobbishly despised such buildings. This room was many floors up, although I couldn't imagine how I knew this for there were no windows.

What on earth was I doing here, anyway, standing in an empty room looking at this un-craftsman like stuff?

'I think I'll go' I decided.

Immediately, the door opened and a very young man entered in total silence. Had I not been looking at this door I wouldn't have been aware that anyone had entered. Certainly there was not the slightest indication that he knew I was there and I wanted at least to pass the time of day, it seemed silly for two people to be in an empty room without even a 'how do you do'. He had closed the door and now simply stood half facing the opposite shorter wall, but never looking at me directly.

So I looked at him very directly indeed, in fact I inspected him from head to foot. That statement needs amending, for in no vision did I ever see feet; we simply assume when we see an upright person that whoever it is must own feet. Like many facile assumptions this is untrue. He was very slight indeed and I fancied that he had one shoulder rather higher than the other which made him appear to be leaning slightly. I couldn't assess him properly for he was dressed in a suit of a mid-blue heavy tweedy stuff, with fine white and pink hairs woven into it and I felt rather disdainful about this. Whoever would think of dressing a youth in such unsuitable clothes? If I'd had the dressing of him he wouldn't be wearing that stuff, I decided. But I had not had any choice of clothes, so it was none of my business. It was a pity, all the same.

His hair was palest gold, but his head seemed a little too large for so slight a frame although it was well shaped. He had a broad forehead and blue eyes, but he didn't seem to be focused on anything, strangely withdrawn as if he were unaware of his surroundings. Certainly, I felt he was unaware of me. The lower part of his face tapered rather too much for the size of his head so that it appeared triangular whereas for real beauty he ought to have been more square jawed.

Without warning an emotion began in me, which developed rapidly, powerfully. I wanted to cross the room and take this young man in my arms, to cuddle him and say:

'There, there love'.

I was beginning to love him, was loving him desperately but for some reason I could not cross the intervening space for a barrier was there, quite invisible.

Then and only then he moved without turning his head to acknowledge my presence. He moved along the line of the long facing wall and I assumed he was going to leave by the corresponding door from which he had entered. But it was only as he reached the right hand end that I saw my casual assumption to be wrong. There was no door, it was an open aperture and beyond it lay complete darkness.

Choking now with fear, with love, with anguish I was crying desperately:

'No, don't go, don't go' but he did not give me a single glance.

Now I knew the identity of the aperture, it was a grave and with no pause he moved straight into it. Blackness.

I was awake instantly, gripped in remorseless dread. Pictures flitted through my mind like a mad kaleidoscope, shifting and flashing. I saw again the two twigs lying on my hearth and cursed myself for a complaisant fool. I had known all along what these symbols meant and refused to bring forth the knowledge. Coward. Fool. Some part of me had agreed to this misery when I agreed to the decision. It was my own fault. This son I was carrying would also die and I would have to put up with it as best I may. I thought back to my ignorant seventeen year old self; I had known then that I would have a hard life and it was here and now. Would I even be able to cope living day by day in the knowledge that death lay at the end? Well, I'd have to, there was no choice in the matter. Four months to go and each day of those months brought death a day nearer. Not life. Death. It was so much that I felt self-pity, I wallowed in it, fool that I was.

One afternoon Eli called without Gwynnie and I told him there was going to be a death. I did not describe the details, only that it would be. His face was dark and sombre, but he said little – indeed, there was nothing to be said – but the Celt knew it to be true. Weirdly I saw the knowledge sink remorselessly through the upper layers, his nationhood, his training, his position in the world, the implacable teachings of his church were all porous and the truth sank through the facile layers to the true human being below.

Following my first idiotic maunderings a curious phenomenon arrived, invisible and I spoke of it to no one. It was as if I were cocooned in a measureless dark blanket, which never diminished, never altered, yet it seemed to act like an enormous cushion, insulating in boundless stability and I could see my person, sick and wretched, in the centre.

Sick and wretched without doubt, I was ill and became more ill. Came the day when I had to attend the clinic and the wind had arrived undiminished from Siberia. The kind nursing sister, whom I knew well, said:

'You silly girl, why have you come out in this weather?'

I did not say that the new young nurse to whom I had said the previous week:

'I don't think I can manage these visits' had replied acidly 'If that is the case I can tell you now that if I'm on duty when you go into labour I shan't come.'

So I had wearily dragged myself to the clinic thinking that if I didn't get help then I would be up the creek and it was just my luck that she would be on call when I needed help. As I cannot tell these names without permission I will name the sister as Molly and Molly knew my history. Matron came in:

'What's she saying?'

Molly said 'She says it doesn't matter. I've been telling her she shouldn't have come out in this weather and she says what are we bothering about, the baby's going to die anyway. I've just told her that if she says it again, I'll slap her.'

Matron said firmly 'I'll slap her myself.'

I looked at the two lovely, loving people and smiled. Matron said gently:

'This isn't going to be another Simon, love. Lightning doesn't strike twice in the same place. You're going to have another lovely one, just like your girls.'

The sweet concerned faces mirrored their sympathy, so I said no more. But it was my last outing on my feet for months, for the following day I was confined to bed and there I stayed. Ill and getting several other illnesses too, one of which brought a specialist from the new hospital who insisted I be admitted and only the intervention of my kind doctor saved me. But I had to promise that if there was a reoccurrence of the problem I would tell at once, so I gave my word.

Christmas passed and the day arrived when I knew without the slightest anxiety, that I was dying. When my husband came from work I asked if he would help get me upstairs to my own bed. In utter bliss I lay there, seeing clearly dark, smoke-like tendrils of darkness gathering and enfolding, wanting no more than to sink gratefully into this peace. A peace to be shattered as the door flew open and my lovely elder daughter flung herself beside me weeping uncontrollably: an appalling argument had begun between my husband and my family and she had heard my mother say that I was dying and that he should call my doctor, which he refused to do. I shall not write the wounding words, but simply tell that of which my daughter cried:

'Mummy, you won't die and leave me will you? What will I do if you die? Promise me, promise me you won't die' and I stroked her lovely head saying, 'I promise I won't die' and she knew I would keep it, for I never made them a promise which I did not keep.

The trouble began and I kept the promise I had given the specialist. Ten minutes later I was being wheeled along a corridor and the face above me was Cherry's. Cherry saved my life. And the circumstances were equally miraculous; indeed she repeated them over and over throughout that night:

'Kathleen, if I hadn't been here you'd have died, for nobody would have known how you give birth and they couldn't have dealt with it. I was actually leaving because I've got a new job and when I finished my last shift they asked if I'd come in tonight as a favour because they're short handed. So I did, but I shouldn't be here, but if I hadn't been you'd be dead' and she muttered this over and over, 'It's a miracle I'm here.'

During the early hours she returned:

'Kathleen, your baby is very sick, but I'll do all I can, you know that, don't you?'

'Yes love, I know. Don't worry; I know what's going to happen. I've know for months' and the tears came as if from my very toenails.

Terrified, she did that which no trained nursing sister should do; she flung herself on the bed beside me and wept also. My thank you's to my daughter and Cherry are hopelessly inadequate, but I record them here, for they saved my life.

Visitors arrived with differing messages, all of which were meaningless, but most were given in deep sympathy and for that I was grateful.

Eli said, his face dark and unfathomable, 'Kathleen love, would you like me to baptize him?'

I replied, 'Thank you, no. I forbid it.' Then added, 'Eli, d'you suppose the God in which you believe would refuse a new baby because it was unbaptized?'

He said with difficulty, 'I wish I was as sure of my own salvation.'

And I never felt so sorry for anyone in my life. He was living within strict conventions and I was living outside those conventions. His were formal and socially acceptable, mine were decidedly unacceptable. The difference was that I was living mine and they were true; socially disdained, but they actually happened. And a deeply buried part of him knew it.

A dichotomy here: the churches forbade all practice of precognitive utterances, labelling them as unnatural and devilish whilst holding before their congregations mysterious delights which were precognitive in essence yet improvable in character. My mother was as devout a believer as any minister could wish for and believed implicitly that precognitive statements not only could be given by certain mediums, but were also reliable, were indeed a truth. In this Eli and she were allied, so whilst professing very publicly the church's teachings, each in their own way demonstrated that they believed precognitive statements. It couldn't be said that I reached any satisfactory conclusions as yet, but at least I could recognize the existing dichotomy. Which was more than they did themselves.

Ensconced now in a small ward, aware that news must have travelled concerning my history and my present, but no one mentioned the deaths of babies although a mute would have realized they knew. I did not disturb the charade, but when the truly wonderful ward sister approached me I asked:

'Can I see him?'

She looked at me with profound pity and said gently:

'my dear, do you think it is wise?'

Answering firmly 'I am sure it is not. But can I see him?'

She said reluctantly 'If you insist, but I'd rather you didn't.'

I said simply 'I have to.'

Acquiescing, she wheeled me to the nursery. My son lay just as I had seen him four months or so earlier, dressed in the heavy twill of hospital clothes. A barrier lay between us of clear glass, so I could not take him in my arms to say: 'There, there' and cuddle him. I realized that I had had to see him partially grown for he had to cross the room in this new hospital with its meagre architraves, its cream coloured walls, high in this concrete structure. As a tiny baby he could not have crossed the room, but the tiny pink and white flecks in the blue suiting had been symbolic flecks to show that it clothed a baby.

Obliged to leave him there he died two weeks later. I was told he had a collapsed lung. It was an explanation of sorts, no doubt, but the true explanations lay far deeper.

Six months later my husband agreed we could go house hunting. I could hear my sons crying in the night and although he would have died rather than admit it I believed that he could also. Eventually, we found a house.

Chapter 8 – Escape To Reality

In retrospect I shall always think of our new home as a Galatea, for the very prosperous man who caused it to be built owned the business which provided the materials and craftsmen. Because it was for his own use he bankrupted himself in the building of it and could not leave it. I saw him in microscopic detail, even though he had been dead for many years (the house was a hundred years old). Except he wasn't dead; he occupied the big curving staircase which rose from the long hall to the second floor. As according to social ethics he was dead and could not therefore argue I will give his name: Garner.

Taking as a yardstick the average semi-detached house, this house was very large indeed and in quality of building and materials it made even the best of semis look like a pathetic shack. Our problem was that a staggering amount of work needed to be done and it was just what was needed for I was too tired every day to think. Re-wiring had had to be done and as the walls were like marble avenues they had been chiseled to accommodate the conduits, which in turn meant more cleaning work. I was on hands and knees scrubbing the floor of the first landing and having begun at the end of a passageway I was now working on the landing proper. It was a lovely day and light poured in from the door at the passage end. Above a half landing to my right was a huge aureole window and behind me was a vast room with three windows, so all in all, the landing was bright with light. For weeks I had felt a presence in the lower staircase, so strongly at times that I had turned my head quickly in the hope of seeing the watcher. As I scrubbed I became intensely aware of a watcher and turned to my right.

Garner. It could be no other. He was standing on the landing at the top of the first flight of stairs and the look of perplexed concern on his face instantly set me laughing. His alarm and anxiety were so ludicrous it was impossible not to laugh and by comparison with his appearance it was even more ludicrous. For here was the classic example of the prosperous Victorian gentleman, country style. A tall man, appearing even taller with the long stovepipe trousers and high buttoned Norfolk jacket, all beautifully tailored in a revolting pepper and salt material. Garner had quite a long aristocratic nose, thin, above a fairly thin, rather gloomy mouth. In spite of his what would have then been sartorial elegance, his mind and thoughts were of an agitated elderly hen. If he could have spoken he would have cried:

'What are you doing to my lovely house? Why are you chiseling my perfect walls? Tearing up my floorboards and disturbing the sawdust I made them pack in to keep the house warm. What are those things you are using? Who are you anyway, this is mine. Mine. Go away.'

But if such noises could have been heard they would have emerged as clucks.

'Oh dear,' I thought, 'don't be so cruel. He's worried out of his mind and you mustn't laugh. Coax him. Comfort him. He's a very unhappy ghost.'

He was in some curious limbo, which nothing could reach. Idiotic as it all seems I couldn't forget him (it was impossible to forget him for he haunted the staircase perpetually) and very quickly I began to mourn the deeper implications, which were here involved. This was but one example of a truly staggering aspect of human approach to life and death and it is really very simple: if one chains oneself to one's possessions in life, the reverse chaining will occur after death. That is exactly what Garner was suffering. Yet it need not be so, for there are realms of delight when we no longer occupy a body … but I must not flout chronology here.

I bought at auction many things at prices no one now could believe possible. I filled the vast rooms with beautiful pieces, using my small earnings for the purpose – for now I had taken a part-time job – it was only in the knowledge that sooner or later I would leave all behind and go to find my space, my cottage. It was a need greater than food, clothes, status or possessions and by now there lay inside me a large glowing furnace of need, not want. Not the fulfillment of some idle desire. Nor was there any obvious reason, however bizarre, that could explain this all-consuming need. It appeared to be purposeless for I had not, at any time, known why this need burned so terribly; and on the face of it, it appeared to be an aberration, but I had learned a little by now, not much, but enough to know that the obvious 'faces' were deceptive. Truth, real truth was something else, something entirely different. Every question begs another: 'Different from what?'

Friends said, with the frankness of old friends:

'All these bare walls; you need some pictures in this house.'

Those who had known me since childhood said:

'Why don't you paint some yourself?'

Rusty as a piece of old left over iron I began to paint a little, aware that whatever miniscule amount of talent I had once possessed was unlikely to return. It was a start, no more.

During this period when we had settled in the big house and begun to accumulate some rather good 'pieces' my father had begun the habit of strolling down through the park on Sunday mornings for a shortish visit. Any new (to us) piece was shown to him, for I well knew his liking for craftsmanship of beautiful wood, leather, stone – any and all natural materials however simply designed were his forte. He owned a very beautiful watch chain of rose-gold and it had been agreed years earlier that I would inherit this chain. For the past eighteen months he had been trying to give me the chain and my reply was always the same:

'Daddy, I will take that chain when you have no further use for it.'

Meaning of course, that I would only take it when he was dead.

Defying statistical analysis, my father had served in the RFA for almost the whole of the First Great War, returning home with a body littered with shrapnel and a duodenal ulcer and the latter had made him into an irascible man. Of country stock, he was a tall man with a huge skeleton covered by skin and little flesh. For some time his ulcer had been giving increasing concern together with undoubted pain to which he did not refer.

It was a beautiful Sunday morning in July and he was sitting on a couch near the big mullioned windows of the south-facing sitting room. He had long legs which were stretched before him and it is this sight which is indelible in my memory of him.

Casually he said:

'I can't work any longer sweetheart and I don't want to live when I can't work.' Then he added 'I want you to take your chain.'

There was a small silence.

Now I write the conversation, which was unheard, could not be heard for to human ears it was silent. He said:

'I am going to die soon and I want to give you your chain with my own hands. I've had a good innings and there are things I wish I had done. But I love you and you have been my favourite child all your life. Let me give you the chain myself. It's a part of existence and it has to happen to all living things. I took life by the throat and shook the hell out of it. I know you understand and you understand what I'm telling you. Don't grieve for me. I've done more living in my span than a thousand I could name.'

Even for this I could not and muttered,

'Daddy, I can't. I'll have it when you've no further use for it.'

It must be admitted that for a second I was tempted, picturing the feel of the wonderfully wrought links flowing through my hands, but it could not be. Why, I did not know. Of a certainty it would come, but not yet, not this way. He did not argue or remonstrate, but rose to his long length and departed.

Increasingly and in conjunction with Parkinson's Law which roughly interpreted means that available space becomes occupied, we began to live a quite full social existence and time passed with what appeared to be an accelerated rate of knots. Perpetually I was busy, frequently working an eighteen-hour day. It was a day in September when I admitted my mother, hoping I would not have to listen to the vagaries and idiosyncrasies of members of her numerous committees. But no, she was almost agitated and this was unusual.

She began, 'You had better be told, your father is going to see a specialist. He's getting worse Kathleen and I'm worried. I don't know what to feed him on, for it's getting so that he can't keep anything down, not even Complan. I've made him egg custards all these years and he can't even keep those down now. Something will have to be done soon for he has to eat, but he's sick all the time. Sometimes I've caught him being sick, but I think there're times when he is and he doesn't tell me.'

I wanted to say abruptly: 'Mother, haven't you realized he's dying?' but I could only make conciliatory noises, thinking all the while of the silliness of all this superfluous conversation. Didn't she know? Couldn't she see? He knew. Why was she fussing so? For she was not normally a fussing indecisive woman, rather the contrary, she was tough and clear-headed where illness was concerned. She left in indecision, for I could not make placatory assurances that yes, he would be cured. And she was not happy.

Anyone who demands that a date will be given for any particular event will be filled with chagrin, for since the deaths of my sons I have been unable to remember dates. I know the birth dates of my daughters and no one else's. I cannot remember the birthdays of my sons, nor the dates of their deaths. It was as if a shutter fell in my mind and now I remember eras, small and large. For this I offer no apology. Consequently, I can only say that the following vision occurred either late September or in the first weeks of October. It was sometime during the night and my body was in bed.

I was not. I was standing with my back to the kitchen sink facing the dog leg section of the hall. I discovered wearily that I was wearing my blue working dress and a pinafore. I thought:

'Oh, for heaven's sake, what else is there to do? I thought I'd finished work for today and now I'm back again. What have I forgotten now?'

The only light to supplement the hall had been in the vestibule so we had installed a light in the ceiling at the foot of the staircase. All inner walls of this house were built of stone, but I saw, with no surprise, that I could gaze through the walls and I did so with shock, instantaneously deepening into alarm, which was followed by choking terror. A figure, immensely tall, was standing motionless beneath the light, a figure of pure horror, but as I, with my impaired sight, could not distinguish outlines clearly, it knew. Dreadfully, unspeakably, it knew I couldn't see it clearly and I had to see it clearly, so it began to move. There was something inexorable about this developing scene, which transfixed me with an unreasoning fear, which seemed to melt my very bones. Whatever I felt, whatever I suffered here would have to be, irrespective of any feelings or thoughts I might entertain. This figure was going to come and I was going to have to see it properly and I would have given all I possessed not to have to know this figure.

It stood at the end of the hall, seeming to dwarf the kitchen door, but from this stance the light was now behind the figure, so it stood in silhouette; and for an infinitesimal fraction of time I knew relief for I could see no details. It knew. Oh my God, it knew. And in the knowing it moved so that the hall light fell full on its face and its face was the face of hell. Was it then that I began to scream? I, the icy self-contained? Was it then I began to weep torrents of tears? I, the frozen mask? Yet even then I could not see in detail for the figure was in profile and it moved soundlessly, moved to its original location.

Frantic with terror: how to get out of the kitchen? To run, God knew where, to flee it matter not where and I realized with sickening despair that from this one site in the house there was no escape. The keys were in the sitting room to my left and the small annex to my right was locked with keys on the same ring. To go out into the hall to get the keys in the sitting room and unlock the French door in that room was unthinkable, for I would have to see that figure again. Nor to leave by the front door, for the ultimate horror would be having to pass the figure and flee along the hall. Then I knew with a certainty bordering on insanity that this had only been a respite, it was going to return and when it did I would have to see it.

As if on cue, for it knew what I was thinking, it moved to the end of the hall, passed the sitting room door to arrive at the end of the kitchen full face. Now I know I was screaming like a banshee, weeping so that I could feel the water clouding my face, hair, neck and clothes, for it moved toward me and light must have arrived from somewhere for I could see it now in detail.

A skull, not dead, this was a living skull. Sparse hairs clung to the great white dome and the great forehead. Beneath the ridges were two blood-flecked eyes, which stood proud of their sockets, so the orbs were huge, rigid, yet soundlessly screaming. I could feel the screams coursing through my own body. A prow of a nose, stripped of all flesh, the great nostrils flared into dark caves which yet issued screams and which did not seem to lift or breathe. The skin covered cheeks were a grimace of skin through which the whitened skull protruded, yet even that decay was a screaming decay. But lower, what should have been a mouth was a rictus, a wolf's snarl, gaping and bloody and from it the howls which could not be heard, but only felt, emerged foaming and blood flecked. Beneath, lay another mouth, bloody and snarling. This living skull had had its throat cut.

Of immense height it moved soundlessly toward me and my body dissolved into unimaginable terror. It was cloaked in a dark filmy material, finer than smoke and obscenely, defying all known laws, defying all known reality, the filmy stuff flowed out before the approaching figure which I now knew would engulf me. Now I knew its name and its name was Death.

I became enwrapped in the forward flowing folds, then a strange and wonderful thing happened: my father's big brown hand was holding my right hand, his courage flowed into my hand and up my arm like tiny darts of blue flame and he was speaking to me, urgently, over and over:

'It's all right, sweetheart, its all right, sweetheart.'

Bemused I heard and saw my husband, hurting physically now for his hands were grasping my shoulders as he shook me into consciousness. He was shouting in anger:

'What the hell is the matter with you, woman? You've been yelling and shouting like a mad woman. Can't a man get his sleep without you carrying on like a lunatic?'

Furiously he turned away. My head and pillow were soaked, so I must have wept in my sleep. That was all the sleep I would get this night. Now I knew what was going to happen and it would be too terrible for words, so I told no one.

Two days later my mother arrived, breathless with news:

'Your father's been to see the specialist and the specialist says he'll operate if your father agrees. You know our old doctor said he'd never do it because it was too dangerous, well this chap says they know more now and there's a chance. Your father asked him what sort of a chance and the chap said about fifty-fifty was the best he could promise'. So he came home and told me and he asked me what he should do.

I said: 'It's a decision you'll have to make for yourself. You can't possibly make a decision like that for anyone else.'

So he went for a walk to think about it and when he came back he said:

'I'm going to take a chance. I've backed horses at a lot worse odds and I can't go on living like this.'

My mother concluded 'So he's going to have it done, Kathleen and I've come to ask you what you think?'

For a moment or two I could make no reply. Stunned, I thought: she knows I know the answer, I don't know how she knows, but she knows I have an answer. Equally surely, I could not tell her. It would be too frenetically brutal. I had a burden now and I would have to carry this burden alone, it was not one I could hang around anyone's neck, although I felt like the Ancient Mariner loaded with a dead albatross. It would be too cruel. My mother was a born worrier, there was no way I could give her this worry. Carefully I replied:

'Oh, I agree with you. It's a decision for him to make, no one can make such a choice for anyone but themselves.'

It was not the reply she expected so she departed dissatisfied without quite knowing why. She wanted to know the outcome of the matter, not the mechanisms which would form the outcome, nor could she say,

'I know you know the outcome.'

Nightmarish conditions began the night following the surgery performed on my father and part of the nightmare began that evening because I had stupidly not read that vision correctly. In total trepidation we walked into the ward and up to his bedside. I had expected to find a dying skeleton and to my utter amazement he was sitting up in bed grinning from ear to ear, his intensely blue eyes sparkling with charisma and full of plans. He said to my mother:

'I'm absolutely fine love and I tell you what we'll do next spring, we'll go to Canada to see Shirley.'

The latter was my younger sister. Dumbfounded, I could barely mutter a greeting, managing to give my congratulations, which I knew sounded hollow and insincere. My mother gave me one swift sideways glance, but made no comment. Our visiting hour passed quickly; given his gregarious nature he had made the acquaintance of many of the other patients and regaled us with their social and medical histories. Later, outside the hospital, she said tartly:

'You didn't sound exactly overjoyed to find him so well.'

I replied, 'Of course I'm pleased, it's incredible. I couldn't believe he could have made such a recovery.'

But she was not deluded and gave me a look of distrustful dislike. Thus we parted and I chose to take the long walk home, hoping to meet no one, hoping not to have to speak to anyone, for my world had crashed about me. Never before had I realized the full extent of my belief in those visions. It had been implicit. That I was lacerated into bleeding shreds by them was of no consequence; they had informed me of a truth which did not exist in the world I knew. To suppose them now to be a lie, a mockery, a distortion of a truth was knowledge not to be borne. If these visions were untrue, deceitful, then no truth existed in the world and by extension, the universe. I seemed to be walking on a tilting planet, all values a hideous sham. Literally, I walked through an earthquake, for the measure of my belief had been totally absolute and I wanted to die, to be gone, my mind could not encompass the destruction of my faith that the truths I had seen were a reality and not a cosmic joke.

When we walked to his bedside the following evening he was dying. Unable to speak, he was struggling for every breath and death was written in huge letters over his head. An old soldier in the adjacent bed told us painfully,

'He's a game 'un, your lad. They were run off their feet this morning and they asked him if he could do his own ablutions. So he took his tackle and set off down the ward, then he fainted and he's burst the wound open. He's been like this ever since, poor lad. But he's a game 'un all right. They should never have got him up in the first place.'

I whispered to my mother, 'Come, let's go' for I knew now that those visions were never wrong, it was I who had been the fool. But if he died now, tonight, which he was visibly doing, he would be spared the agony-to-come. She drew away as if my touch was poisonous and literally snarled,

'Shut up, don't say another word.'

There appeared a curious phenomenon, for I seemed to shrink and dwindle to a formless bleating nonentity and she grew in stature, in awful wrath like some avenging angel, towering in implacable power, which could not be resisted. In seconds she had summoned the male nursing sister:

'What are you doing? What are you doing lurking in your office when my husband is here dying before my eyes? Who is the damned doctor for this ward? Get him here, now.'

In a remarkably short space of time a doctor arrived and she applied her rage to him:

'What are you doing for my husband? Is this how you treat a dying man? Where's the specialist? I want him here, now, for until you see to my husband I will not leave this hospital. Move yourself. Now.'

Bemused by this virago they moved and she amassed the services of seven doctors in a remarkably short period. Had she owned a tail she would have lashed it, but her tongue and fury served her well. Somehow, heaven knows how, they brought him back from death.

At last we were able to leave and stood outside the hospital, but she was not done yet. There was me and she spoke the words I had always felt:

'As for you, I tell you now you disgust me. There isn't a kind feeling in your body and I've watched you for years. You are as cold as ice and as heartless a bitch as it's possible to imagine. You'd have walked out and left him to die and not lifted a finger to save him. Oh, I only hope to God that he never finds out. You hell cat, he worshipped the ground you walked on, you were his sun and moon and stars and you'd have walked away and let him die without a backward glance.'

I said quietly, 'I loved him enough to leave him. He'd have gone peacefully and without what's to come. You don't know what you've done this night.'

But I knew. It was going to happen. It was never, never wrong. He would die in unimaginable agony and I didn't know how I was going to bear it and I wouldn't be able to bear any of it for him, I was just a spectator.

Drearily the days followed each other, sodden with a gloom which acquired a weird kind of substance of their own and my father lay dying by agonizing millimetres. Somewhere about the Christmas period my mother had 'flu' and I visited, for some reason, alone. Sitting beside his bed I did for him that which he had always done for me when I was ill; I held his hand. He had not eaten for a month and was now but a gaunt spectre, the little which remained of flesh peeling, dissolving before my eyes. For the first-and-only time he spoke of his suffering, muttering:

'Sweetheart, I have had a month of torture.'

And my tears fell on the big, once so capable hand; like the great splashes we used to call 'thunder drops' as children.

I said 'Daddy, I know, I know.'

As I walked home I thought of the appalling irony of his dying, he who had been one of the most courageous of men, taking chances with his life which a hundred men would have fled from. I remembered one short crisp conversation when I had asked:

'When you agreed to become a bomb disposal officer, did you ever think you'd be killed?'

(There had only been two such in the County and my father had been one of them). He had replied immediately:

'Of course not. I knew I wouldn't be killed. D'you take me for a bloody fool? I shall die in my bed, I've always known that.'

I thought: he had a Sixth Sense just as I have, that's why he could take the reckless chances he used to take; it was because he knew he had a charmed life. But he doesn't deserve this prolonging of torture, no one does, it's an offence against reason and sanity. Nothing else in Nature would be so cruel; that which seems to be cruel, as animals fall upon and devour the weak and old and dying is the real mercy. It is mankind who is merciless and it's all sheathed in a syrupy glue of various creeds and ideologies, but when you get down to reality and watch someone tortured, all the fondant phrases are just so much whitewash over truth.

January. The dread month. The month of death and indeed it seemed as if the land itself had died, gripped as it was in a hell of mist and black ice which hung motionless in the petrifying air. And I, too, had 'flu' and was sitting beside a great fire, wrapped in wool and impenetrable gloom.

My mother arrived and she looked unspeakably weary and for the first time, old. It was Monday afternoon. Instantly, I felt sorry for her. Gone now the flaming power of righteous anger, drained too of her inexhaustible energy, she seemed to be composed of flakes like the broken stems of wheat, dry and in danger of imminent dispersal.

She said quietly, 'I had to come, Kathleen. Your father is very ill indeed and they've moved him to a side room of his own. I asked the doctor if he was in pain and he said yes, he was afraid so, but he said they're doing all they can. I had to come and tell you. You have a right to know.'

I said gently, 'You shouldn't have come out in this weather.'

'I had to come' she said simply, 'I had to tell you myself.'

'Well' said I, 'you mustn't come out again', then, uncannily, another voice spoke through my vocal chords, I only recognizing them when they were actually spoken:

'He won't die till Wednesday.'

We gazed at each other. A truth had entered.

Very precisely now for I looked at the clock on the mantel: four o' clock on Wednesday afternoon. It was as if I moved without conscious volition, impelled only by a dark irresistible force, which dictated my thought and actions. Like an automaton I prepared a meal for my family, one that would keep and re-heat if necessary. At six-thirty I was in the hall struggling into my thickest coat when my husband arrived.

'And just where d'you think you're going?' he asked grimly.

'I'm going to see my father' I said.

'Oh, no you're not' he replied.

'I'm going to see my father' I insisted.

'You are not. It's hell out there and in your state? I tell you what, if you go out in the ice you'll have pneumonia by morning' was his parting comment.

It was as if his voice was a rustling of leaves and of as little account. Beyond rational thought or argument I was propelled now and only

Kathleen Fraser

physical force or broken legs could have interfered with this imperative. I had to see my father and like an account now, my world consisted only of imperative. I had to see my father.

The suspicious and hard sister at the door of the Intensive Care ward asked for my credentials and on being told that I was his daughter she grudgingly allowed that I might see my father and led me into a large room. It was dark; the only light was above a curtained cubicle in the centre of the room. She said with hostility:

'The doctors are with him, but you may go in. Be silent here. We permit no noise.' And so saying she drew aside a curtain which proved to be the one at the foot of the bed. With two doctors leaning over the occupant it became immediately obvious to them that I could not see, so they silently motioned to me to come around.

It lay there as I had seen four months earlier. Almost unrecognizable as a human being and this travesty of humanity was my father. Sparse damp hairs lay over the great-whitened skull. His forehead ridged in silent screaming agony. The great prominent nose stripped of flesh, yet the cavernous nostrils flared, issuing screams. The mouth, his mouth drawn into a bloody foaming rictus, a snarling screaming torment and above it the sparkling sapphire eyes protruded from the skull, naked now, fully exposed staring orbs, bloody with unimaginable pain. And below lay another mouth beneath the great jutting jawbone. This nightmare from hell had just had its throat cut and it gaped in screaming bloody foam.

When did I begin to weep, uncontrollably, to cry out in this darkness where noise was forbidden? I do not know, only that I was like a mad woman, being shaken and pushed as my husband had shaken me four months earlier.

Words hissed, 'Control yourself. Get out of here. Out, out, you are disgraceful.' And I could not tell her, any more than I could tell my husband.

My mother's home lay very near this hospital and to that I rushed, weeping in terror, the ice about me, encasing, shattered now. My dear brother-in-law and Betty stared at me in alarm as I burst in and the pent emotions of years spilled in a raging torrent:

'You wouldn't listen, would you? I tried to get you away, but your damned sanctimonious conscience and your bloody Christian charity condemned him. I knew what would happen. I saw it, I lived it months ago and to spare you, I never told you. I have lived in a hell knowing what was going to be. For you it's been now, just, but I've had to live with it every day for months. Hard, am I? Cold, am I? I loved him; damn you and I loved him enough to let him go. Love? You don't know the meaning of the word. He wouldn't have let a horse or a dog suffer like this; he'd have taken a gun and shot 'em. But who would save him? Not you, damn you. Is this what your so-called religion means? They promise an ultimate heaven to their believers, but they'll sacrifice anything not to get there. Mercy, you don't know the meaning of the word.'

It was unforgivable. Outrageous and some part of me wondered, detached, how it was possible to weep so much. Where was all the water coming from, for I wept for them, now, for Simon and Andrew and my father and it seemed I would weep myself away for the tears were torrents. Harry, so kind and loving, moved swiftly to hold me against his broad chest, to coax and comfort me into some sort of quiet which was, in the end, achieved. Throughout this tirade my mother sat, stricken and unspeaking and at last Betty and Harry departed.

Timidly my mother asked, 'Kathleen, what should we do?'

And I, who did not pray, answered, 'We have to pray for him. There has got to be an end. He can't die and he must be helped to go' and I asked for and obtained the service of a minister. A futile gesture, for he reiterated worn dogma, knowing no other way of dealing with this situation. At last we sat quietly, my mother and I. She bore me no resentment for my disgusting outburst: indeed she was strangely subdued. Tea, of course, but we had barely begun to drink when I opened my mouth and words emerged. I looked at them in dull surprise. They were:

'I'll have my chain now if you please.'

Without a word she went upstairs to fetch it and laid it in a heap before me on the table. It lay there richly, beautifully, glowing beneath the light. I made no attempt to touch it, but knew that indeed, it was mine now. My father had come to present it to me. Five minutes later there was a knocking on the front door, a kindly neighbour had taken a telephone message from the hospital that my father was dead, but I already knew that and although my mother did not say so, I believe she knew also.

Januaries. It is always a relief when they are over, although I cannot tell of any day that is an anniversary of those deaths. All the physical details which were present in the vision, corresponded to the actual scene that occurred four months later.

Truth. A reversal of time itself.

Chapter 9 – Why?

There followed months of dread questionings, which were conducted in my head. Of satisfactory answers there were few. But I reached one implacable conclusion and it was that I was being punished for something. That some implacable Deity was visiting a punishment on me for some dreadful evil which I myself had committed and I racked my brains to try to identify what monstrous evil I could have performed which would inflict upon me this savage punishment. It was not enough to have my family die, I had to live those deaths before they happened and die a little myself, daily, before the actual deaths. Yes, there were many improvements which could be made in my character; I had a swift temper; I was impatient with fools; I owned a cynical tongue which could lash and lived a life I knew to be superficial and false. In short, I disliked myself intensely. Somehow, somewhere, there lay inside me a standard against which I measured myself and perpetually, by comparison with this implacable standard – which never altered – my shortcomings were measured. By comparison I was odious.

Examining my life with meticulous scrutiny I tried to assess, in worldly and social terms, the wrongs for which I was being punished and thought that in a wider sense they were little greater than the people gathered about me. This did not make me produce excuses because I felt that many behaved in much worse a manner. I thought of the murderers, rapists and torturers whose violent acts filled the media in increasing proportions, but it was no use to attempt to assuage this standard by such squalid means as inferring that because I did not murder, rape or torture I was any better than they.

This implacable standard was not assembled because of any conventional religious belief, nor did it seem to exist because of any prevalent social ethics or climate of opinion. It seemed to exist by itself, as a thing-in-itself, which was wholly unidentifiable. Yet beside it I was an insufferable degraded creature, shamed, despicable. At last I decided that I had committed some unimaginably evil act in a previous existence and was being obliged to live this life in reparation. For I knew I had lived other, earlier lives and now I must pay.

In a purely physical sense I felt that I had been flattened, paper thin, by a gigantic steamroller. I resolved to try to improve my character. To atone. In a monetary sense I could not surrender much less for I personally owned almost nothing, denying myself all but the minimum of the small luxuries which so many of my friends seemed to demand or expect. But there is more to character than physical luxuries.

On outraged townspeople the news broke:

'The Pack Horse Yard To Be Demolished'.

A week earlier I had given up my job thinking that I could make up the loss of meagre earnings by doing everything, making everything we needed myself, although the truth was that I did all those tasks anyway. Now I knew exactly what I would do; I would fulfil the promise I had made to the Yard as a young girl, I would go and paint it. So I stood in the Yard one dark and louring afternoon in teeming rain, gazing at the Pack Horse pub, wondering what to do. I wanted to paint stone as stone, well aware of how the pundits regarded such intentions as provincial mediocrity. One was supposed to paint the thoughts one owned concerning objects, record one's feelings regarding the object in question, render all such symbolically as the observer's truth.

But I had been looking at pictures for most of my life and thought very seriously that some of the symbolic thoughts thus represented reflected very dire states of mind of many artists. Stone. The very fabric of the earth itself. Stone was beautiful. I had consulted much in the library, but could find no instructions or advice as to how to paint stone as a living entity. I had gazed at great pictures, but none could tell me how to approach the painting of stone in the manner I wished to portray it.

So I stood, that day and looked. Then I 'saw'. These ancient stones had arrived from the quarries in their natural state, honey coloured, interspersed here and there with the pure blaze of raw sienna. What could be seen now upon the stones was the detritus of history, the wearing of various weathers, the patchings of pointing, yet beneath were the clear colours of the earth. Now I knew how to begin. But I was rusty and of meagre talent. Still, for good or ill I would try, with no expectation of success. But I was not thinking in terms of producing a masterpiece, I was simply keeping a promise.

Very naturally, my small venture aroused much comment. This was not a town considered to be of beauty attracting artists; it was a working town, overlaid by centuries of lanolin-laden muck. Repellent to many. Being essentially a practical person I could only paint what I could see, so I had to stand and suffer the comments (varied) and the questions (varied). Time was short and I quickly learned that monosyllabic answers were the quickest way of deterring the importunate.

Came the day when an attractive lady with a mass of tumbling red curls planted herself behind the easel and began:

'I've seen you here a lot and I've come to ask you why you're painting. It isn't everybody's cup of tea, after all. So why are you doing it?'

I replied with chill, 'I like it, that's why.'

'Yes, she said firmly, 'So do I. I think it's a disgrace that it's to be demolished and a lot of other people do too. Have you read the letters about it in the paper?'

'No' was my dismissive reply.

Undeterred, she went on, 'There've been loads of complaints. Everybody's angry; you can hear people talking about it all over the place. Have you written a letter?'

My reply was abrasive 'No.'

'Well' she said 'I think you're doing the best thing. At least there'll be some record of it when it's gone.'

Then she went on conversationally, apparently oblivious to the fact that she was getting almost nothing from me,

'I used to live there, you know.'

I said 'Oh.'

She continued, 'Yes and I loved it. When I was a little girl you know. My mother was the landlady there. It was rather funny at the time, having a landlady of a pub, there were always just landlords then, but my mother had it, by herself.'

I repeated, 'Oh' and continued to paint, wishing her at the bottom of the sea.

She continued inexorably, 'What will you do with the pictures when you've painted them? I know you're painting more than one because I've seen you over there. Will you sell them?'

Obliged now to answer I said 'I haven't the faintest idea.'

She persisted, 'But you're doing the Tap now, aren't you?'

'Yes' I replied irritably.

She said 'It was my favourite part. I loved it. I still do. When you finish the picture will you sell it to me?'

I thought: this is impossible, but I answered cautiously:

'I can't promise. I don't know what I'll do with them. Ask me when I've done. There'll be four altogether because they won't all go into one. I had to do a lot of research first to find the histories. There are five distinct buildings here and the Tap is the oldest. They built from back to front and kept adding on. But all this used to be a big empty space and it's where Charles the Second granted a charter for a market, so it's why it's still known as the market place. And the weavers brought their cloth here to the Tap and it was loaded onto pack ponies.'

She asked, 'You love it, don't you?'

I said 'Yes, I do. Here is the heart of a town and it isn't often you can point to a place and say 'there is the heart', so when you remove the heart the body begins to die. There is an end here, the end of an era.'

She said 'There's more to it than that though, there is something else, isn't there?'

At that I laid down my brushes and spoke that which I never spoke to strangers, I said:

'I have a Sixth Sense. I saw it when I was a young girl, saw its beauty. I promised then that I'd come and paint it and I'm keeping the promise.'

To my amazement, to my curious sense of déjà vu I heard her exclaim with a tone of triumph:

'I knew it. I knew it when I first saw you here. I knew you didn't want to talk to me, but I couldn't go, I had to make you speak.'

Then she said the words I had known for years would come and come from a stranger:

'Come with me. You need me. Come with me.'

With a strange fatalistic sense I went. Never would I have gone of my own volition, but she led me to Emmie and Emmie I needed.

Joan, for that was the red-haired lady's name, took me to a spiritualist's meeting. It was a small, shabby room with a number of smallish shabby people in it. Regarding the prevalent belief which society in general imposed upon all matters relating to spiritualism and its allied mysteries, my attitude was ambivalent; on the one hand I was prepared to believe that some possessed a Sixth Sense, were 'fey' as the Scottish called it, but there was an element of skepticism too; I was not prepared to accept the charlatans. As it proved my apprehensions were groundless, for although a few smiled at me, no one other than Joan said a word.

But my attention was compelled by a plump lady of indeterminate age who wore a kind of plushy lacy snood on her head, although her clothes and appearance were of no consequence. It was her eyes that caused me to stare for they didn't seem to be gazing at anyone or anything in the room. Inward looking eyes. What my mother would have called 'yonderly' as if she continually gazed at something which no one else could see.

Joan whispered, 'She has a little church and I'll take you there next time. She's good, you know. She's very good.'

Without demur I agreed to go to another 'little church' although the description was far too splendid as I found myself in another small, shabby room full of small, shabby people. It was of no consequence. I have entered vast cathedrals and felt nothing but awe at the talents of the craftsmen who built them and none for the ritualistic dogma performed within them.

Of dogma here there was a dearth. Proceedings began with a formal, very short prayer and the last and first verses of a hymn and I got the feeling that this was simply an obligatory move, a kind of pacifier, for as soon as it was over Emmie (for it was she of the yonderly eyes) began systematically, row by row, to inform the seated assembly what their futures would be, her address prefaced by the admonition that no person to whom she spoke must answer with anything other than a simple 'Yes' or 'No'. With complete self-confidence she added the rider that no one's life history would be given freedom and if her addressee did not recognize anyone she was speaking of that person must answer smartly. There was no time to be wasted.

Her voice was rather low-pitched, but very clear nonetheless and she had great command of language, articulate and precise. Hearing the drone I sank into a rather lazy reverie, only coming to a start by Joan nudging my arm. Emmie was speaking to me and I gaped foolishly.

'You,' she said, 'I'm speaking to you. Pay attention. I don't have time to waste. There's a young girl here with very dark hair cut in a fringe across the forehead. She has rosy cheeks and lovely dark eyes. She died of consumption when she was twenty-one years old. You were at school together and she was your friend. Her name is Kathleen.'

And she paused for a second, then went on, 'and that's your name, isn't it?'

Dumbfounded, I muttered, 'Yes'.

Not enough for Emmie.

She said sharply, 'Speak up. That's your name isn't it?'

I said rather louder, 'Yes' and burst into tears.

'Stop crying, you're upsetting her, she was your very dear friend and she loved you. She loves you yet and she's brought you a beautiful sheaf of red roses; those mean love. She's also showing me something; it's a cardboard box with 'Stork Margarine' on the side. It's a bit odd this, she's taking loads of stuff out of this box and there's a little cake here with a frill around it. Its got robins and things on top, there's white icing. There's a lot of stuff, little boxes and things. D'you know anything about all this?'

Barely able to answer for sheer amazement I managed, 'Yes, yes I do.' 'Good' said Emmie, 'Now I can get on. I am to give her love and you are not to cry for her because she's happy, she has a garden now and those flowers are from her garden.'

Shattered, I sat and remembered Kathleen, my dear, my lovely friend and was humiliated, sunk in remorse for I had not thought of her for years. Every word Emmie had said of her was true and there could be only one or two people alive today who would know of this, of the box and its contents. We had been sitting in the park one evening after walking together and she had suddenly said:

'Kathleen, I've got consumption I think.'

Alarmed I had said 'Have you been to the doctor's?'

And she admitted that she had not. Angrily, frightened, I more or less ordered to go and it became official; she had tuberculosis.

It was possible to visit the hospital on Saturday afternoons and I went almost every week. After some months she was allowed to go out and we did that which we had done as schoolgirls, we spent some time in the library. Let it be clear that although I shared some of the top honours with her, there was no doubt as to who was the true scholar; she had a brilliant mind and taught me to like poetry as she loved it. Following our library stint I used to take her to my home for tea. Without exception my family loved her and with good reason, for she was a saint.

Prior to Christmas, Auntie paid us a visit.

To me she said 'Are you buying a present for Kathleen?'

I replied, 'Well yes, I thought I'd buy her some nice writing paper and envelopes. I can still get some of that grey deckle edged stuff and she writes quite a lot of letters.'

Auntie said 'Well, when you take your present will you take one from me?'

'Yes, of course I will. She'll love that.'

Immediately the rest of the family caught fire, yes, everyone would like to send something. My mother went to visit an ancient aunt who, at the beginning of the war, had squirreled away stuff which was now unobtainable and it was time to relieve her of some precious goodies. So a tiny fruitcake was made and I iced the top of it. Our own cupboards yielded some tiny pretty ornaments and a red frill. Thus we all filled the box, magazines, talcum powder in a pretty bottle, soaps, etc; and I took it to her parent's house. A letter arrived which my mother would not read until we were all assembled. All wept at the beautiful words of a poet and one line only I remembered: '... I did not know I had such friends.'

A few weeks later she died and I, callously, had not remembered her for years. It had been a privilege to know her; a very rare person had been my friend, so truly pure that I had always been inadequate beside her. I was so now.

But from this incident I gave my trust to Emmie, for there was no possible way she could have described Kathleen with stunning accuracy other than by actually seeing her. Later, she gave me several other instances of mediumship, which was and is unequalled and we became friends. Overall, those small, shabby people – Emmie apart – somehow generated a most glorious peace. It became so evident that I could see it hang motionless in the air, softly silvery and it fell upon me like a balm. I did not know what it was and I knew most surely that they did not know they generated it. But it began to heal me, for I was sorely distressed.

For all their apparent insignificance in worldly, social terms I admired these people for they unselfconsciously made no secret of their beliefs although they well knew of the epithets which were attached to their beliefs, knew of the hostility of and by, the formal church doctrines and the opinions of those who held power of government in the various aspects. It could not be said that I was thinking clearly for I was not, I was hurting too much for clear objective analysis, but I was beginning to see the dichotomies.

Nor did I myself emerge as a particularly honest person, for these very ordinary people had the courage of their convictions and their lives were permeated by their beliefs. In contrast, I led two distinct and separate lives, one which lay upon the surface of the social scene and which portrayed a rather sophisticated, cynical character and another entirely different person who lived unseen truths. In the meanwhile I thought a great deal, but it also has to be admitted that much of my thinking went around in circles and no very clear distinctions could be drawn.

Circles, my goodness yes. It was a lovely day and I was sitting on the broad step outside the French door. I was eating my lunchtime sandwich and gazing with pleasure at the sunlight catching the crazy paving which floored the big walled garden. In the burgeoning trees along the avenue birds were making an incessant racket, for they were all busy rearing young and the trees themselves were 'dressed for best' as the massed leaves were in their flush of youth, soft yet brilliant in their greenery. It was very quiet here, isolated. The immense walls surrounding the garden made it an enchanting private world, exploited only by the numerous birds which were astonishingly tame and which found ample pickings in the rich loam which surrounded the paving.

Circular, I thought with a sense of shock. Of course, everything is circular, right to the limits of the Universe. It's a natural shape, the shape of everything we know, everything we can observe and it's so natural to us that we don't even notice it, we take it completely for granted. And if it were not circular we'd go mad.

Imagination ran riot then and I began to see the circularity from the smallest seed to the limits of the Universe, beyond the galaxies, which were themselves either round or ovoid. Ovoid, yes. A seed could be ovoid and so far as I knew most of them were. Shapes, the beginning of things, the beginning of living things. Flowers, plants, trees all inherently curving. Splintered rocks would inevitably assume a rounded shape, for weather would erode all sharp angles irrespective of the fact that the original splintering created cubes or straight edges. My mind began to make ludicrous comparisons now; what if? What if one looked in the bathroom mirror and saw one's face in rectangles or squares? One would go insane on the spot. What if trees grew with rectangular trunks? If plants grew like boxes, children grew like cubes? On and on, the lists were endless ... what if the sky were filled with square stars, the moon a rectangle?

Then, very simply, I saw what we were doing to ourselves. Across the land, across the globe, we were building vast rectangles for people to work in, to live in and the ever increasing violence which was emerging from the huge rectangles which were flats and in which so many were obliged to live, their aspects equally rectangular, were disturbed in mind by alien shapes. No wonder malcontents were emerging from these vast housing units. No wonder that people feared, were locked in disillusion and misery. Cheap, they were to build. How cheap? They were expensive, not cheap, for the increasing violence was a direct result of the unnatural shapes in which people existed. For the natural shapes, the circle and the ovoid were being obliterated and unnatural behaviour was on the increase. I thought: We were happier when we lived in rondavels. It wasn't conclusive as thinking, but it was a start of some kind.

Far from being perfect, which I well knew, the Pack Horse pictures were finished and to my surprise they raised a lot of attention and I had many offers for them, none of which I would accept. If they were sold it would be as a set, for they contained all the history I could manage to discover. I painted a fair number of views at that period, lurking at the rear of old properties, for I wanted none of the tarted-up frontages. On the whole they sold quite well, although it cannot be said that there was any real monetary advantage in it as they cost such a lot to paint in the first instance.

It was a short-lived notoriety and the denouement arrived from two entirely different quarters, the first of which was a vision. At this juncture I will elucidate rather more carefully as to the nature of what I have written as 'visions' as it may be supposed that I am presenting myself as a 'visionary' and I am most surely not. Rather it is that I have called them 'visions' simply because although to date in this narrative I was asleep in my bed when they occurred, they later occurred when I was fully awake. The effect of all was identical: they were truths and truths which could not have been deduced from the circumstances preceding their arrival in physical terms. Precognitive in nature. Unacceptable in social terms. Yet they happened in real physical existence. Science in general denied the possibility of living events prior to their emergence. Very simply, Science was wrong. In combination scientists owned then and now, a lot of 'clout'. I had not, nor have now, any clout whatsoever. But I am disturbing chronology…

In the most charitable way I learned something I needed to

recognize and it happened as follows: I first saw the shop counter and it was one of the worn, smoothly shabby counters, which most shops owned in my youth. A thick slab of mahogany, pale in the centre by much wear and tear. Looking up I saw that this was a shop of a kind. Not large, but it could have stepped straight from a drawing by Phiz, it was so old. To my right was a large window, iron barred, dusty, cobwebby, which didn't look as if any part had been disturbed for years.

No light of any significance penetrated the grubby panes, but the room itself was clean and quite bright. On the opposite facing wall was an open doorway to the left, which gave onto a room, which was obviously brightly lit. It seemed to be a workroom of some kind, for I could see a worktable there and a man sitting with his back to me busy making something which I felt to be a piece of jewellery, but as I couldn't see clearly I may have been wrong. Certainly and for some unfathomable reason, I felt that whoever was working at this table – and there were others, although not in view – they were making artifacts of immense and rare beauty. However unspectacular the venue, they were artists who were the cream of their profession. To the right of the doorway was a long trestle table of no interest, being merely a useful object of a kind one may find almost anywhere. Functional, they were, but useful too. There was no floor covering in either the shop or the room beyond. Merely clean bare boards. Altogether, it seemed as if I was in a working establishment. But that was to change dramatically.

With a rapidity which should have startled, but did not, people appeared. On the other side of the old counter was a big, powerful, grizzled man in tweeds of some indeterminate hue, but there were leathers on his sleeves and I formed the instant opinion that this man had been a teacher, no, a headmaster, for he wore that indefinable sense of authority which those who teach so often assume effortlessly and which seems to permeate their clothes. He wasn't scruffy, but he wasn't smart. From a large squarish face he observed me quite levelly, drawing no conclusions as to my character for he knew exactly who I was and why I was there. Which was more than I knew.

Beside him was a lady. Perhaps I ought to have written 'lady' with a capital L, for if she had not, in life, been titled, then I was a crass simpleton. She was the world's conception of the classical English lady, perfectly groomed, perfectly mannered. Her beautifully shaped head swathed expensively in a style which hugged the pale gold into a pleated coil at the back of her head. Her suit – Chanel at her most restrained – could not have achieved such perfection in moulding the tall slenderness with some cream coloured material which looked like shantung, but wasn't. Beneath the suit was a jumper of the identical shade, decorated by something in fine gold. Fashion-wise, it ought to have been disastrous to be all-over cream coloured and gold, but it was simple perfection. Her face was a perfect oval, perfectly featured and ageless in beauty, but she was not young.

How much time passed whilst I assimilated these details I cannot say, but I suppose it would not have been very long. No sooner had I absorbed the scene it became combined into an instantaneous nerve centre. I could see the whole set-up charged with something like translucent light, which was communicative, a kind of energy, which was totally charged with information. Speech was unnecessary; there were people in the back room and this instant communication subsumed them all, all at the same time. None needed speech; they all knew and they knew it all together. To me they said 'she's ready now, we can begin.'

From the back room several women appeared like a relay team. All were different from each other, but all wore pinafores and overalls. It looked like a cleaning women's outing. Yet in some indefinable manner there was no hierarchy here, no spurious class distinction whatsoever. They all had differing features and differed in dress, but in combination with the elegant Beauty and the Grizzly Bear before me all were exactly identical. One mind. One action. One intention. The relay women each carried some object with which they very quickly heaped the table at the rear. 'Now we can begin.'

It was silent. Sound they didn't need. A lady in a flowered overall approached, then I noticed the shelving to my left. I'd assumed that the old counter stretched up to the wall. It did not. Tiers of shelving rose, each different from all others, each designed with a perfection which would have caused Nash to take up knitting and each shelf designed to reflect and combine with the object which was placed upon it. What the shelving itself was made of is impossible to describe and I can but say it was not stone, not marble, not any material exists to which it could be likened, but it was perfection. Quite light in colour, but not creamy coloured or soft grey, a new colour but not one which will ever be discovered on earth.

For, of course, all these people were – in worldly terms – dead. Except they were so brilliantly alive that they would have caused what we believe to be living people appear to be dead. Now a continuous stream of relay women and as each placed her object upon the shelf which had been created to hold it, the object and the shelf melded into a perfection of proportion which is impossible to convey simply because nothing exists on earth which is totally perfect. Each object was so beautiful I could feel myself melting inside: colours, shapes, blue, red, gold and green all wrought into exquisite shapes, some similar to vase shapes, some curving, some bowl shapes. As the shelves filled I also filled with utter matchless beauty, with awe, for these were the creations of the gods and goddesses.

The very last one remaining shelf was unoccupied and a small, bustling, dark haired lady in a blue wrap-around overall carried toward it a small vase of gorgeous shape and made of some intense blue material laced with gold and she set it down slightly out of alignment. Unhesitatingly and rudely, without asking permission I moved it into its correct position. Instantaneously they were all alight with joy. I had been tested and I had done the right thing. So now they would show me their real treasure. It was brought from the back room by two of the women and as they approached my bones began to melt. It was moving … They set it down upon the old counter, it's silken hair still swaying, folding, lifting and falling as if each fine hair knew what it had to do, knew how to swirl with its fellows in ripples, dancing and curling.

It was a dog, but not even similar to any dog I had ever seen. Quite tall, perhaps two and a half or three feet in height, its proud glorious head erect and lit with intelligence, as were the great jewel-like amber eyes. From the top of this dog's regal head to the silken swaying tail, hair moved, swishing and swirling about a narrow arc which was its body and which was the most perfectly proportioned curving arc I have ever seen, either in vision or in this world. And the draping moving folds and arcs of hair, as was the dog itself, had been wrought in a metal so fine as to make even baby hair appear coarse as ship's rope. In colour it was a kind of amalgam of copper, of gold, of russet, of sunlight, but it was no colour which is describable, as the whole utterly peerless perfection is indescribable. This was the acme of creation. They had created this dog and it glowed with life although it was composed of an unidentifiable metal.

In utter ecstasy I gazed at this wondrous creation. Then I awakened, saturated by inexpressible beauty. Time to cease painting: I had seen supremacy of creation; nothing ever created upon this earth could equal such wonders and all were the work of people deemed to be dead except they were more brilliantly alive than any person deemed to be living.

As she wanted it so badly I painted a picture of Joan and her sister sitting outside the Pack Horse Tap, but it was difficult work for as the ancient walls came into being a figure intruded, crossing the yard. A sailor, no less, accompanied by a huge Alsatian dog. Handsome, agile, crowned by a lovely head of dark waving hair he intruded so often I began to despair of ever completing the picture. At last I told her impatiently that it did not seem possible to finish and described the intruders, whereupon she exclaimed:

'But that was my father and our dog. He was never the landlord, that was my mother's job.' We stared at each other in amazement. A ghost, no less.

Although reduced to a cipher by such peerless creations the most prominent factor was the communication facility used by those true artists for it was Light. They had no need of words, light flashed between them all apparently instantaneously, so what one knew all knew and all at the same time. I did not then know the immense importance of this factor, but the fact remains that although I was never able to describe the wonders of those creations I was always able to describe the astonishing quality of that Light.

Chapter 10 – Collapse

'Pride goeth before a fall' and similar Awful Warnings used to hang upon bedroom walls when I was a child. 'Thou God Se'est Me' was not conductive to sleep when something lay upon your conscience and there was usually something fairly weighty on mine. But the former Awful Warning became, in my case, an only too dreadful truth and I fell all the way.

It arose because of the Pack Horse pictures, for I had been in a small group and the topic had been introduced into the conversation. To be explicit, I was asked if I would ever sell them and a young man, on hearing my views – although he was not part of the group – supported my views wholeheartedly and proceeded to illustrate his point with a description of his reactions when asked to release something of his own creation. It was an amicable conversation and we parted cordially.

The following evening, without anger, but with chilly disdain, my husband told me of my insufferable behaviour, lack of dignity and overweening pride. As my mother had cut me down as a child, so he cut me down as an adult. The dreadful part of it was that there was an element of truth in his cold analysis of my character. Yes, I was quite proud of the pictures and more proud still to own something of my very own and which dozens of people wanted. Added to this was the fact that in general I disliked myself intensely, holding my person always against that unseen standard and continually knowing how inadequately I matched that standard I went 'over the edge' and had a nervous breakdown.

It lasted three weeks but I did not tell anyone. When anyone other than myself was in the house I behaved as normally as possible and the moment I was alone I wept incessantly. Of this episode I will say little other than I believed myself to be so vile a creature that there appeared to be no uninhabited corner of the Universe which I would not filthily soil by hiding in it and I prayed continuously for death. I was lying on the rug in the back sitting room, face down, unable to live with myself any longer when I felt a slender gentle hand laid across my forehead and without exerting any pressure the hand lifted me to my feet and moved me to the kitchen. Tea, I needed tea.

Then I 'saw'. Over my head, so near that had I lifted an arm I could have touched it, was an immensity of white cloud. It had no boundaries and some part of me felt that it extended to unimaginable distance, limitless in extent. Glitter was there as if it were admixed with powdered diamonds and from it there issued an unmoving effortless power unmatched on earth for strength: Benignity. It descended through my cells to that I was suffused entirely by this colossal power. And it cured me.

The same evening I walked to Emmie's shabby little room and a stranger stood before me and said:

'I have seen an intense white light flash on behind you. You must know it, you must have seen it. Tell me you've seen it.'

I whispered, 'Yes, I've seen it.'

She said illuminated by white light, 'Oh God, I've never seen anything like it in my life.'

And I watched her face transformed into rapture. I also was transformed for it cured me.

Without regret I ceased to paint. There were, after all, sufficient numbers of indifferent pictures in the world without my adding to the number. In that dusty old shop I had seen what the so-called 'dead' artists could create and their creations were of matchless beauty. No more would I refer in any possible instance to my meagre talents and that promise I made to myself I have kept to this moment, but years later there was a change. Now I know what I am, but explanations must be held in abeyance. Later, I sold the pictures as a set to pay off a debt of honour and felt a weight lift off my shoulders.

I was walking across the back sitting room and the sun must have been shining, for it was filled with soft coloured light when I was, literally, stopped in my tracks. There arose before me, as if from a bottomless pit, three capital lettered words, white light against a black background. Stunned, I could only stare: 'WHO AM I?'

My mind went into instant over-drive and my first innate response was to say, 'I am me, I am Kathleen,' yet so fast was everything moving that as I thought the words I knew also that they were no answer. It all became a chaotic tumbling-churning torrent of descriptions of myself, instantly recognized and just as instantly discarded. For none would answer. I am English, middle-aged, mother of two daughters, wife of Neil, a daughter myself, sister of, reside at, friend of, cousin of, like, love, read, laugh … any and all adjectives, nouns, pronouns all crumbled into chaff and I watched them fall into a torrent to be carried off as detritus on the fast flow, all useless as answers for none could answer that one simple question which remained: 'WHO AM I?'

Crass fool, I told myself. A puling idiot and I think you're losing your marbles. Then I wondered seriously if I was schizophrenic; one would have thought that to identify oneself would be the simplest thing in the world, but it was not, for no identification I could muster would answer the question. With a feeling of empty alarm I at last admitted to myself that I did not know. Nor could I forget the encounter. I was really very stupid. There were, there are, no mitigatory excuses to be made, I was a fool.

One evening I was sitting in Emmie's little 'church' as she so grandiloquently called it, letting the lovely peace these people unwittingly generated sooth my tattered mind, lulled also by her voice. I was not asleep but interminable thoughts of my sons and my father coursed through my mind.

At once, a most remarkable situation developed: it was as if I had control over my disorganized thoughts and with great precision I toured my head from the inside closing down the operations section by section as a thrifty housewife would tour a house, switching off the lights.

Suddenly, I thought with immense satisfaction: 'There, I've quietened that lot down' and it was simply lovely to sit gazing at what now appeared to be an empty peaceful state. Opening my eyes for a second or two I noticed that I was breathing quite beautifully and smiled to myself. How silly to call breathing beautiful. In utter peace I closed my eyes again and immediately I saw another 'I' – one which I had hitherto not known existed – rise up before me. Then the right hand side of my head blanked off into impenetrable darkness and I saw the light and darkness side by side. The 'I' disappeared into the darkness and I followed, then knew no more.

How long the interval I cannot say, but an interval separated my earlier experience from that which I could now see; I was before what I knew to be a tunnel and knew somehow that it was of great length, but the entrance was obscured by a pair of filmy curtains, finer than smoke, yet wholly opaque. I put out my hands and drew the curtains apart only to find an identical, but slightly smaller pair of curtains. How long I traversed the tunnel I cannot say, but it seemed to go on interminably yet as I parted the curtains which stretched its length I realized that as the tunnel narrowed, so the curtains became smaller and smaller until they were almost indiscernible. There was a lightening flash in which I would have known terror had it not been that it ended before it became recognizable. Free. I was freed into light and knew a miniscule moment of fear which dissolved as I knew it.

Before me an Elephant. Vast. Superb. Enormous. It filled my whole vision. Gazing in utter wonder at the enormity of this wonderful creature I could see draped over its mighty head a triangular shawl of open square sections made of pure gold. At each intersection of the squares was a jewel, a sapphire or a topaz and each gem was as large as a pigeon's egg. This mind numbing display should have detracted from the immense majesty of the beast, yet did not, was merely an adjunct, a fitting covering for that which was Pure Goodness. Every cell of this enormous beast radiated Goodness and as I knew this so the trunk moved to grasp me about the waist. I could feel its warmth, the coiling goodness and warmth seeping into my body. Then silently, effortlessly, that utterly gentle coiling was lifting me, upwards now, higher and higher ...

Briefly, swiftly I could see the land stretching into vastness, hazy with heat, the colours attenuated by heat into soft sandy shades, this was a hot land of great distances. Even the sky in which I was flying was not the clear intensity of Northern Blue, but admixed with haze, the tendrils of cloud buttered by the sun. Down, now, I could see below me a great palisaded area containing many people, their skins darkly rich, their clothes a moving kaleidoscope of riotous colours. A slender brown arm flung toward me in a farewell and the owner was a young slender woman dressed in a swathe of brilliant blue. Then I was freed of the enormous trunk and flying, flying into the hazy tendrils of gentle colour, flying into utter, utter bliss ...

With the abruptness of an icy douche I opened my eyes to the grey shabbiness of Emmie's place and mourned: Why had I had to return? Why couldn't I go on in bliss? Why have I to exist in this dreariness? But there were no answers.

Discarding, temporarily, the demands of chronology I write now of a suspicion which dawned many months, probably years later, a suspicion which deepened.

I believe it was my own death that I 'saw'. More. I believe that land to have been India. I was in a garden and found that growing flowers was not easy, for the big old trees along the avenue shaded the greater part of it, but I tried, of course. In front of the windows were two flowerbeds filled with roses and I must have been weeding, for when the vision ended I was staring stupidly at the grubby gardening gloves and the trowel in my right hand. Nor can I say how it all began, only that I started to hear music. No radio was playing. There were no musicians. This was music of a different nature. Nature's music.

A sound. A chord. A swelling, rising crescendo of sound, gathering in volume until it became a symphony, an irresistible pealing of differing harmonies all combining into one vast upswelling expression of what? Of joy. Riotous, yet united. One enormous sound which was not a cry nor a bellow, simply one vast sound as if a thousand orchestras had decided to shout their Joy in one fantastic moment which was developing into an ecstasy to which all contributed and in which all were united irrespective of the note each individual produced. Irresistibly the thousands joined into one huge cry, a shout, a declaration: I am living.

Swept up within this indescribable unification of peerless sound I could hear the individuals: along the avenue the great trees rumbled a deep ringing base; I could hear the gliding of the sap, see the sap rising up the broad trunks, hear and see it carousing into the branches and leaves, feel the myriad leaves waft the sound into the one vast singing chord. A clump of London Pride were chattering their joy like small castanets, yet even these complacent little flowers mellifluously combined their chatter into the one glorious note. Before me the roses preened their self-satisfaction, mellow as cellos, joyous with beauty.

Worms burrowed in the rich loam and the miniscule fallings of miniscule particles which fell behind them as they tunnelled made fractional thudding sounds as they fell to the floor, yet even these tiniest of drums all added to the rising splendour. Somewhere nearby was a nest of baby mice and the brushing of their fur as they jostled each other for position simply added to the immense volume of joyous music.

All about me, all the earth with its living creatures was united into a peerless music, which was inexpressibly wonderful. The whole planet was ringing like one great bell and I too rang with the Joy of Life, for it was Life itself, which rang and it seemed as if the sound would reach out to the stars in one vast peal of glorious sound.

Then I was caught up in the sound and swept up, turning to girdle the Earth, seeing below me great deserts, glowing golden; vast tracts of jungles, green as emeralds; sapphire waters dusted with clouds and I circled the globe enclosed within a sound no words will describe. Aghast, I looked at the grubby gloves and the trowel. Ungrateful as I was I mourned now, why did I have to return? I ought to have been suffused with gratitude for ever hearing the world live and cry out its Joy of Life.

That which I am about to describe was the 'clincher', which formulated the decision to write of the strange life I led. There were many anomalies present, but one sentence spoken by my husband had pricked uncomfortably, rousing me at times to deep resentment and it was:

'Proof is what I need.'

I thought often: what more proof could there be than living three deaths and knowing minute details of those deaths, before they happen? Who could lie about such agonies? Who could be such a monster? Who could even fabricate such stories? One would require to be a genius and a genius I was most surely not. I was an intensely practical hardheaded housewife.

Before attempting to describe this vision certain aspects must be established: I can but use words, for they are my only tools; black letters upon white. Searching my brain, which is not that of a poet, nor a writer for that matter I will attempt to summon all my descriptive talents (meagre, I admit) to portray some glimmering of that which I 'saw' and knowing full well as I write that no words can, or will, convey the most remote picture of the picture I 'saw'. To illustrate this point I will suggest that whomsoever reads these words extends their imagination to offer description of a rainbow. The latter can be seen, for they arc across the sky following certain conditions after rain. Beautiful they are, but they cannot be touched or handled in any manner whatsoever. Science can and does render explanations as to the physical processes during which rainbows are formed and offer minute and detailed explanations as to how light is broken into the seven glorious bands. But a rainbow cannot be weighed or measured; it is not conducive to discovery of its end for as one moves towards it, the rainbow retreats. Here my problem commences for I am about to try to describe that which is as elusive as a rainbow, knowing well that no words I can summon will be adequate.

Now to the tangible and the intangible, as is the rainbow.

To a house in Union Street, in my old village. Elaine's old kitchen, well, of all places to be! How had I got here? Somehow it didn't matter. Anyway, here I was and I hadn't been here for years, yet it was as if time had stood still for nothing seemed to be changed significantly. There was but one difference in this kitchen which otherwise seemed to be suspended in time, for to the left of the window there had been a well-worn brown leather armchair in which had sat Elaine's father. Nostalgia now, as I recollected this lovely, charming man who was almost always to be found sitting there, book in hand, but who never failed to lay down his book and talk courteously to you whenever you called. He had been that rare creature, a gentleman. Not a 'gentleman' in the classic social sense which merely describes wealth, power, isolation and usually an indefinable yet impervious arrogance, but the true meaning of the coupled words: gentle man. He had died when I was at the beginning of my teenage years and Elaine had been devastated by grief, for she had adored him and no wonder. He had been one of the most delightful men I could ever remember meeting and certainly my own father, often brusque and irascible, would never have laid down his reading material to talk to my friends. Children then were seen, but were instructed frequently not to be heard.

To the immediate right of the window was the white porcelain sink, which I had so admired as a child. Sinks then were made of stone or some dark red shiny stuff I never knew the name of.

With a little start I emerged from reminiscence: Why had I come here? I had supposed myself to be alone and I was not. Had I been asleep, drowsing in nostalgia? By now I was to the right of the window and to its left a figure was facing me. Oh, ohhhh, a god, it couldn't be anything but a god. Yet he looked man-like enough and, beset by my eternal curiosity I subjected him to intense scrutiny. Beautiful, he was. Gloriously, perfectly beautiful, yet a beauty without the smallest hint of femininity. About five ten in height, I thought and from the top of the softly waving dark hair, to the tip of the perfectly proportioned chin, the only similar example I could think of was Michael Angelo's 'David' except this man was more beautiful and alive. Throughout, the dark eyes smiled at me with great gentleness and I knew that he could effortlessly read every thought in my head.

Clothes. A formal lounge suit. What a pathetic description. It was a suit fit for a god, it looked as if it had been moulded by a god and oh, the cloth, this was cloth of the gods. Almost navy in colour, yet of no colour which is truly accurate; and the cloth itself was the cloth of dreams.

With no sense of movement I found myself in my original position and there, before the window was a large shining silvery white sphere, glinting on its translucent perimeter with tiny flashes of rainbow coloured light. Within it, in sleep my weary, careworn body, a shabby creature, a woman of straw and I wanted to die of shame at the person I was fretted, harassed by the banal mediocrities of existence, consumed by self-loathing and wondered how this glorious, flawless being could bear to be in the same room with me. Yet he glowed, knowing exactly what I was, who I was and not judgmental in the smallest particle. Uncritically, he gleamed even more intensely.

Unrejected, indeed, the very opposite, for now he indicated, communicated without words, to look, to look to my right and where the back door should have been to the right of the sink was no door, it was dark glittering space. In the space was a world composed entirely of incandescent white light. It hung in the darkness like the hope of the world. Incredibly, I could see a huge city, tall buildings of superlative heart-stopping beauty fashioned entirely of light. Figures moved through the city, themselves composed of incandescence, flowing freely in a harmony I could not hear, nor describe, yet which was a rhythm to which all were attuned. No light such as this exists in the Universe which is visible to us. No ecstasy comparable to this supreme wonder. Transfixed in wonder I could only gaze …

Eventually, although how long I was transfixed and transformed I cannot say, only that I was conscious of the old shabby kitchen and the god-like man was still gazing at me with boundless pleasure. Once more he indicated without ever showing evidence of doing so and there lay between us a circle of this light glowing like melted pearls. There were no words, for words were irrelevant. This was for me, a gift. My own circle of light.

Then I was awake in my bedroom and the circle hung before me in the room. Truly, a gift, I had brought it away with me and I owned it for many weeks. Meeting people who were troubled I found I could manipulate it, so I put it about them. During those weeks I gazed at this shimmering circle every night, amazed that I should have been given such a miraculous wonder. Inevitably, my crass curiosity overcame sense and one night I put out my hand to touch it, wondering if I could hold it, was it hot or cold and it shivered into nothingness in a trillion tiny points of light. Numbly, almost paralyzed with horror, I realized I'd destroyed the most precious gift anyone could be given, realized also that the god-like man had known exactly what I would do and had not minded.

Months later I realized who the god-like creature had been in what we ludicrously suppose to be 'living existence'. It had been Mr. Johnson, Elaine's father and he had shown me his new home. He had been a wonderful person and deserved the miraculous home.

For some weeks I had been conscious of a feeling of impending change, the suspicion that the ending of an era was approaching. It cannot be said that I knew what turn my life would take for I did not, only that there would be a difference. There was actually nothing new concerning such similar feelings for as an era ended and a new one approached I could sense these changes as animals sense the approach of storms and natural disasters.

Predictably, it began with Emmie and as she turned her attention to me one particular evening she unaccountably became – not hesitant, for she was never hesitant – but very intense and she spoke slowly, but with great emphasis:

'Kathleen love, I have a lady here, all white and she is very beautiful. She is telling me that you will barely remember her, for she passed on when you were only two and a half. But she says you will know who she is because you will have heard her name spoken all your life. Kathleen, the lady was known to you as 'Auntie Grace'. Before I go on you must tell me that you know who I am talking to.'

I said with great conviction, 'Yes I do.'

Emmie continued, 'Good. That is good. This is Grace and it was always said of her by those who knew her that she was the only person they ever knew who exactly matched her name. I must be very careful here, for this is important and I must be very careful to tell you exactly what she has come to tell you. She says that you have other relatives in Halifax. True?'

I nodded and said 'Yes, that's true.'

'This other lot have twitted you for years about reading, haven't they?' asked Emmie.

'Yes always' I replied.

Emmie paused and asked me directly, 'do you read a lot, love?'

'Yes, I do' I said.

Returning to her normal delivery Emmie said briskly, 'Yes, Grace is telling me they are an ignorant lot, they don't read a book from one year's end to the next. And they've made rather nasty fun of you lots of times. Called you a book worm, haven't they?'

'That's true,' I said with a spark of resentment.

'Grace says you're not to bother love, let 'em talk. They're not going to learn anything just by talking, so forget 'em. They live in ignorance and they'll die in ignorance' said Emmie who paused dramatically, her head lowered.

This was so unusual I could not stare. When at last she did speak she seemed curiously altered, curiously hesitant:

'Kathleen, Grace says I must tell you that you're going to read some kinds of books such as you've never read before. She's been showing me these books and I have to tell you that I can't describe them, I don't understand them. So I can't tell you this clearly, because the books are beyond me. But you must read them. It's very important and again I can't tell you how important it is because I don't understand this.'

Emmie suddenly stood very straight and it was as if she had gained height. In some imperceptible manner her face changed and she said, looking at me with immense concentration:

'You're looking for something, aren't you Kathleen?'

And in that very instant something coalesced in my head.

I replied, 'Yes, I am.'

But I did not speak the rest of the sentence for it simply ran in my head: 'I want to know if there is a God or not?'

Emmie reverted instantaneously to her normal being:

'Yes, Grace is telling me you're looking for something and she says that if you go on reading you will find what you're looking for. She tells me it won't always be easy, but whatever you do you must stick at it. Whatever happens you must not give up or give in. Will you promise, Kathleen? Grace is very insistent about it, you must not give in and if you go on you'll find what you're looking for.'

I said, not knowing what I was letting myself in for, 'Yes, I promise.'

Later that evening I thought carefully about Emmie's instructions from Auntie Grace and wondered what might lie ahead concerning my reading matter, but concluded with no alarm that no doubt I'd learn sooner or later. More immediately I was struck anew by the fact of Grace impinging upon my life. That she had been universally loved was true, but she was of no real blood relationship for she had been the sister of my mother's cousin's wife and had died at a young age; thereafter mourned always and had remained like a shining beacon in the lives of all who knew her, my parents, auntie and auntie's daughter Agnes. To them she had owned the quality of saintliness, but I had only the faintest recollection of this lovely lady for in truth, I was two and a half when she died.

Six weeks passed and on a day when the library was filled with sunshine I paused to surrender the books I had read then moved beyond the wicket. Suddenly I 'saw' tall shining figures composed of white light and turned, impelled by no conscious decision to a section labelled Physics and the books slipped off the shelves into my waiting arms. Needs are fulfilled. It is wants that are the deceivers. My earlier existence changed completely. The end of an era indeed.

It must be emphasized that when I began to read the abstruse subject of Physics it was the last subject on earth from which I expected to learn whether or not there was a God. As with so much of the flat surface appearance which we delude ourselves as being reality, that expectation is also a delusion.

Chapter 11 – A Little Hope

Description of the next few years will not be given. There was a time of flux and all needed to settle into appropriate channels. We had left Garner's house (I had felt as if I only lodged there during the eight years we lived there) and but one experience of a Paranormal nature occurred in the next premises. As it was an example of a learning experience I will describe it.

It was Sunday morning and the whole of the morning was to be occupied with an activity which had been arranged for days and which could not be postponed. Yet from the moment of leaving my bed I kept 'seeing' my brother-in-law, Harry. This was odd, for very unusually I had had a serious disagreement with my elder sister and for the first time in our lives we had been separated from each other for a whole year. It must be said that we didn't see each other too often, but we had always had visits from them during intervals of six weeks or thereabouts.

Harry was standing in a large terraced garden in Buxton, of all places and he was alone. As I was seeing this scene it was interrupted by my husband and the whole of that morning followed the same pattern. We had a man to meet and as conversation continued incessantly I began to feel a sense of déjà vu, for I was involved in the talks, yet distracted by seeing Harry. In the end it felt as if I was living on two levels and not successfully operating on either. At last we were home again and the telephone rang:

Betty said 'Kathleen, I'm in Honiton with Doreen and John. I have to tell you that Harry died suddenly this morning at five o'clock.'

And I thought: 'Yes, I've known all morning. That's why I've kept seeing him in Buxton, standing in that garden. That's where I was before Simon died.'

Of course, all disagreements ended and we never referred to them again. Many arrangements had to be made, were made and we brought Betty home after the funeral, eventually getting her settled in her own home. Throughout the distress and involved arrangements, I felt strangely ill at ease, uncomfortable inside my skin and this was nothing to do with my previous disagreements with Betty.

As time continued this sense of being ill at ease within myself became more and more pronounced. Quite ordinary jobs, which I normally tackled without a moment's hesitation were becoming disturbing chores and I couldn't perform with any of my usual competence. Absurdly, I thought: If I were a car somebody would be saying I was operating on one cylinder – whatever that might be, for of cars I knew less than a five year old.

My life became a considerable problem. This curious discomfort, an alien incompetence, was so unnatural to me that I began to seriously worry. Quite clearly I knew that although I was able to tackle many jobs, at no job was I an expert, or even academically qualified. A jack-of-all-trades, but master of none. Now I couldn't do anything with even reasonable success and it was beginning to affect my life for I had to be competent, there was no one else to do these jobs and it was as if one hand had been immobilized. At the end of three months I knew the reason. Harry was with me all the time and I knew the reason too.

That ludicrous incident in the railway carriage when I was young and had seen inside the curate, actually entered the curate, could just as easily be reversed. Did I suppose that my mind could not be invaded by another mind? It was invaded and by Harry. Not only that, he had brought with him his physical inabilities also. Now I began to think: he had been a man who had tried very hard (too hard perhaps) to accumulate domestic talents and to have married into a family who took such talents for granted must have been a sore trial. There had not been the creativity in his fingers and now there was almost none in mine.

Only one thing now to be done; I went to a Spiritualists' Church. This was an acknowledged Church and well maintained. Presently an extremely elegant lady approached me:

'You have here a man and his name is Harry.'

Having been well schooled by Emmie I merely said 'Yes.'

She said 'He has passed on, but fairly recently.'

Nodding I answered 'Yes.'

She said 'There is a connection with Halifax, Harry came from Halifax didn't he?'

'Yes.' I said.

She gave me a small smile, 'He doesn't go, does he?'

'No,' I returned with feeling, 'he doesn't.'

'He will,' she said simply, 'he'll go tonight. Before you leave here we will be gone. He didn't know where to go when he passed on, so he came to you. He loved you, you know. He loved you very much. Nothing ever passed between you, for you wouldn't have accepted him anyway, but he couldn't leave you. It's been difficult hasn't it?'

Sadly I said 'Very difficult.'

She smiled, 'Don't worry, it will be all right.'

After the proceedings in general ended I was making my way out as soon as possible and the lady followed me, catching up in the vestibule. Taking my arm she led me outside and began hurriedly:

'I couldn't say too much in there but I couldn't let you go without explaining more. He was your sister's husband wasn't he?'

'Yes, he was.' I said.

'I knew,' she returned, 'and I had to be careful in there for some of them might have drawn the wrong conclusions. But he'd loved you for years and never said a word. You knew he did, didn't you?'

I replied simply, 'Of course I knew. But I wouldn't have entertained him even if we'd both been single and I certainly wouldn't when he was married to my sister. It was just hard lines for him, that's all, but never by one word in my life did I ever give him cause to think I loved him, except that I thought he was a very good person and I liked him for it.'

'Yes, I knew all that. But he was drawn to you, you see and he didn't know where else to go. It's been spoiling your life, for he had two left thumbs and he's been robbing you of your dexterity hasn't he?'

'You can say that again.' I replied.

'Well don't worry my love. We can do that, you know, we can summon someone to fetch them when they're lost like he was.'

With an enormous sense of freedom I replied, 'He's gone now, I'm free. I want to thank you very much, you can't imagine what a relief it is to be myself again.'

She smiled, 'Oh, it happens sometimes, so we do what we can. It's because they're not mediumistic when they're in their bodies, but they always find out later that they don't die. But you know that, don't you?'

I smiled 'Oh yes, I know.'

And thus we parted and I never saw her again, but I'd never seen her before then for that matter.

That small story has been written for two distinct reasons, one of which must follow in chronological sequence and the other is that I would not offer the offence to my sister of knowing that her husband loved me. He was fond of her and behaved toward her with every kindness and circumspection, but I fear that I was the love of his life and it was a love I neither wanted nor would permit to develop. Silence only on the subject. Unfortunately, he was not the only husband to be so afflicted and I found this phenomenon distinctly distasteful. I wanted no man. I wanted answers now and was up to my neck in learning.

On the spurious flat face of reality it might appear to be utterly illogical to be learning what the scientific world was presenting as truth, for no discipline was more rejecting of, more dismissive of and more disdainful of the events of my life. Two opposing poles and apparently there was no possible domain in which they would ever be reconciled. So why did I read astrophysics? I did not know, is the simple answer. And to spend all available moments (together with moments which I made available at the cost of ignoring other jobs) reading such abstruse literature appeared to be irrational, ludicrous.

My brain seemed to go into over-drive at times and very naturally I was trying to learn with no supervision or careful channeling. When young I had read because I wanted to know what 'made people tick' and now I was learning what made matter 'tick'.

In general, regarding the fabric of my flat surface existence matters were in apparent disorder. I am not relating my existence on that deceptive plane, for such events were banal, repeated in thousands of similar lives and as of no interest to anyone there is no requirement to supply details. I told my husband I was leaving him, but we came back together after a while. Knowing it would not last I simply resumed the conventional apparatus for a while, then we parted once more. Space and my cottage lured tantalizingly near, but another factor entered the melee; my mother was betraying unmistakable signs of Alzheimer's disease and this was an obligation which could not be dismissed. My goal, my hope, my desperate thirst for I knew not what seemed now to recede inexorably and there were times when I felt utter despair.

I was house hunting, had very little money and the task seemed impossible. Prices were rising and as it was obvious that as I would have to care for my mother, no shack would do. She had to be comfortable.

As this is pertinent I will describe the episode. Fruitlessly I had wandered about my native village in what appeared to be a hopeless quest for a house I could afford to buy. I was getting off the bus at the town stop and on my way to an agent I knew when I 'saw' figures of white light. Go to ……..'s. This man had the reputation of being something of a shark, but it was from him and the howling mistake he made that day (although he did not lose on the overall deal) that I got my own house. Not a cottage, it was one of a terrace of stone built houses and in excellent condition, south facing and with a tiny strip of garden. I was sent there. Let there be no doubt on the score, for in normal times I would never have chosen to deal with that particular agent. There had been direct intervention from another domain.

In one of her ever-decreasing moments of lucidity, my mother said pathetically that yes, she'd like to live there. It was as I was decorating the ground floor room for her that the news was brought that my husband was in hospital. He had had a heart attack and I realized that I would have to care for him also.

Betty called and I spoke forthrightly:

'It's the greatest irony I've ever known. I've wanted to live alone since I was nineteen and it's been the dream of my life to live in my own house. Now I've got it and it's going to be filled with the two loving tyrants who have dominated my existence. I shall have to care for both of them and it's a fifty fifty chance whether I'll survive or not. There's a fine old chance that they'll kill me between them, because I'll have to work as well and I don't know how I'm going to do it.'

In complete mystification she said 'I don't understand you. I don't know what you're talking about' and I realized that of course she couldn't be expected to know for I had not told her about this terrible need.

There being no choice I had to make the best of the situation. At no time did it occur to me to ask for any help because I simply did not know that any was available. They were burdens and I was used to being loaded with burdens of my own and the burdens of friends and relatives. It seemed to be my life's work. Capable. Strong. So I was a pack pony. My husband had been self-employed, had refused years earlier to buy insurance for himself, therefore it was work or starve. I worked. Up at five, in silence do as many chores as possible, rush to work, return at five and begin to cook whilst they watched me in patient anticipation. Since setting foot in the house, my mother had never known who I was and said disagreeably that she had never liked me for I had been a nosy neighbour. Every evening after clearing up after our meal I installed her in our upstairs sitting room in front of the television and at precisely nine o'clock she thanked me for allowing her to visit for the weekend and said regretfully that she'd have to leave:

'Frank doesn't know I've come, you see, so I must go. And there are the children to see too. They'll all be wondering where I am.'

After ten minutes I went down to find her dressed in her outdoor clothes, bundle beneath her arm containing spare undies, etc. and then followed her along the silent streets until she gradually wandered to an uncertain halt. Possible then to lead her home and get her settled into bed. Day after interminable day.

Sunday was fully occupied with the big cleaning chores and the washing. Many, many times in my life I had read of people who, impelled by a need to investigate, have wandered the world with no visible means of support and wondered always how they managed the necessary chores of feeding, obtaining the monies to feed, cleaning their persons and their clothing, to say nothing of their surroundings if they chose to stay in their homes. Such stories have always, for me, owned a strong element of superficiality. Essentially, I am a practical person and if one does not pay the rates bill one is prosecuted, so to pay one's bills and keep oneself out of the courts or jail one must work. It is that simple. I have never lived in an airy-fairy world and have had full confrontation with the harsh realities of life. It is impossible for a woman to take off and find her destiny without financial support. I had no such support, therefore I had to work. The latter paragraph may appear to have no bearing upon that which has gone before, but I would have it noted that I was not, at any time, an adherent of the 'wandering through the wilderness' persuasion. In my physical existence I was subject to the dictates of society and both my feet were firmly on the ground.

On this very ground I was presented with an appalling decision and none of the solutions were acceptable. My husband had been told he could work again, but he would not be able to unless I helped him. This meant leaving my mother unattended and so bewildered was her mind she actually needed constant attendance. If I did not help him he would have another heart attack and may have died, but if I left her she may do something drastic which would harm her and many others. The decision I reached was made purely on the question of age: my mother was eighty-six and my husband in the later fifties. I decided to help him. Whatever I did was potentially disastrous, for if he had an attack whilst driving alone terrible consequences could result. I felt as if I were being squeezed by a scold's bridle.

Inevitably, the day came when I could no longer deal with the situation. We had followed the usual evening procedure and I had gone to my mother's room to find her fully dressed and waiting. But that night I could not go walking the streets and tried to persuade her to take off her hat and coat. Persuaded she would not be. Go she would and she seemed to swell and inflame, her face became distorted and as I watched she seemed to slide into some kind of brainstorm. In exhaustion I took the keys and left her and at that she raved and it took hours to settle her. At five a.m. she was shouting to my husband to take her home and reiterating that Frank wouldn't know where she was etc. My husband, furious, turned over.

Down in her room I sat, in utter despair, knowing I could not deal with this any longer. She could not now be left alone and equally he could not either. Then another mind entered the situation. I could not see him, but the very air in the room was electric now with his presence. My father. He talked soundlessly into my right ear:

'Let her go, sweetheart, let her go. You can't do this any more, you must get help and let her go.'

She stood, fully dressed, glaring at me, hopelessly insane because I had thwarted her. I wished myself dead. It was my own fault for being a coward when I was nineteen. I should have left home. A rotten coward, I thought with disgust.

My doctor said 'Let her go, she'll get very much worse.'

Betty said 'Let her go, Kathleen.'

And the social worker said 'What are you on?'

Not having the slightest idea as to what she meant I said, 'I don't understand.'

She repeated impatiently, 'What are you on? Which drug do you take?'

'I'm sorry,' I answered, 'What makes you think I take drugs?'

She said 'You must have been taking something to live like this. What is it? Valium?'

I could not explain to her what caused me to function, so I returned simply:

'I don't take any pills at all.'

Later I reflected on this curious attitude. Obviously, I was out of touch with present-day solutions. It seemed to me then, as it does now, that it's no use in trying to blanket misery in your brain, because it only clouds your mind into soporific porridge and whatever drug it is will only last for a while in its effects, so you are going to have to find some way of dealing with your problems sooner or later. It may be simplified, but that's the way it is.

Within four days my mother was ensconced in a home for the elderly and I felt bad all the time. As I never felt 'good' there was little difference.

My younger daughter suggested we start a business together – in a small way. I asked my husband if he would employ someone to help him and he agreed. Thus it was that she and I began working together and sometime later, entirely predictably – he had another heart attack which stopped him from working altogether. However, our little business grew quite well and kept us.

During the springtime of that year I had a curious vision. I found myself standing on the top step of the lower staircase and I was looking at the quite heavy paper I'd used for the ceiling. Above were the attic stairs and so constructed that the curving stairs above corresponded to a slight curve in this ceiling. I hadn't put that paper on any too well and decided I'd alter it a bit when I had time. As the landing light was on I could see my miscalculation very clearly. By this time the relations between my husband and I were strained badly and I had chosen to live in the big attic bedroom, which meant he had the rest of the house to himself. Therefore it was a shock when I transferred my gaze from the ceiling's slight miscalculation, through the wall, across the landing and through the bedroom wall beyond. Now I was looking about the bedroom and was astonished to find that my possessions were in it. My clothes hung in the fitted recess and unmistakable small personal objects were about. Then I had an even greater shock for I realized that I was alone in my house. No one else lived here. How had it happened? I didn't know, but I was living alone after all these years. There were continuations of this vision, but they related solely to my private life and will be omitted.

In the July of that year I had a swift, serious illness, was transferred to hospital for surgery and on my return to my home my husband and I separated finally. Neither wished to live with anyone else; we could not live together.

At last I was alone in my own house; and it may be supposed that I went mad with joy; I did not. As I explained earlier, one cannot live in this world without financial support. If the bills went unpaid I would be in a sordid situation and as the only financial support I owned was work, I had to continue working. An invidious position. In September I had 'flu' and stayed, somehow, on my feet. There was no time to be ill.

Sometime later, as I was shampooing a client, the first of the daytime visions began. It was a tunnel and the enclosed space was round, seemingly to stretch to an impossible-to estimate distance, but at the end of the tunnel was Infinity, a glorious amalgam of colour and an inexplicable 'Awareness'. The sides of this tunnel were dark, rounded and faintly gleaming as if dully polished. For an infinitesimal fraction of time I saw Infinity wholly but then, equally in an infinitesimal fraction of time I was within the tunnel again. Now I knew the nature of this tunnel: it was Time. Time itself. Flooded now with strange knowledge.

The next second I was stupidly gazing at the foaming head beneath my hands. Where had I been? Did the client know I'd been away? I seemed to have been gone for ages, yet realized that it could not have been long or she would have begun to complain.

In a peculiar wild excitement I realized I had learned something of what seemed to be inexhaustible value. Of course, one could go back in time, one could remember past experiences, relive them if necessary, but to move, to go on, one could only move forward in time. All living, all future experiences were in future time. Knowledge came flooding in: it was no use anyone declaring that future time could not be known, because there was no other dimension in which one could exist, there was no Now. The next breath one would take was in a future dimension of time, as was the next thought one was about to have, to think. The future was the only possible avenue and at the end was glorious Infinity.

I wanted to shout 'Eureka' but of course I did nothing of the kind. But I thought now, deeply and from many aspects. One's future, anyone's future was open for there were no barriers in this tunnel which was Time. Therefore it could not be claimed that it was not possible to move into one's future because it was possible and the events of my life had shown clearly that it was possible, for it had happened, many times.

Brooding like a pregnant hen I tried to examine this knowledge from all angles and say with regret that I missed entirely the crucial factor. But, it was a start.

Never having truly rid myself of the 'flu' I got it at Christmas time, full-blown, but with the clamour of people begging for appointments there was no question of taking to my bed. I worked, not knowing how I managed to stay upright. Haunted always by the pressing: I must give up and start to write, yet unable to see how there were any means by which I could do so, nagged eerily by the feeling that if I could not find some financial support I would simply go on being ill. So, of course, it happened and in January I had to enter hospital for surgery again and was away for a week. In February I had 'flu' again and worked on. By now I could not eat and the flesh had melted from my bones. Came the day when I ate one half slice of bread and went home knowing well that if this went on I would die and caring little as to whether I did or not.

Making myself a cup of coffee I added a spoonful of honey, feeling drearily that it might restore some lost energy. I had been a strong woman, well nourished in my youth, but now after years of punishing work and illness I was spent. I went to bed at eight thirty hoping now never to awaken, thinking wryly that I had known for years I would die at fifty-six years of age and that was now my age. Ironical, that having lived so much I would die in this squalid fashion and no one would ever know that a world of light existed. Moreover, it was open to very ordinary people. It did not follow that people of wealth and power would be a part of that incredible beauty, indeed, they were less likely to reach that pinnacle of perfection, for arrogance and disdain were not the keys to admittance.

Amid such tumbling thought I lay down on my back and no sooner had my head touched my pillow than the rocking began in my head. With no anxiety I thought: I am going to have a stroke or something and I hope it's fatal. I'd have to lie like a log and have the girls be obliged to wash me and feed me with a spoon. That's disgusting and it would ruin their lives. I shall try to die. So violent was the rocking it seemed as if my whole head was shaking, but from the inside, then quite quickly it seemed to settle then into a pleasant rhythm, which spread painlessly down my body. By the time it reached my feet the sensation was lovely, similar to lying on water which moves gently in a lulling motion and I lay in utter peace, content to be lulled.

With no sense of alarm I looked down at my body, thinking: You poor bewildered thing, why do you worry so? Why do you let yourself be tortured and frayed by things which don't matter in the slightest? You're fretted and shredded by stupid irritations which have no value whatsoever. This is so lovely, so lovely, why can't you be at peace? This is peace. I'm not confined; I can go anywhere if I choose. Floating now, still lying on a horizontal plane I turned lazily to see on my left my small bedside cabinet and thought: It's time I tidied that up a bit, I'll do it tomorrow. Turning effortlessly in an almost full circle I looked at the doors of the wardrobe section. One of the handles had loosened and I thought: I'll get a screwdriver and fasten that on properly or it's going to be off.

For a moment or two I moved without volition up to the ceiling beside the window, seeing effortlessly the town two miles away, entering the library, then casting about the well known thoroughfares, but there was nothing to see which I did not know well so I returned again to consider a new tack: Why don't I do this more often? I know exactly how to do it, I've always known. I've done it oh, thousands of times and it's so easy, so peaceful. I'll do it more often.

Only one area was barred to me; I knew I could go anywhere in the world if I wished to, I had but to go, there were no barriers to travelling, except, except I couldn't turn in a circle of 360 degrees because the head on the pillow below could not be, for some reason, traversed. Still, it didn't matter, nothing, nothing mattered ... and I was sucked into a whirlpool of darkness.

On the moment of awakening I was cured. Fit as a flea. My old self, bouncing with energy. Yet I lay, remembering, deciding I would do that again for I knew exactly how to do it, ohhh, I've forgotten. Frantically I searched my memory. It was so simple, I knew how to do it, I'd done it thousands of times ... In the end, with reluctance, I admitted to myself that a shutter had been lowered and I couldn't remember the mechanism which lifted it, yet it had been so simple.

Another bonus however, I had a resource, I owned one half of our little business and I would ask my daughter if she would buy my half. It was no great sum, in fact it was really quite small as resource capital, but I could begin to write and I could live on it for a while anyway. She agreed at once and I bought a secondhand typewriter. As a typist I was a disaster area, but I'd manage somehow. For several weeks I impressed upon pristine white paper the black miseries and resentments, the griefs and idiocies of my life. Then I took the lot out into the garden and burned it.

I began all over again. It was July and a lovely day. So my life began.

Skirmishing was ended. For years I had thought: I will die at fifty-six and it became true, there began a death, but there are more kinds of death than disintegration of the body.

The dog it was that died, but it was a protracted demise.

Chapter 12 – 'Eureka: Greek – it is found.'

It was a lovely morning in July and the sunshine was already bathing my room with golden light. Even the tinkling of milk bottles sounded somehow mellowed and the chatter of women a pleasant murmuring. Children's voices rising and lowering, their giggles added to pleasant domesticity all compounded now into the humming of life beyond my window.

I was writing when I became physically conscious of a strange developing phenomenon. My feet had disappeared. I could walk on them, but I could not see them. Without the smallest alarm I realized that they had become invisible. How I knew the invisibility was going to spread, to rise, to engulf me I did not know, but I knew with utter certainty that this would follow and it was time to begin moving whilst I was able to move.

Space was required. As much space as was obtainable in my room. All moveable furniture had to be pushed as nearly as possible to the walls and it was going to be quite a task for now my lower legs were disappearing into darkness. All dining chairs were pushed with great effort, painfully and the last item was the typing table, which by now had assumed the proportions and weight of the rock of Gibraltar. I leaned my now invisible hips against it to the uttermost reaches. My last physical act was to draw the last of the dining chairs into the space created in the centre of the room and sat down. Somehow I had just managed the whole operation in the time available, for now my body was darkness and only my head was free. I faced the hearth and looked at the little gilt mantel clock: it was precisely nine thirty am.

A swooping sensation, a falling into a vortex of utter darkness. Then I knew no more. How long this lasted I do not know, but as some period, some nameless period of time I could see again and what I could see defies all description. I will try, but words will not suffice.

Before me lay a Void, an immensity of Space. But the Space was filled. There is the fleeting recollection of my mind, of my person. Oh, oh, ohhhh. A gasping sensation of indescribable wonder, of awe, of limitless intelligence, of an intelligence so vast, so supremely the pinnacle of all understanding, all knowledge, that no puny human mind could ever grasp, ever know. A MIND. An intelligence from which the whole Universe had been formed. This MIND was the source of all which had ever been created within this MIND. Light was the MIND's creation. Love. Everything nameable and knowable, everything observable and unobservable. In that one fleeting fraction of time I could 'see' and what I saw is as beyond understanding, as unreachable, as unknown as the rim of the Universe, for this MIND had created the whole of the Universe. I knew, I saw. There is a recollection of wandering in vast filled Space knowing exactly everything which could be known, but I am unable to recollect it, or tell of how everything was created.

When my eyes opened they were observing the clock. It told eleven thirty. Two hours had elapsed.

Eventually, with no recollection of how it was accomplished, I moved and now I was clinging to the architrave of the kitchen door. My body was composed of palest golden light of no physical substance and I could see within it and through it. It was as if a force was lifting me as I held the architrave and I knew that if I released my hold I would fly and be gone.

The golden light became submerged now with another realization: Joy. A Joy so pure, so limitless I was dissolving into it, a Force so irresistible that it consumed like a vast golden flame without boundaries, all-encompassing; beyond rapture, beyond ecstasy, a consuming for which there are no words, no feelings, only a subsuming Perfection in which I drowned.

Of what followed that day I have no recollection. Did I eat or sleep or even breathe? I do not know, for I was lost in a wonder that I cannot describe. All I may tell is that the following day the whole experience was repeated.

Now I know that even if I could remember that which I saw and knew within that immensity of MIND, that Void which contained everything knowable, it would be useless in the world for if all the world's knowledge or the capacity for knowledge were to be fused into one dynamic concentration it would be no more than one drop in one ocean, for we do not have the ability to comprehend the enormity of the MIND itself.

All I may write is woefully inadequate; all I may say is that I saw It, knew It and that I have given all I own to write these words. I will not embroider or attempt to convince. This I lived and saw.

For three weeks I lived in a paradisiacal haze of golden light. Did I eat? Or sleep? Or perform physical functions? I do not know. My first coherent memory is of my younger daughter knocking at my door, so I must have locked it for some reason.

She said in wonder, 'Mum, what's happened? You're, you're different. I, ...' then she stopped abruptly.

I could not explain and strangely she questioned me no more. So what she saw I do not know.

But the following day I acted. To the library, where else? Knowing exactly where to discover explanations, or at least some descriptions of that which I had seen and it was to be found in the ancient eastern writings. It was called 'The Supreme Enlightenment' and I read that to those who were granted this incredible experience, an edict was laid that it was too precious to be described. Indeed, it was considered to be offensive to so attempt. I thought: that edict is unnecessary, for it is impossible to describe the Indescribable.

To infer that I thought much is ludicrous: my head was so filled with answers and explanations I could not isolate any of the whirling, teeming knowledge in my head. Yet from that chaos arose the implacable, Why me? Why had this happened to me? I was no saintly creature, immolated from the world. I was as ordinary as the bread and butter which was my staple diet. Never in my life had I meditated; I did not know how to meditate. I had heard of the transcendental theories which were being increasingly practiced, very much in vogue in the West, but no lure would attract me to that net. Nor was this priceless bestowal because of my character, for I had a swift temper and a cutting tongue. It was understandable that gentle seekers-after-truth, true mystics, would and did sit for years in contemplation, meditating on what they knew to be true, or believed to be true. They and I had as much in common as the Pacific Ocean to a cup of cold tea. As for natural goodness being the reward of knowing the MIND, I was a one-legged horse in that race. So, 'Why me?' There was no logical explanation; I was a provincial housewife in a provincial town, as obscure as a grain of sand on a long beach.

But I knew now that a God existed, but it was not the God which had ever been described and presented with gospelling. God was a MIND. An infinity of Intelligence. Creation.

Some weeks had passed. Not being a calendar watcher I cannot say how many, but it must have been sometime in mid-autumn when I awoke one morning very quickly. Usually – as with many others – I drifted upwards through many misty layers, sometimes half remembering dreams, sometimes not. Often content to lazily adjust to the new day and savour the last moments of idleness. Not this morning, at one moment I was asleep and the next moment I was fully awake; there was no interim period.

In the same instant I knew I had missed something, something I wanted to remember; was it a dream? Could I have been dreaming of something and the dream had been interrupted? No. It wasn't quite like that, different somehow. How different? I did not know, except it didn't feel like a dream, but what could it be if it wasn't? There wasn't anything else, for it was not a vision, I always knew them. What on earth could have wakened me up so quickly? I'd missed something, something precious. At last I got up feeling as if I'd been deprived of something and laboured under a sense of loss. Would it return? I didn't know, but I resolved that the next morning I'd try to wake up sooner; perhaps it would return and I'd see it, whatever it was.

The following morning I awakened at what I felt to be the speed of light. Asleep and awake during the same breath, but I wasn't quick enough. Only the most brief of glances, certainly insufficient to detect anything. It was like seeing the end of the hem of a dress moving behind a closing door, so that you couldn't see the dress or the colour and certainly not the figure that was wearing it. Now I felt truly deprived as if something incredibly wonderful, something magical had been snatched from me at the very last moment. I got up mourning and mourned for the rest of the day. Pervaded by an inexplicable sense of loss. Could I possibly have awakened any faster? It was unfeasible on all counts. Now it was an imperative that I see this thing, although I hadn't the remotest idea as to what it could be, only that if I didn't see it I'd be in despair.

From sleep to full consciousness with no pause and I saw. It stayed and the world exploded into an incredible awed wonder. I saw, through translucency, yet with crystalline clarity, pure energy and it had a name:

Pure Life.

Pure Energy.

Imploded into a concentration so intense that it seemed to radiate like radium. It was as if the Atlantic had been distilled, with all its mighty power intact, into an egg cup full of water. Like the unimaginable force which is deemed to exist within a black hole.

Intelligent energy.

There burst onto my bemused mind the reason why I had lived my future before that future evolved into what we supposed was reality.

Incredibly, this lived with me. This had known my future, informed of my future, it was a Mind in itself, but it was not my conscious mind, it was another Mind. Why? Why did this live with me? How could it bear to? It must have chosen to, but in no sense whatsoever did it belong to me.

It knew.

It knew all that needed to be known.

It had dragged me into my future because it had known my future. There was nothing which it did not know and suddenly, without warning, I looked through the mind straight into the library. I was there and the books, some of them vast volumes of which I could see every word on every page and know exactly the nature and meaning of all, all in one glance. Each book, thousands of them, I could see and know without ever reading one.

Pure energy, I would not have known it was allied to me without the outline of my own person, for it was transparent and I could see the capillaries, blood and bone of my body. Yet within the outline this colossal implosion of Life and Life which Knew.

At last I rose, seeing it no longer, insensate with Joy. And as had happened after entering the Void I lost all knowledge of the passing of days for I lived in a trance of utter Joy.

Later, much later, I began incompetently to write. Who on earth would believe this?

Thousands of the questions that I had read, thousands that I had lived, all answered now and I did not know where to begin.

Effortlessly, I could see the whole of mankind, the whole of its written history. See and know where we had stumbled, formed erroneous conclusions, seen that which lay hidden in the minds of men and women. It was as if the whole world had opened like a great multipetalled flower, each tiny leaf an answer, each tiny petal a solution; and I knew that if I were to live for a thousand years I could not, would not, be able to elucidate each and every instance which required explanation.

From a world of laborious questioning I had moved into a world in which there were only answers. So many. So many I could not write them. As I incompetently struggled all other explanations intruded, all jockeying for space, for all were compounded now into one vast Whole, I could separate none for all combined. No subject, no answer, no question could be isolated from any other except one:

Why me?

A thousand times I asked and to this there was no answer, nor is there now, as I write. Which did not end the one-sided dialogue: Why was this not given to a better brain than mine? Why not to a trained mind which could have formulated this immensity of knowledge? I'm not clever enough. I'm not good enough. How am I going to tell of this when there are only words to use? But to all those plaintive wailings there was no reply. I had to go on, to try and I who had read billions of words could not release this immensity of knowledge.

It was November. How I know it I cannot remember, but it was a day in late November as I was sitting before the typewriter when the next vision began and it began so suddenly I actually jumped in my chair. I thought: 'Oh heavens, a water main has burst' for there had erupted by my right side a great gushing column of what I supposed to be water. Then it settled into a continuous silent upward flood and the column had a name, it was:

'Time.'

Instantly I knew the identity of this column, its nature and its functions. It was:

'Energy.'

Time was energy as life was energy. As the column was transparent I could see within it and there was a great deal within it. Houses, lawns, children, adults, buildings, plants and animals, all the occupants of the flat surface material world, together with the attendant creations of mankind moved steadily within the energy in which they moved and it was the diurnal clock by which the whole planet moved and was constrained. But I was on the outside, looking in.

In one brief flash I saw how the energy which is Time could be isolated and discovered: you removed the concept from all you observed and knew in the physical world and then considered what would be the result, the future of all matter, if time were obliterated.

As I concluded this, the torrent faded and I typed as fast as my fingers would move in order to record the concept before I forgot it. Then I saw what the result would be: matter could only exist within Time because Time itself was the energy which permitted the existence of matter. If Time were removed all matter would halt and a frozen world, a frozen heavens and a frozen Universe would be the result. Everything would cease in one infinitesimal instant. But But…

If Time was a necessary component, in that matter required time, the energy of time in order to exist, then another dimension of time existed also, for I was outside that column when I saw the energy…

It was as if Pandora's box had opened. For all that I had known, read and lived instantly assumed a new complexion. And as I began to consider the implications my mind reeled again, for it meant looking at everything from a different standpoint. How on earth was I ever to make sense of all this, let alone write it? I tried of course, but what resulted were disorderly meanderings.

Some little time passed, but it was not long after the experience of learning the nature of and the dimension of Time that I was crossing my living space when I left the world again. Prior to description, I now write that what is to follow was repeated throughout that whole winter. It is the only vision of my life, that was repeated and because I am unscholarly I do not keep written records of events. For that omission I make no apology. I do not care to see butterflies pinned to cards. Nor do I choose to be pinned to days, to months, to hours etc. For I deal in eras and it was during this era, in this house, that I learned.

Further to that I will add that the vision which I shall describe, has been repeated throughout my life, is repeated as I write and I see this sight in all locations and in all circumstances. It is not so much that I re-live it; it is now an indelible part of my being.

In space, dark and looking to my left. Hanging in the velvet was the spiral arm of the Milky Way seen more clearly now than I had ever seen it. It looked as if a giant's fist had hurled diamonds and diamond dust across the sky and I wanted to move nearer, to touch, to move amongst the exquisite clusters; and eerily there was a tiny sensation that if … that if something … but it was gone. But, oh the beauty of this sight, how utterably wonderful.

For some reason I transferred my gaze and was assailed by immense shock. I had expected to see more of the heavens, to view star clusters, fantastic distributions of diamonds which appeared to be strewn by casual arrangement, but which were present in their very casually abstract designs of great beauty. It was not so, for at a distance, but not so distant that any stars or dust lay between, was an Immensity of darkness. It was as if the right hand view of the sky had been blanked off from me. But there was nothing here of the impersonal grandeur: this limitless darkness exuded Intelligence, massive, all consuming Intelligence. It lived.

I lost thought, lost all power of thought. Simply stared in one all consuming awe. Rendered immobile in every human function. A tiny aperture appeared and within was light, was a combination of exquisite colours, rose and white and gold. Tiny as the aperture was by comparison with the unimaginable immensity I could see quite clearly and I saw a tiny tendril of the Immensity detach itself like a fragmentary plume of smoke emerges from a burning candle, yet which is still bonded to the candle.

Behind me and to my right, but at a distance was the earth, our planet; I could see it clearly although I was not facing it. Wonderful it looked, striated banks of blue, of gold, of greens, browns and white. As I watched, the tiny plume effortlessly and without losing its own integrity of formation glided gently and inexorably through our planet, then returned to its parent formation.

And that is how living intelligent energy subsumed our planet.

As I gazed (only in awe, for thought was impossible) I was invaded by information from the Dark Immensity: It knew I was there. I was so much less than atom size, but It knew I was there. Bereft of thought or the power to think, but stood in my room consumed with a wonder and awe which has never diminished.

Much later, tiny implications began to stir, to surface. Implications which grew into majestic truths; comparisons; explanations; until I was submerged in information that it seemed as if I would drown in facts. Answers to questions which had been demanded by humankind and which had remained unanswered to perplex human kind. It seemed as if I had been dumped into an immense forest, each individual tree a truth, but I wandered helplessly among the thousands of truths wondering hopelessly how I would ever extract them all and construct them into cohesive thought.

At this juncture, a pause, a clarification and explanation as to the nature and function of these visions; and I will use as parallel example that which I saw a-building at the time. It was as if my life was an enormous tapestry, which was being assembled – as tapestries are – stitch by stitch. Anyone who has ever seen a huge tapestry will concede that the number of stitches required to complete a picture the size of a carpet must be colossal, almost uncountable. Yet every single microscopic stitch has a function and is a necessary part of the whole in order that the finished tapestry portrays the story, which it is intended to present. Likewise, these visions contained a truth in every microscopic aspect and sometimes (almost always) I would see some microscopic stitch which contained its own truth emerge years later. At times, one single stitch of truth could transform the whole picture. This is not written in order to plead extenuating circumstances, nor to offer excuses for my own ineptitude; for I have made no secret of my lack of scholarly talents. There was too much information for my brain to absorb and clarify and I wished a thousand times that I owned a better brain, one which could collate all this information. So although I did not plan this writing (an admission any writer would deplore) I find I am brought quite neatly to a vision which appeared to be almost childish in its simplicity, but from which I learned an amount which has increased over the years and from which I still learn.

Disliking sordid squalour but also disliking cleaning chores at an equal rate I did a premises cleaning every week. Certainly I must have been dusting prior to the vision I shall now describe, because when it was over my first physical sight was of a yellow duster clutched in my hand. The popular over-view of persons who claim to have mystical experiences is, perhaps, deceptive; certainly I lived on no lofty plane detached from banal functions. In the interim periods between these astounding visions I functioned like the rest, in soul-destroying mediocrity.

A severed brain. My mind reeled. A human brain, living and in complete order except the upper layer had been trepanned and I could see the twin lobes in microscopic detail. I knew, of course, that the brain feels no pain, it being an organ, which processes the fact of pain from all parts of the body, without itself feeling any. It lay there, filling my vision. To whom this brain belonged I had not the smallest notion, nor did it occur to me – weirdly – to ever wonder as to the identity of the owner. It was a brain and I could see it in infinitesimal detail. Axons, dendrites, individual cells as if the whole were under an electron microscope. Transfixed in utter amazement I could only stare. I knew the outer layers of a brain were a rather unpleasant grayish colour, as unappetizing as cooked, uneatable tripe, but these inner cells and capillaries were not unpleasing and appeared to be a creamy pinkish colour. (Having never seen the inner cell of a brain I cannot vouch for the authenticity of the colour.) Very obviously no one can vouch for the colour, for although trepanning of the skull is possible, trepanning of a living brain would cause instant death and the colour would change automatically.

Subtly, without warning, a change in colour began on the top right perimeter of the brain. One or two cells became suffused with a delightful roseate light and the effect was stunningly beautiful. Each cell became a minute beacon of living light and as the suffusion spread – which it did – but not with any haste or the smallest hysteria, merely a gentle inexorable merging, quite a large section of the brain was a glowing carpet of roseate light to the extent of the individual cells losing their crisp outlines.

Without warning, the truth, the identity of this light was known to me. Each miniscule cell was invaded by knowledge of its true identity. Each cell had become aware that the invading light was its own soul and this hitherto mysterious identity was, in fact, a direct result of the MIND's intelligence pervading the planet. It was Life itself recognizing the characteristics of Life, living energy. Therefore, Life was not simply an energy, but bore characteristics of its own and was not simply a force, a force which propelled a body, there was more to it than that. Abruptly, I saw the duster and had to sit down for a while wondering what all this meant. Now there was more than ever to think about, to collate. Each of these visions appeared to be so disparate I could see no conjunction between any of them. It all appeared to be haphazard, illogical. Yet somewhere inside me was a persuasion that it was not. If only I could arrange the pieces of this fabulous jigsaw puzzle I would see the finished picture, but my brain reeled for each vision was so filled with information that I was stupefied with answers.

It is only now, years later, as I write these words that I finally know the identity of the brain's owner; it was my own brain. At the age of fifty-six I would die and I had known it for years. But that was only one half of the truth. Yes, a death had begun, but it was not the death of the body, it was the death of the ego. I tell, without remorse, that there was a lot of ego and a long lingering death it proved to be.

I wish there were another medium in existence to describe the Void. Neither sculpture nor painting will do, neither music nor dance, neither scent nor touch, for there was, there is Pure Energy, Pure Comprehensive Intelligence, Pure Creation and from it came:

Matter
Time
Life

There are no absurd concepts such as 'God the Father' for it was within that MIND that the male/female conjunction was conceived in order to perpetuate living species.

Chapter 13 – Risk Takings

At the time of deciding to write I had also realized that I might fail. Comparable to my father's decision, I thought: there's only a fifty-fifty chance of my succeeding and I resolved that if I did not succeed it was not because that which I had lived in those early visions was untrue. Indeed they were only too harrowingly true where the deaths were concerned, but my own incompetence was such that I did not think I would be able to write convincingly. I had to prove that precognition and the existence of a Sixth Sense was true and what better proof could be offered than the deaths of one's children? It has to be admitted that I was 'green' in this respect, for Science in general has precluded all such precognitive assertions as figments of distorted and defective intelligences, behaving generally as brutally implacable as church doctrines on the subject. It might be supposed that these polar opposites were disunited on all fronts, but on this subject – without ever quite realizing the fact – they were actually united. I often thought wryly: they ought to devise a banner for themselves with a large caption: 'If we say it doesn't exist, then it doesn't exist.' Which is about the acme of implacability. It was of no help to me.

Indeed, there appeared to be no help from any social quarter. I could not, of course, seek help from the State, for apart from begging being anathema to me, my early resolve had been that if I failed, my life, the taking of it, would be the penalty. Succeed or die and the fault would be in being unable to write that which I knew to be true. It was crass stupidity, but at times it appeared to be valid and logical, given what I knew of myself. Actually, I knew very little; ego was the barrier. 'A little learning is a dangerous thing' it is said. I had done much learning, both by academic standards and actual experience. But as Edith Cavell said of patriotism, 'It was not enough'.

My perspectives had changed irrevocably, for no one who ever entered the Void emerged unchanged. I conceded that which Emmie had always serenely claimed and which I had vehemently denied: I was a medium. Not in the superficial sense of conveying messages from departed relatives to pleading relatives still in their bodies, for the visions I had seen were not of mundane quality, they were too vast for comprehension. Yet the greater part of my existence was spent in analyses and in these I was aided for at times I was actually struck by bolts of lightening and new perspectives were suddenly illumined which clarified old questions. During my daily life I was aware that these visions did not follow one upon the other in haste; I was given time during the interim periods to absorb, to think, to clarify this enormity of new knowledge and to make comparisons with that which I had read over the years: for this knowledge encompassed the myriad aspects of human existence together with the myriad experiences of humankind.

Frequently I experienced the strange sensation of being suspended in space and watching the Universe expand, radiate from this one central point of which I was the centre. But the point was so infinitesimally tiny, so immeasurably tiny that I seemed to be no more than an electron and I could not understand how anything so small could see such unimaginable vistas. Inevitably, this clarified the sense I had of myself as being almost a 'nothing' a point of consciousness, no more, yet a point which could see the limitless vastness and it was strange beyond measure.

Learning from the astrophysicists the nature of matter – or as much as had been learned concerning the mysteries of Nature – I had read of the researches into many other disciplines: zoology, biology, vulcanology, study of the earth's composition, studies of native peoples and their adjustment to their habitat, studies of sleep, of time, of anything and everything I could absorb, sponge-like in the nature of researchers. Einstein had been permitted, with condescension from lesser minds, to proclaim his belief in a God; likewise Jung, after studying for years concluded that a belief in a God was necessary for the mental health of humans. Laboriously I had ploughed my way through some (not all) of philosophical dissertations, which had analysed to decimal point the aspects of the human character, some of which outline 'the-thing-in-itself'. In none had I discovered an answer to the simple question which had racked my being: 'How it is possible to live one's future before that future arrives?'

And in none of the often tortuous written explanations which fairly encompassed human and natural experience and being was there an answer. But an answer now existed, for I had lived the answer; one owned another mind. There was a secondary 'I'. Even then I did not see the ramifications, but it was a beginning.

Earlier I had been halted when crossing the sitting room of the big house to wonder at the words, which had, risen, unknown and unbidden, in my mind, 'Who am I?' During the evening I sat in Emmie's shabby little 'church' and saw the magnificent elephant, pure Goodness, I had also seen briefly, arising from some darkness in myself hitherto unknown, the 'I' which lived with me, yet which had been for all of my previous existence unknown and unrecognized. This had been the other 'I', the mind which had known what my future was to be. Recollection was cleared now; for this 'I' was the Sixth Sense, the prompter, that which told the truth because it knew the truth. So many instances, important and unimportant ...

How often had I gone into the library to find, without conscious impulse a book which I had needed at a particular time? How frequently had I opened a book, apparently at random, feeling eerily that the volume had seemed to open itself at a particular leaf to see perhaps one paragraph, one line which appeared to leap from the page? Coincidence? No. There was another mind that knew which book I needed at the time.

Sixth Sense? Absurd. This was another mind.

Letters had arrived and I had known before even seeing the printed address the identity of the writer. I remembered once handing a letter to my husband which had been addressed to him from a man I had never met and had without hesitation described the writer to my husband (which did not please him) but he had admitted that the picture was accurate in all respects.

Silly incidents which I had dismissed without undue consideration, such as setting forth with a clear image in my mind of someone not seen for perhaps years, yet meeting that person with no surprise, for this other mind had known the meeting would occur. Freud had tortuously attributed this small phenomenon in his usual tedious manner, but Freud had not known his own identity, nor the identity of the prompter. For, together with many of the supposedly 'great thinkers' he had, male-like, considered objectively, but this was knowledge that was entirely subjective. One must know oneself before making arrogant pronouncements. Freud had attributed almost all human foibles to lust, but lust was not its true name.

I thought of Jung's theory of synchronicity, the apparently random assemblage of coincidences, which he seemed to feel were anything but random and which he called 'Synchronicity'. That purpose and intention must be involved, which lowered his status in the eyes of the scientific community. He further compromised status by insisting that a God existed, a most unscientific theory, but they had not satisfactorily explained that the laws of chance did not govern the apparently random assemblage of coincidences.

Throughout apparently banal instances in our lives this 'I' emerged, perplexing some, refuted by others, accepted serenely by many; and I thought of the sociologists who studied the beliefs, habits and physical stature of what remained of the 'native' peoples. It had appeared to me that to make a study of human beings who qualified for some outlandish appellation such as 'native' was an insult of the first order. Curiosity I well understood, having been its victim all my life and it has to be said that many approached such studies with no apparent hostility to, or disdain of such natural people living in their natural habitats. If some of their practices appeared to be bizarre to sophisticated eyes that still was no excuse for examining their lives and persons with intense scrutiny. Now I saw with great clarity that objectivity was the culprit. Even with sympathy and compassion such studies were flawed, because if the investigator did not know him or herself (usually a 'him') then any results or conclusions which might be drawn would also be flawed. Partial truths, not whole truths.

One single factor emerged from all such studies and it was that all native peoples employed, without hesitation, or self-consciousness or apology, Sixth Sense. It was and had ever been, homogenous throughout the world and throughout our history. I thought of the Inuit living in some of the harshest climatic conditions anywhere to be found. I thought of their innate belief that the animals who provided them with all their requirements for survival, clothing, heat and food, were animate creatures to whom they owed their deepest respect and to whom apology must be made for their capture and slaughter. Thought also, of the condescension awarded to these people for such unsophisticated beliefs; but the proof of a pudding was in the eating: such people lived in their environment without despoiling the earth. Did we?

Similarly, the Australian aborigines, trekking as they did over vast spaces, existing in conditions which would destroy any casual sophisticate in days, perhaps hours, yet who lived with an intimacy with their land of such intensity that they could 'read' the earth as the casual read a magazine. Not only read it, but also know themselves to be in unison with it. Truly so. This planet is a living entity. I had watched it become so. Their religion, their beliefs compounded of a strange theory they called their 'Dreamtime' and I thought how apt was this description. It signified an existence, a dimension which was incalculable by any physical means of detection, it existed in their collective consciousness, dominated their existence. A factor. A sense. One in which all participated, all without hesitation accepting as a truth and which they regarded as sacred, not to be defiled. And rightly so. Nor was it confined within their persons, for this intelligence moved across distance, so that any malcontent who left the tribe could and did die, of no apparent physical injury, but died by mind, for his own was allied to the mind of his tribe. All, of course, to Western conclusions was viewed with disbelief and some contempt. Nor was this phenomenon peculiar to the Aborigine, for similar instances had been recorded in the ancient heart of the planet: Africa.

There had been at time when Africa had been an obsession of mine and all books which described the land and its peoples had consumed me. Centred in focus were the Bushmen of the Kalahari, tiny in stature, immense in knowledge. Regarded by sophisticates as ignorant natives, yet surviving in the killing conditions of parched earth. They, also, owned a belief sparsely described, yet of a power and intensity which equals any present day fanatic, but which was to them a natural acceptable component of existence. Baldly, it could be described as 'not so much thinking their belief as being their belief' and there is a great difference between the two concepts.

Of course, Africa yielded huge amounts of that which investigators found inexplicable and which many scientists also found inexplicable and therefore dismissed as fantasies of native origin and the products of infantile intelligences. It was easier to claim the non-existence of a factor to which one has no answer than to admit one has no answer, for the latter would diminish the stature, the important self-recognition of the person. To scientists in general this factor is of great importance. Consequently, when stories emerged from Africa of offenders being punished, sometimes by death and by inexplicable methods, no great investigations were conducted for the simple reason that the movers and shakers, the plausible analysts, did not know why they were supposing themselves to be a unity, one person, one mind. Again, objective. And, of course, the witch doctors with their amulets and dried remains, their pebbles and mysteries, held much clout. Some were undoubtedly 'seers' but power always corrupts (as Lord Astley would have it, power can corrupt absolutely) and undoubtedly many of the ilks were dangerous people. Discarding individuals, there remained and remains, an awareness which is beyond the layers which successive Christian missionaries had imposed (at time by sinister means) onto the native peoples. Innate and indestructible, it still emerges …

And I thought of the Native Indians of the Americas, with their belief in a 'Great White Spirit' and considered that they, together with the peoples of the East who, with charming courtesy, believed that all living forms contained a soul and to which they paid their homage, were as nearly truly intelligent people as could be described.

With a deep anger I considered the howling disunity, which had resulted from the emergence of Newton and the consequent establishment of the Industrial Revolution. Information, knowledge, talent, the manipulation of machines, which inevitably manipulated those whose lives were governed by their use. From this had emerged loss, loss of individual identity albeit that the natural awareness had been suppressed and overlaid by centuries of ideologies and nationalism; all, as I thought with increasing anger, to support and promote a small section of humanity in power which submerged natural knowledge; but could not, in spite of threats and often vicious punishments of varying kinds and degrees, wholly dismantle that which was beyond suppression, that which Knew. I thought of Eli and the Celt below the foggy constitution of his church; when I had told him of the real truth he had known it too.

Trivia, I considered. Premonitory flashes of knowledge which flicked so many into awareness and which were so largely discounted, taken for granted as being part of the general scene, woven into the fabric of the mundane. Hunches, prior intimations of something, which was to occur; who bothered to analyse them? And I performed small analyses of such trivia. What were we really experiencing? Exactly where, from whence did we draw our information? One could read, of course and draw parallels based upon past experiences of one's own, or similar experiences related by another. One could base reasonable predictions based upon logic one already possessed. It was possible to predict what a person would do or say in a given situation – especially if one knew the person well, even with strangers certain body language was a direct indication of what was to follow. But suppose no physical touchstones were to hand? Suppose that a situation were to arise where no physical indicators existed to enable one to make any assessment as to what might follow? Ah yes, one would be relying entirely on that tired old concept: Intuition. What was intuition? Another mind. A mind that was not constrained, not limited by the field of vision, of touch, of awareness of the world about one, but a mind which could reach beyond the body's circumscribed capabilities. Yet an active intuition could save one's life, as many who had been in danger of losing theirs could testify.

As is obvious, my mind raged for months over one topic after another, darting through the maelstrom, noting here, noting there, sifting, analyzing, drawing comparison, unravelling mysteries in field after field of human interest, the lives and occupations of human kind. Nor could I, when sitting to type, form coherent explanations with meagre skill and meagre training, do little more than offer protest rather than solid information, retreating perpetually to 'my sons and my father died and I knew those deaths before they came to be and it was because of this other 'I' the soul which lives with me, but is not mine'. Perpetually, it was not enough. Information was there, knowledge was there, but I could not bring it out of myself. Truth, truth that was absolute. Then came that which stopped me in my tracks.

Quite literally, out of the blue as I walked on some errand or some purpose across my living room, it flared in purest white capitals:

'PURITY'

What the...? What on earth?

And it wouldn't go away. I couldn't remove it, for it came between me and everything I did for three days. At last, reluctantly, I paid it my full attention, only to discover that the concept of purity was an enigma and very difficult to analyse. We use the term freely: pure cream, pure beauty, pure living and still it is meaningless because we use it as an adjective in order to describe something which already exists. As a thing-in-itself purity has no substance, for to describe it in any manner whatsoever one inevitably attaches it to some physical or material object and that, of course, negates its own status. Inevitably if one described a person as living pure love, one still had to maintain that the person was of utter purity, but that explanation could not be supported because whoever it was would be composed of atoms and atoms were material substances, therefore the argument collapsed. For to describe purity unalloyed and combined with no other subject was a task which seemed impossible to fulfil; it was a measure, a yardstick, a concept only that something existed which would fully explain the concept. Even analysis of a gas yielded no more than that atoms existed in what appeared to be nothing more than a vapour, tenuous like smoke, but still containing atoms. With a sense of shock I realized that Purity did not admit of explanation as a thing-in-itself, it was simply a conjecture, but and it was a very big but, we were always seeking it and it danced tantalizingly before us. It could not be pinned to a card like a butterfly; we just yearned to find it although it had no substance. How did we conceive such a concept? We once knew the concept to be a reality.

And the only concept to which purity could be truly allied was the concept of a God, howsoever you visualized that concept. I knew it to be a MIND and herein lay the concept of purity. Twin concepts. Twin energies. Purity may appear on the flat deceptive surface, but it was infinitely more than that. A whole new can of worms was opened ... I had to think again, although in truth I never did anything but think.

Months had passed, how many I have no idea of, nor is it of the slightest importance. A soundless, painless, violent explosion occurred inside my head, throwing all thoughts into jeopardy, indeed, no thoughts were even possible now. It was as if two enormous magnets clashed and again I knew and in knowing became immobilized.

The mind which lived with me, but which was not my own, was of the identical nature and quality, was the same as the Void Itself. It was part of the Void. And I was back where I had begun. Living in an indescribable haze of golden rapture.

When at last I surfaced the questions began, very slowly at first, then with increasingly insistent vigour. Stunned, the first question was, 'How could that incredible Perfection, even the most infinitesimal portion, an atom's worth, no more, bear to live with me?' There was no reply, nor has there ever been a reply. I asked, of course, I must have asked the question a thousand times in my life, but I have never had a reply, yet it still seems inconceivable.

Once more all my perspectives altered, throwing all that I previously experienced into new light and this in turn reflected on the writing so that all that which was previously written was, more or less, obsolete. Having learned this new knowledge I could, at least, attempt to convey something of the Void. It would not be comprehensive, but there would be something. Or was it even feasible now to make the attempt? The unpleasant flat surface reality was looming larger on the horizon; financial problems in that I had very little money left and no prospect of obtaining more. Although having lived parsimoniously it had been insufficient.

I have made no mention of it, nor will in the future, I felt that I knew how to depart this life without leaving physical evidence and as I did not wish to embarrass my family I decided to seek confirmation. But where? From whom? Dying held no terrors for I often wished I could leave the eternal problems of what we supposed to be reality.

Crossing my room one day I was halted by a bolt of information: 'A Buddhist' and realized that I had to meet one. Not an English Buddhist, I had to meet the genuine person; it had to be a Tibetan and one as near the top of the hierarchy as possible. I would have liked to attempt to see the Dalai Llama, but knew such ambition was impossible. In any case I couldn't afford bus fares, let alone the unimaginable cost of long travelling, even supposing such a personage would permit an audience. But I could try for a lesser personage and forthwith walked into the town. Details are unimportant, but that afternoon an English Buddhist visited me. He knew of a Geisha and could make the arrangements. Loosely, a Geisha is equivalent to an archbishop, certainly a person of great importance and as I was to learn months later, the chances of meeting such a person are almost nil. But I was in need and the need was fulfilled. Three weeks later I was driven to a large building in a setting of great beauty.

Chapter 14 – Avalanches

As I stepped from the car I smelled the aura of holiness and it is useless to offer any comparison to an earthly scent, for non exists. The most pungent rose, the most gloriously rampant of Regale lilies may as well own the odiferous reek of a dung heap beside this exquisite fragrance and it was with this all pervasive scent in my person that I met Rosa. She was the equivalent of a nun in the Buddhist hierarchy and told me that she was to take up residence in Buxton. Fleetingly I thought: this is no coincidence, for it was in Buxton that I saw Harry, my brother-in-law after his death and it was in Buxton that I stood in the lovely garden before Simon's death. Is there some significance in the area I wondered?

Many people resided in this large building, most of them quite young, all wearing a similar expression of curious withdrawal and I concluded that they sat in mediation for long periods. Indeed, I received the impression of an other-worldliness, but all were extremely quiet and courteous. It was a mixed gathering of varied nationalities; rightly so, for nationalism is one of the worst barriers to self-recognition.

Later, I was escorted to the Geisha and my heart seemed to stop beating. Here was true Holiness. The only time in my whole life I was to meet it. He was slight and beneath the heavy robe I could not suppose a body. Ageless. Dark eyes like serenely glowing lamps in a face of ivory. He could have been fifty years old or five thousand. Time was meaningless in this face. Holiness. Effortless. It radiated from him yet was without movement. No clawing here. No reaching out to 'bring you in' which is such an evangelical characteristic. By simply being one knew the true meaning of innate, all embracing holy beauty.

He sat beside me and I told an extremely abbreviated account of that which I had seen, the Void and his interpreter, young, dark and glowing, relayed my words to the Geisha. I told him of my intention to end my life and asked if it was feasible. The very air became charged and the young interpreter, himself lacking dexterity with my alien tongue burst out:

'Please do not do this. Geisha says you are so lucky, so lucky – I cannot tell how. And will you please – from me – be told that I, I must add too. For you are so lucky, lucky.'

There followed a rapid exchange of their language, of which I knew not one word and then the interpreter spoke again:

'Geisha says I am to tell you that you are reincarnation, you have, you have been monk, one of our monks in our home. You have lived with us before.'

Without surprise I accepted these words, for some years earlier I had been obsessed by the remote magical land and had read every scrap of information I could gather concerning it, although not a great deal was known. Its brutal ravishment had devastated me and I had felt a deep anger that the world had made but conciliatory meaningless noises in Tibet's defense. To me it had seemed the one pure and holy country on the face of the earth. Certainly I had lived other lives and to be told that I had lived an earlier existence there I could accept without a qualm.

As the Geisha was sitting beside me he turned to face me, as I faced him. There commenced a conversation between us conducted in no recognizable language, yet I understood all that he was saying, yet cannot now write any of the words we exchanged apart from one phrase in English: 'Look the other way.'

We stood together before departure and the Geisha took my hand between both his hands, palms flat and we gazed at each other for a moment or two. A blessing. A benison. I loved him simply, as one human being to another.

As we retrieved our shoes my companion said uncertainly:

'That's seemed like a bit of an anticlimax. It's a pity you've come all this way for that. I hope you don't think it's all been a waste of time. After all, you don't seem to have been told anything.'

I replied with utter confidence, 'Oh, don't think that. I got all I came for.'

And it was all contained in that one simple phrase: 'Look the other way'. From that opened a whole new world of astonishing ramifications. Not all at once. The ramifications continued over a long period, but the core, the brilliant core of analysis remained the same: 'Look the other way'.

Before leaving, Rosa gave me the hospitality of her small house, told me a little of her history and what she hoped to achieve. As she had listened to my history in the Geisha's room, repetition was unnecessary, but I asked the inevitable question:

'Why me?' and she smiled with great sweetness, replying 'Why not?'.

I could think of dozens of reasons 'Why not?'. I was not 'good' as they were good. I was half educated, barely that; I was nearly penniless; could not write that which I knew to be true and was therefore incompetent and felt obscurely that had all this knowledge been bestowed upon some worthy person with a far better brain this ocean of knowledge would, by now, have been reduced to lucid prose. Why me? Well, I'd just have to go on trying.

As I stepped into my living room I had a moment of revelation: there were possessions here I could sell. What a crass fool I'd been. There was nothing of any great value; I did not own Meissen or Dr. Wall's early china pieces. But I could live without most of this stuff and hopefully it would raise enough to keep me for a few months. At least, I could try again. My elder daughter, realizing that I was about to strip myself, brought a piece that I had once given her. I protested, but she insisted and it helped. It was all-sordid in the extreme, but necessary, for beg I would not. Having begun this venture it behoved me to suffer for it myself and not to whine or scrabble, expecting or demanding others to support me. My parents had shown me well the arts of survival and it was up to me to use them. Thus, bit-by-bit, I shed possessions, keeping only my gold chain. If I had to die because of my incompetence, then my girls would not have to bear the expense of burying me, for the chain would cover the cost.

Inevitably and predictably, human demands intruded. Betty rang in the child-like slim voice I well recognized:

'Kathleen, you'll have to come. I'm terrible. My back's gone again. You'll have to get down here because I can't do anything. Come now.'

Sometime earlier I had lived with her for six weeks, sleeping on her sitting room floor and waiting on her every whim, because of her back. Determined not to repeat the process I arranged for her to be brought to my house and she was confined to my bed for a month by our doctor. At this juncture a very limited description of my sister is necessary as she was to be involved in an experience which was to throw an entirely new perspective on my understanding.

Betty had never borne children although she was physically capable of doing so. The barrier had been because of a previous illness suffered by Harry. Betty had privately admitted to me that she was delighted by the outcome. Being essentially a selfish person, she contentedly lived her widowhood following her own whims. She had taken care not to learn any of the survival techniques and freely admitted that she had loathed all forms of work since childhood (a fact our old headmistress had noted with disapproval) yet in spite of this curious anomaly she actually owned a very good brain and a comprehensive memory, ending her school career as head girl without trying in the least to achieve anything. Consequently, she now fielded all her banal problems onto my shoulders with a casual disregard as to my feelings in the matter.

'You can do things' she announced airily, therefore I could 'do' her things. So when she was ill she demanded constant attendance. Fool that I was, I succumbed to my mother's ultimate form of blackmail, I was disarmed by tears. Below all this surface superficiality lay a very tough character; she had protected her own interests for almost all her life and this had resulted in a will of steel. No Queensbury rules governed her methods of getting her own way; she was very like our mother. If she roused herself to war, then it was all-out war, no holds barred: it didn't happen often, but when it did the big bright scimitar was unsheathed.

Again, I will be obliged to write another small history: Agnes was on the scene again. She had married at the age of sixty and lived nearby. Loyal to a fault, she did not admit that she had made a howling error, but I deeply felt that she was unhappy in spite of the fact that she never complained about his treatment of her. She called on me regularly and now Betty was confined to bed she called almost daily. For a while they enjoyed themselves, reminiscing about earlier days, earlier 'howlers' and to some extent I enjoyed the company for we had so much in common family history. One day Agnes said abruptly:

'My hand's gone. It's gone dead and I can't feel anything with it.'

Instantly I was alarmed, for it looked like the hand of a corpse.

I said roughly, 'Have you been to the doctor?'

'No' she replied 'and I'm not going.'

So I answered firmly 'Oh, yes you are. You're going if I have to drag you kicking and screaming.'

She said amiably: 'I might have known you'd start hell-raising. I wish I'd never told you.'

I persisted 'You're not going out of this house you stubborn little mule until you promise me you'll go to the doctor's.'

She said 'Oh, all right, I'll promise.'

And I knew she was lying in her teeth; she had no intention of doing anything.

Betty said 'You're too little to be awkward.'

Agnes said, as she had said for years in this kind of repartee: 'They don't make diamonds out of bricks.'

Betty filled the gap, 'And poison lies in a little room.'

It had been exchanged so often that it was a ritual. But I was worried. Two days later Betty was allowed to rise and life became a little easier. But the following morning Agnes's husband arrived.

'You'll 'ave to come. Your Agnes 'as 'ad a stroke. I tried to get 'er moving, but I think she's paralyzed a bit. 'Er mouth's all funny and she can't talk right. Anyway, she's your family, an' you'll 'ave to look after 'er. I can't do it. She's your responsibility, it's nowt to do wi' me.'

I thought with disgust, 'You horrible little creature. How could she have saddled herself with you?' But I went. Agnes had indeed had a stroke and her right side was paralyzed, but her mind was clear. She looked at me with great love; it shone from the huge brown eyes.

I said gently, 'Would you like to come to me, love?'

Her twisted mouth could only mumble, but her eyes said 'Yes, oh yes.' 'Right, I'll go and arrange it' and I did, installing her in my living room, for if she had been upstairs I could not have heard her if she needed anything.

Amid the arrangement an uncomfortable memory had surfaced and it was composed of self-guilt. Months earlier Agnes had called and for the first and only time had spoken, very guardedly, of the awful life she was suffering because of this man. The rise of pity often emerges from me as anger and I had upbraided her for 'putting up with it'. Words had arisen in my throat and congealed into an impenetrable barrier. I had wanted to say, tried to say,

'Leave him, love and come and live with me. It's freedom hall and you can do what you like.'

I could not speak those words and she had said quietly: 'Don't be cross with me, Kathleen. I have loved you more than any other person on this earth.'

Totally disarmed I could only look and pity. Now, at least, I could make her happy and as comfortable as possible. Some old friends visited her and there were many comings and goings. There was laughter, that quintessential facet of living, which is discounted in all supposedly serious discussions as being a frivolity, a diminisher, a sure and certain method of having one's viewpoint irrevocably tainted by so errant a characteristic.

Each evening Agnes's unpleasant husband arrived, drunk and aggressive and I froze as the story of her life with him surfaced. Paralyzed as she was, he sat upon her bed demanding her share of some household bill. It was unspeakable, an outrage, but it was happening. His nephew called and there issued information which froze my blood:

'I've come to tell you love, that we're sorry he's knocked you about so much. We've tried to talk to him, but there's no changing him. You were a lot too soft for him; his first wife was tough and she kept him in order, but you're far too nice. I want you to know we're all sorry. We did try, but he wouldn't listen to any of us. Anyway, you're safe now, Kathleen will look after you. He told us he'd shook you till your teeth rattled, but he couldn't bring you round again. I am sorry, love.'

And it was then that the killing fury began inside me. I said nothing, but I made a huge, unforgivable mistake, I did not warn Betty and Betty had heard this too. I should have spoken, explained the situation and I did not. This evil little man had to be appeased no matter if my tongue was bitten off in the process, for he had a husband's jurisdiction over Agnes and I had none. I had assumed, stupidly, that Betty would have assessed the situation also, but she had not. Then disaster struck.

He arrived one evening as Betty and I were on our way to bed. Agnes had been settled down and all seemed peaceful. Banging on my door was the man, drunk and abusive, demanding entrance, demanding to see his wife and Betty's scimitar was unsheathed. A virago now. An unstoppable sword of vengeance with which she described his antecedents, his present and his undoubted future and weirdly the one improvable facet in all the tirade was to evolve.

He took immediate revenge. The following day he summoned his doctor and exercising his rights as a husband caused her to be installed in hospital. The great brown eyes blurred in anguish. During the following week Betty went to her own home and I was left alone. The killing fury arose, enveloping me in an alien convulsion of fury such as to be unrecognizable. It was as if I split apart and one part of me watched as the other devised methods of killing the malignant insect who walked by my house every night, drunk and vile. In my cellar was a big tyre lever and I wanted to wait for him in the darkness and beat his small foul skeleton into shards, shards no larger than matchsticks, beat and beat until nothing recognizable as a human form remained. In terror I went to bed, as if by the act of lying down to sleep I would rid myself of this possession.

From the moment of Agnes's removal I had wept incessantly and again it was as if another mind watched the weeping creature I had become. Betty said, with more than a hint of ice:

'I have never seen you cry like this in your life. You didn't cry when Simon died. I might as well tell you I thought you were as hard as nails. What are you crying like this for?'

I could not reply. I just wept.

During this period I had one of the most terrible visions of my life. Knowing of the deaths of my sons and my father had riven me, yet throughout there had been an element of naturalness about them, impregnated as they were with appalling agony of mind. But this was to reveal an unnaturalness I had hitherto not encountered. This was the unnaturalness of evil and I tell of this whole incident for one purpose only: in the microscopic there is to be found the macroscopic. This affects many.

I was standing in Agnes's bedroom and the rather dim light in the centre of the ceiling had been turned on. A brief glance at the window showed darkness and I knew that this was sometime in the middle of the night. To my left was the double bed, with a section of the covers thrown triangularly as if someone had just left it. Someone had, for I was standing just behind the malignance, so near I could have touched him; he was facing the window. There are extremes of horror which are difficult to describe, for the blood freezes and the mind becomes strangely incapacitated causing the body to lose momentum, be unable to maintain direction over its movements. One becomes immobile in the face of that which is truly unspeakable, the antithesis of all that is naturally associated with living forms. I could only watch.

He disintegrated before my eyes and as he was illuminated fully by the light I saw the whole in microscopic detail. The sparse hair which covered his skull was plastered wetly, for sweat was springing from the skull to form rivers of water which gathered and flowed over the ridges which constituted his forehead and as water collected within the ridges new rivulets formed and ran down the sides so that his whole head appeared to be under water. It poured from the ugly narrow jawbone in a continuous stream, unspeakably vile, as if contaminated. His eyes had protruded from his head, glaring, as if they were gazing at that which I could not see, but which had terrified him into madness, for undoubtedly this creature had gone insane, was gibbering from a mouth which was shrieking, unable to contain what the insane eyes were seeing.

Worst of all, the whole skeleton was rattling, shaking itself to pieces remorselessly and the jaw's dripping waters were spraying as the ceaseless horrific uncontrollable rattling disjointed it from the skull. In a horror, which seemed to halt the beating of my own heart, distantly, yet which I could feel and know, I watched a pit open before him, black, bottomless and he toppled into an unimaginable hell of evil.

Shuddering, trembling, I awoke, knowing what was going to happen to this vile creature: he would die as a gibbering lunatic. But what could possibly encompass such an end I could not even begin to know. But it would happen. This was truth.

Agnes lay in hospital for three weeks before dying. And the malignancy ordered her the most expensive funeral that could be obtained. Her friends, Betty and I waited in the small, beautifully appointed ante room and uncaring as to whether I would be believed or not, as to whether I was considered to be stupid or not I spoke out freely, describing the end I knew the despicable travesty of a human being would suffer. And as my words were heard no voice rose in either protest or disagreement. There existed in them all that, which knew absolute truth, recognized it clearly.

It was July, a beautiful afternoon and as I walked to my gate I suddenly knew freedom and the world was lovely again, my roses preening in the sunshine. Free. Now I knew whose anger, whose desire to kill, whose thirst for revenge had subsumed me: Agnes had occupied me for three weeks and now I was free, my own person. I thought rather ruefully that being a medium did have its drawbacks. Both she and Harry had fled to me, but of course the advantages outweighed the minor disadvantages.

A new character must be introduced, an old friend of Agnes, a contemporary and a lady I had known all my life. She and Agnes had lived side by side and she and my mother had been close friends. We were both of old families and a rapport exists in such relationships which is now rare. Earlier I had been allocated the job of saving Sylvia's life and in persuading a new doctor to attend. She had known well that she was dying and told me frankly that she cared not the slightest at the prospect. The medical staff had given her a new lease and knowing that she was now at home I paid a visit.

She was deeply and unusually agitated, beginning at once:

'Oh Kathleen, you'll never guess what's happened. Agnes's husband was here this morning at half past eight and I'd to get out of bed because he was banging on my door so much I thought the panels would come in. I don't get up till ten and he knows I don't so I opened the window and told him to go, but he was yelling like a madman and he started banging his fist on my window. I thought: Oh my God, he's going to smash it, so I had to put my dressing gown on and go down to let him in. Kathleen, you've never seen a sight like it in your life. He sat on that sofa and sweat was pouring off him. He was rattling all over like castanets and gibbering. He said he'd been up all night walking the streets and I said "You can't stop here, go into your own home" and he said he daren't go in that house. So I asked him why and do you know what he said?' She did not wait for a reply, but rushed on, 'He said he wakened up about one o'clock and Agnes was beside him in bed.'

I left quite quickly and as I walked to my home I could see the whole incredible story reveal itself. Agnes's revenge, pure and simple. She could not make me kill him for her, so she had killed him herself without violence by merely demonstrating to him that whilst a body may be slaughtered, a mind cannot. A mind lives on and it was this knowledge which had encompassed his descent into lunacy. Omitting brutal details I merely tell that he wandered far and wide for weeks, salvaged by the police, salvaged by social workers, dismissed from a hospital for insane cruelty to another patient and systematically destroying their home during the interim periods. He died a raving madman the following February. And the ramifications of this small obscure domestic disaster spread in my mind into a thousand ripples. Before analysis of the ramification I write the sequel.

A small brief vision, encapsulated in clarity, as ever. I was in my living room with my back to the hearth when Agnes entered soundlessly and twinkling. No words of explanation were required; I knew exactly what she had done, just as she knew exactly that I knew. With no reproach, but unable to prevent grinning, I said:

'Oh, Agnes, you are naughty.'

Then I awoke.

The malignancy's descent into madness was caused simply because he had no faith except the conscious faith that the small could be cheated and bullied, robbed and misused to support his own greed. Nor had he any belief that the body only dies, but that the quintessential 'I' that was Agnes could or would survive. He lived solely for the purpose of obtaining all that could be grasped in any material sense to support his material person. Insensate greed was his characteristic. So long as he did not injure her to the extent that she would need medical assistance he could terrorize her without fear of retribution in a physical sense and to discover that he had not escaped retribution and moreover, retribution he was powerless to obviate or destroy, drove him insane. One may see a ghost, but one cannot obliterate a ghost. Only another can exert such influence, but I did not know it even then.

One fact emerged from this tragic drama with stunning clarity: here was a classic example of what could occur to a creature when it filled its brain with selfishness; when it clogged the cells with greed and insensate ambition. Few, pitifully few cells could glow with roseate light, illuming the creature, for the brain was a stinking morass, which no light could penetrate. But even the vile wretch who had been Agnes's husband had owned a few vacant cells in his brain, for the creature had loved roses and they bloomed for him.

This had been one small example of the actual meanings of that vision of an open brain; I was to see many more examples whilst being uncomfortably aware that there were sections of my own which didn't bear close scrutiny. I was trying to love people more, love them freely without criticism; and it was a long painful process, demanding a strict discipline which could never be relaxed. Flashing temper was another 'blocker' together with cynicism. This dying was not easy. Not rapid. A long slow dismantling, in fact.

Inexorably, financial disaster loomed again and I realized that the only asset which remained was the house, so the house would have to go. Perhaps I could find some shack or other, a garage even, in which I could exist. And it was as I was engaged in such deliberations that life took another unexpected turn.

Chapter 15 – Answers to a Multitude of Questions

During this new era and following the realization that something could be described of the MIND, I lived in a quandary for my inadequate brain could see so many ramifications of this knowledge that it was overloaded with the sheer amount. Having sought answers to the question of 'Is there a God or not?' and sought in the most unlikely of subjects: astrophysics and Science in general; I had seen the MIND and the implications were vast, as were conclusions that this knowledge would raise furores amongst many conventional beliefs. Nor was it that I feared upsetting many of such conventions for that the aspect was the very least of my problems. The real problem was in selection: which avenues to choose, which to analyze, which to expose as being mythical or, in some cases, to be deceits, or at best to be but partial truths which were productive of misinterpretations and could lead to very real dangers.

Equally bewildering was the knowledge that the imploded point of intelligent energy we call 'Life' was not only common to all, but also a miniscule (perhaps but a few cells) charged with true knowledge and was independent of the limitations of the body. I had sought answers to what I had supposed was my Sixth Sense, the sense which had impressed upon my conscious mind the deaths of my sons and my father. Now I knew this sense; but myriads of other questions could all be explained and there lay the quandary: What to write and what not to write?

It was an embarrassment of riches. Which aspects of the human condition to elucidate and which to ignore? Hardly any aspect of what are deemed to be civilized societies could be omitted for this knowledge involved such a plethora of aspects; flat surface reality was but a thin, fragile, convoluted and facile mixture that to lift but one thread from the tangle was to find a number of equally facile threads clinging to it. How to disentangle even one subject? I tried. I wrote reams. In truth, I could not see the wood for the trees. Only one factor encompassed the whole: in evolving such complexities we had isolated ourselves, one from another, tribe from tribe, nation from nation and therein lay the true problem.

Cursing my ineptitude I wrote on, knowing, with discomfort, that my resources were almost at an end that I would have to sell the house I had so longed for and for so many years. But this was more important and my own squalid comforts paled into insignificance beside this major problem. Knowing the answers I had to formulate the questions and it could only be done by writing. I could not discuss the strange events of my life for no sooner did I mention any facet relating to what was deemed to be Supernatural than the withdrawn look appeared, the polite but chilly retreat into ill-concealed repudiation.

Startlingly and very rapidly, a new situation arose: my younger daughter had the opportunity to buy business premises of her own and the rest of the property was also for sale. It was all ancient and in need of repair. I would have to sell, so I said:

'If I buy the rest as a holding property and you buy the business it could be divided into an upper flat and a lower salon'.

Instantly she was set alight: 'Yes, it'd be perfect, then I could live in the flat and have my business below. In the meantime you could live with me, then I'd sell my house and we could look for one for you. Would you really do it, Mum?'

'Yes, I'll do it' I replied, thinking that there was little choice in the matter.

My house, I knew, would sell quickly; only the intervention of those glorious figures composed of white light had caused me to get it in the first instance, together with the momentary inattention of an agent reputed to be one of the sharpest of characters.

Thus began a period of extraordinary change. In one day I could have sold my house ten times over and at a hugely greater sum than I had originally paid. But my taking up residence with my daughter became a long and protracted affair due to circumstances beyond anyone's control. My daughter's house, being larger, offered me a choice of rooms and I had elected to occupy the very large and comfortable attic room, underdrawn and pleasant. Only my personal possessions arrived with me, for I sold my house contents together with the property. Two suitcases and two smallish armchairs, my typewriter, gold chain and some workmen's tools comprised my estate, together with a property, which had been neglected for decades. None of this mattered. I only had to survive, however meagrely; I had not to, could not, give up or give in.

Inevitably, there were periods of doubt, periods when it seemed as if the physical world about me, the social taboos and conventions were so impenetrably established that I, the obscure, would never with my inadequate brain, produce evidence that would hold or be acceptable. Even so, throughout my life had run a threnody, dark, immeasurably mysterious, but which would neither be denied nor circumvented: You have to go on. Prove it. Prove that which I had called my 'Sixth Sense' was true, was valid. I could not read the equations for at school I had loathed algebra. Nor could I write an equation; I simply lived these truths, yet what value was my life? Nothing.

With all the inevitability of sunrise, a bolt of understanding exploded in my head. Painless. Causing no physical damage. Yet it felt as if my head exploded: 'MATTER AND ENERGY'

At the time I was sitting in my attic room, laboriously trying to write. No more now. I went for a walk, for the act of walking seemed to clarify ideas. There was a whole world of ideas to clarify now, for the concept was a core and all else divided. Why had I not realized? Not seen? I'd been staring at the truth and it was so simple I couldn't now believe why I hadn't seen this simplicity. Of course, everything that was observable was either matter or energy. The very construction of an atom was matter governed, yet, governed by energy. This was not an equation, for there was a preponderance of value in the energy, the energy was of greater importance than the matter and in more than one aspect. For if you removed the energy the matter, like time, would be halted. Frozen. So the identical rule which governed the necessity of time being an energy, also governed the fact of matter. Matter could not either move or exist without energy and time. Energy had to exist also in order that matter could exist and move.

In a shower of illumination it dawned on me that as the energy, which I knew it to be when I saw that which-lived-with-me-but-was-not-mine was an indescribable intelligence laying within the atom itself. It directed the construction. For heaven's sake, I thought, bemusedly, it, the energy was the dominant factor. There was no equality in the atom because if the matter which was the nucleus, was released vast amounts of energy were also released; the matter was then a deadly shower, but the energy could not be destroyed. It was a scientific discovery that energy could not be destroyed; it could be dissipated in all directions, but then what? It couldn't be tracked or traced because it couldn't be seen. It may re-form in some wholly mysterious manner, but it would be invisible. It was invisible anyway. You could only detect its presence if it caused matter to move, to do something. But if you interfered with the original constructions of the atom, whatever the form might have been before your interference, then you had also interfered with the intelligence, which had caused the original construction. And, of course, as all one could observe was composed of atoms, all of the natural world, whatever the form, animal, vegetable and mineral, if you exploded the construction you also blew apart the intelligence in the energy which had directed that particular instruction: that particular form.

It didn't matter if it was a leaf or a hair, a mountain or a drop of water. It wasn't the size of the physical object; it was the intelligence which had caused its atoms to form in a particular way. Nor, I thought with iron resolve, was there any doubt as to where that intelligence was to be sited, its source was the Void. That was where all intelligence lay. That was the source of all that could be known, for that was the seat of all creation. The MIND.

PURE INTELLIGENT ENERGY in which all forms, all concepts had been devised. LIFE itself. Within the concept of time in which matter could exist, so the construction had been devised.

It seemed as if my head would burst open, for all the new ramifications poured in.

I thought of Einstein's contention (to paraphrase) 'that the most mysterious thing about the Universe was the fact that we could understand it'. I thought of the classic beauty of the atomic table and realized that it was an integral constituent, not a random collection of atoms, but a balanced and beautiful formation. It was logical, so logical that when gaps had appeared in the table they had been filled by logical thought, given that the numbers of electrons attributed to the various atoms increased in numbers depending upon the nature of the substance.

Incontrovertibly, if someone blew apart the atoms of a substance – as with the hydrogen bomb – subsequent forms which emerged from the holocaust would inevitably assume grotesque forms because the forms had not been so designed in their original state. Interfering with designs which had been in balance beforehand, in total ignorance of that majestic balance would thereby impose a new disastrous imbalance. One could not create any improvements on the original designs.

Immediately, because I could never stay on one topic for long as dozens of other topics intruded, I thought of the systems which pertained in the natural world and which were being discovered at an ever-increasing rate to everyone's amazement and with immense pleasure admixed with immense awe.

A purist would say at this juncture that I was the classic example of the under-educated attempting to evolve theories which five thousand years of written history had failed to elucidate. Further, a scholar would say (it was observed of me by a scholar, self-described) that I was as unfitted to present logical theories as the most abysmal of cretins and in justice, I would have to agree with such assessments. But I made no claims either then or now as to academic status and if these explanations appear disjointed they are simply presented as a learning period. Beset by ever-changing volumes of knowledge I could not select one topic on which to write a thesis, for dozens of other apparently unrelated topics immediately jostled in my mind for equal consideration. It was not that I lacked information, it was the contrary, I was subsumed by it; and try as I would – and I tried mightily – to isolate a topic I could not, for the information was so all-encompassing, fitting conclusively into dozens of other topics that I could not separate one from any other. Succinctly, it was like studying all recognized disciplines at one and the same time.

One factor emerged with clarity. There could be no divisions or separations, either in the natural world (living forms such as animals, fishes, plants etc) albeit there are millions of species and many are incredibly complex, for all are united by the one energy, Life. Nor could there be separations such as class, creed, temperament or colour, even though human beings have decided their own classifications (often detrimental) with which to define themselves. All should know that the physical forms which they occupy are fragile and finite. We are animated by one energy and that energy is Life.

It would interest me to know whether anyone who reads these words could discover the absolute truths which lay hidden and which I could not then see or describe. Bearing in mind also, that philosophers and thinkers had been trying to isolate absolute truth for millennia.

With blazing exactitude I could see how the natural world had evolved from the most primitive cells of all; the literature having yielded that the first cells which could be deemed to be 'living' had been named as the 'prokaryotes' and in due process of time these had changed into more sophisticated forms which had been dubbed as the 'eukaryotes' thereby setting in motion a progression of ever more changes; limbs, cilia, eyes and nervous systems, all evolving into an animal filled ocean which teemed with evolving plants. The planet burgeoned with myriads of living forms, changing continuously yet maintaining a strange stability, subject only to the vagaries of climatic changes; although even drastic climate upheavals still permitted living forms to adapt to newer, possibly harsher conditions.

When man arrived on the scene there was enough to support him, but this creature owned an opposing finger and thumb. For the first time in the world's history a creature roamed the plenitude with the capacity to alter it, to remove from the abundance more than he required in order to exist.

It is not my intention to write a textbook on natural history, nor on the origins of man. Anyone who desires such knowledge can find it at no cost. Darwin arrived upon the scene and filled with curiosity supported by training and scholarly aptitudes, watched many animals in their natural habitat; thereby, after some hesitation and much soul searching he produced 'The Origin of Species' which was the result of a vast amount of research. Darwin produced the theory that humans were the descendants of apes, which brought howls of fury from the then socially blanketed Victorians who were willing to adapt to any new invention – especially those which were potentially profitable – but were not only unwilling to have their ancestry described, but were appalled at the thought that it had ever been in question. They knew what they were and the world knew it, they made sure of that.

As I am not writing a potted history of English the subject will be abandoned, for it was not what Darwin said which was at issue, it was what was left unsaid. The unsaid is the point at issue. Yet the answer has run like a silver threnody from the first prokaryotes to any living form now upon the planet. No adaptation is possible unless intelligence exists within the form. Nor is the amount of intelligence at issue, for the form may be microscopic, but if it knows how to feed and reproduce an amount of intelligence must be and is, present. For the larger creatures to adapt to alien circumstances intelligence must be present. The choices are simple, adapt or die. But nothing can adapt or change which is witless, without intelligence.

Considering the forms which exist upon the planet one would require the services of a massive computer and assessing them numerically is a task which I will neither attempt, nor justify as being necessary, for there are estimated to be a million and a half insects to name but one species. The oceans teem with various forms of life, as does the land. But if one individual of each species were to be subjected to intense scrutiny all would be found to be different from all others, irrespective of similarities. Yet there exists the most unlikely symbiotic relationships between many. They could be described as unique binary systems, for each depends for survival on the other. Trees, which tolerate certain insects, are classic cases. Flocks of differing birds which inhabit a particular area, but which all feed on different foods and are so constructed that sufficient exists for all, for the foods available are equally varied.

As I am not making inventories I shall write no more examples. My purpose is to expose and describe that which flows through the myriad forms of creatures, which are deemed to be 'living' and say now that the single common denominator in all the fantastic array is Life itself. And the intelligence, which caused forms to emerge, was prompted within the MIND. To pipe that 'God made little apples' is simply trite. The forms were designed within the MIND and the MIND provided Life.

That is the unsaid issue. It is the one and only explanation, which holds. For Darwin's evolutionary theory to 'hold water' one may only posit that from the commencement of living forms to emerge upon this planet, the construction of the forms and the subsequent adaptabilities of the forms were directed by the Energy, for that is where the order and the prompting were embedded, in Life.

None of the latter explanations were products of my brain. These all arrived when I saw the living energy which prompted my own obscure existence and when I wrote that I saw the answers all at the same time, no exaggerations or hyperbole were involved.

We can reach into five thousand years of written history to trace the accumulation of knowledge. Some do, with immense satisfaction and a feeling of triumph: How clever we are; How superior to all other living forms.

But what if? What if, after five thousand years of history one began with all the accumulation of knowledge in one fell swoop? One would have to retrace backwards, step by step, not being obliged to reach the knowledge, for one knows it, but the obligation would be that one had to recognize the questions. It was a reversal, a mirror image and in the miraculous instant when I saw that-which-lived-within-me-but-which-was-not-mine, I saw all the answers all at the same time.

Regarding the emergence of living forms upon the planet, one stark fact emerged: each knew its own identity. It might struggle for food, for continuance of its species given the instructions, which were in-built, but it had no ambitions to be anything other than its own blueprint.

Even rampant dandelions are programmed simply to produce others of the same ilk, so they don't try to be holly trees or runner beans. I thought irritably: It's useless to simply contend that the structure of a form is programmed into the DNA. and the RNA carries the information like a postman, but one is simply left with further questions: Who or What caused the exquisite helix to form in the first instance? And caused the RNA to deliver the messages? It all boiled down to this:

Purposeful or Purposeless?
Creation or Chaos?

Predictably, my head exploded again and my horizons extended. Equally predictably, I had another vision.

Chapter 16 – Struggles

Before commencing description of the vision, certain details must be established of a purely private nature concerning the conditions which appertained at this period; they are given only in order to illustrate truths and have implications in a much wider field. There was to follow an inextricable mingling of my private affairs with more public, homogenous truths and I cannot visualize any better method of illustration than by citing the conditions of my own life, for I lived them and they are verifiable.

By agreement with my youngest daughter, the promise was that I would buy the house body and live with her until such time as conveyancing could be completed. A flat would be created of the upper floor and she would sell her house, repaying me and occupying the whole premises. I would then try to buy some tiny property wherever one could be found. She was unmarried at this time, having been divorced from her first husband. We lived together in a house, which was near the lower entrance to Plover Road. Such were the flat surface conditions prevailing at the time.

It was approaching Christmas time and the hairdressing salon was very busy.

My daughter said 'I'm sorry, Mum, but you'll have to come in and help us. Julie's off and I can't get any help at this short notice. Will you do the six weeks up to Christmas?'

With some reluctance, yet thinking the money would help I said 'Yes'.

In order to gain some privacy and quiet conditions I had established the habit of rising at three or four a.m. to write. On the morning of the vision I had risen at four, crept down two flights of stairs to make tea and thought: Perhaps I ought to try for another hour's sleep because it's going to be a frantic day. I returned to bed and fell into a hazy doze from which I emerged to hear my daughter leave the bathroom below and then lost count of time. Lost consciousness, for the vision began.

I was walking along the lane behind the houses in Oakes Road and wondered: What on earth am I doing here? What have I come back for? I was passing the third house from the end, so I could see our old house clearly and knew that my husband was in it. Briefly I wondered why, why had he returned to it, but I couldn't find an answer, thinking:

'Well, I know he's there and it'd be churlish to pass without saying 'Hello' so I'll pop in for a minute.'

Before moving any nearer I suddenly felt very smart and instinctively looked down at myself. Dressed to kill, ye gods, where had I come by these clothes? Having made my own clothes for years I had managed to present myself reasonably dressed, although I well knew that my tailoring was not of the bespoke quality. But this taupe coloured cloth had been cut – if not by a master – at least one of the extremely skilled fraternities. One thing was for sure: I hadn't made this. Between the lapels flowed an off white silken cascade and I knew that a such perfectly stitched affair hadn't been made by my fingers either. How on earth had I come by this lot? Again, there was an incredibly swift blurring, which settled into incomprehension, for I didn't know.

Anyway, I decided briskly, I'll pop in and say 'Hello' and if he doesn't want to see me I can always leave. With no more ado, I seemed to pass at a rapid rate through the rest of the lane, through the awkward gate, along the back garden and into what had been my old living/kitchen. Then I halted. Surprised, but unsurprised. Piles of papers littered every surface and on the large table in the centre the miscellany was indescribable. I thought: I might have known he'd get into a mess like this when I'm not behind him clearing up his rubbish. Rather oddly, there were persons in the room who all appeared to be strangers. All were watching me, but there was no hostility, rather it was as if they were all there as spectators, but why they should have come at all was a puzzle. Still, it didn't matter. If they happened to be there it was none of my business and there seemed to be no reason to ask why they had come.

I was standing with my back to the hearth and to my left, in the far corner was the small entrance, which gave access to the cellar on the right and to the front sitting room on the left. In this space my husband appeared and I knew immediately he was in a towering rage. Instantly, I thought: I ought not to have come here. I'd better go and fast. By then it was too late for retreat.

His arm was about a thing, a thing which in some weird manner resembled a woman, but was a travesty of humanity. It lay against him flaccidly, unmoving, unspeaking, as if it was a whitish skin, which contained no substance whatsoever, neither form nor life. The sight of the thing made me heave with revulsion, for it was indeed a revolting sight, corpselike, the colour of death yet without even the dignity of death, for even a corpse has substance, yet the thing appeared to have had everything which it ought to have had within it sucked out, so that the remainder lay limply, curiously folded because even the skin owned no skin-like integrity.

He had an attractive voice, deeply baritone and with clear diction, but it was acid now with fury:

'This is the woman I love and this is the woman I'll have. I want a divorce; I'll have no more of you. This is what I love.'

Aghast, I could only stare, unbelieving. It was impossible. No one, no one in their right mind could love such a Thing. It was revolting.

I said 'I'm not going to argue Neil. If you want a divorce I shall not oppose you.'

But I thought: it's impossible. I can't believe this. Still, it's obvious he hates me, so I'd better go. But that …

Abruptly he left, taking the thing with him and I prepared to leave also. Then suddenly I thought: I can't believe this, it isn't true. If a divorce is what he wants then I'll gladly give him one, if it'll make him happy, but he can't be happy with that, that Thing. I'll see if I can talk to him and make him see. So I went into our old sitting room and was surprised to find several strangers in there also. Yet none spoke or interfered, they simply watched, all ranged around the room as in the kitchen.

My husband was sitting upon our original sofa, which was drawn up at an angle on the inner side of the room, partially facing the hearth and the window and still clutching the flaccid length of inanimaty, which vaguely resembled a woman. I stood before them on the hearthrug and said firmly: 'Neil, I will not divorce you for that, that Thing. I'll give you a divorce on any grounds you choose, anything that will make you happy. But I know you and I know that Thing won't make you happy. I don't know how you can even contemplate it. Look at it, for goodness's sake. It's foul. You can't live with that foulness.'

With the granite-like implacability I knew so well he said 'This is what I choose. This is my woman and the woman I love. Get out of here, I want nothing to do with you.'

Recognizing a defeat I well remembered, I left to return to the kitchen. The sooner the better. But as I passed the table I noticed two objects lying amongst the pile of papers and thought: Well, he won't need these. He can't possibly have any use for them. I'll take these with me, for he can't use them. Two handbags. One white, constructed like a 'Dorothy bag', which had a hanging gilt shoulder strap and the other was black, embossed with an attractive design and made to be carried in the hand, a clutch bag. Tucking them under my arm I moved toward the window side, on my way to the back entrance, but as I reached the area near the window a vast cavern appeared in the floor and as I gazed I recognized it, its name was Death. He would die before me.

I was outside now and standing at the division of Plover Road, looking down towards my destination. The trees which lined the upper side were in full leaf and it was as if the whole area was changed. Certainly, it was very attractive for the rather dangerous old pavement beneath the trees had been replaced by a very attractive walkway. My destination was obscurely distant and I could distinguish no clear outlines, but had the odd feeling that I lived there, it was my home now and my daughter was there. It seemed very odd and I couldn't understand it, yet I was drawn there. So I set off, but I didn't get very far, for behind me was a roaring, my husband had followed. I turned and there he was in the roadway above the upper curve of the garden. Beside the wall stood a man who bore a strange resemblance to him, but there was little time to see him clearly for my husband was now in a royal rage:

'You're a thief. I've always suspected it and now I've got proof. You've taken what's mine you rotten thief, but I'll punish you now all right. You'll go to court and I'll have you in jail for this. Give me back what's mine. Mine, d'you hear? Mine.'

As I moved towards him in a state of remorse I realized I ought not to have removed the handbags without asking permission. After all, they had been mixed in with his possessions, but that still had not given me the right to remove them.

Agitated, I hurtled into explanations, 'Neil, I didn't mean to take them without asking, I simply thought you wouldn't want them. After all, you can't carry handbags about. I didn't mean to rob you, I've never robbed you, God knows. You've … You've always had the best and I made do with what was left. Listen, Neil, please listen…'

No chance whatsoever, he had never listened. He clutched me in his powerful arms and held me in a vice against his broad powerful body, roaring all the while that I was a rotten thief whom he would punish (and who, weirdly had the social power to punish) and my voice was lost in his fury. Then I was awake and heard my daughter begin to move down the lower stairs; one, two, three. Oh my God I've overslept. I was going to be late. Hurtling out of bed I tore into dressing gown and slippers, crossed to the top of the upper stairs and rushed as fast as possible down the flight over the landing, hearing her steps all the while. As I saw her foot reach the entrance by the back door I was down the lower flight and just behind her: 'Oh, I'm sorry love, I'd got up earlier and went back to bed and now I've overslept and I'm late. I should've stayed up, I know I should. I'm sorry, but I'll be ready in time.'

To my own ears I sounded like an agitated hen and she turned in surprise:

'Mum, what're you on about? You're not late at all. I've only just got up myself, so what makes you think you're late?'

I chattered, 'But I've been away so long, I've been dreaming.'

With a peculiar intensity she said slowly,

'Mum, I think you'd better sit down. We'll have some tea and you can tell me about it. I want to listen to this.'

So I told her in detail and when I ended the narrative she said slowly: 'Don't you know what those handbags were?'

'No, I don't.' I replied.

She said very clearly, 'They're ours, mine and my sister's. Mine is the white one and it's upstairs now, it's in my wardrobe. And the clutch bag is my sister's; I've seen her with it. Mum don't you realize what this means?'

Reluctantly, I said 'Yes, I think I do now.'

She returned calmly: 'He thinks you were trying to steal us from him, but I have to tell you now that you can't. I know him, but I still love him, he's my father.'

I replied, 'Yes, nothing can change that. Nor should it; whatever else he was a good father to you. It was he and I who couldn't get on.'

And I knew what the barrier had been: I owned a Sixth Sense and he couldn't accept it, nor could I abandon it. The Sixth Sense. The soul, as I now knew it to be, the mind-which-was-not-my-property. He had rejected it on the devious and deceitful flat surface reality, which, of itself was a compound of blatant prejudice and implacable hostility. It was a sad irony that we should meet each other in sleep, for that is what had happened. It was not our physical persons who had met, it was our souls.

Then, of course, another shower of considerations invaded my head. First and foremost I considered the time factor and it appeared to be insoluble. I had awakened to hear my daughter leave the bathroom and to her left was a narrow section of wall which was also the upper wall of the lower staircase. She only had to take three steps at the most in order to descend the stairs. During the interim period when I had the vision-of-the-future the physical reality would have occupied at least twenty minutes of time. Yet when I had awakened again, it was to hear her footsteps on the stairs; one, two, three and I supposed myself to have overslept for it seemed as if I'd been away for ages. Yet in measurable time there could have been no measurable interval, for she was walking on the landing below when I first realized she had got up and left the bathroom.

What did I know of time at that juncture? I knew there was an energy which was time and it was within this energy that the visible world existed. I also knew that another dimension of time existed and that it was within this immeasurable dimension that the soul, the Sixth Sense existed. What I did not realize consciously was that I had just lived a demonstration: it was insufficient to know what moved in its own dimension, but I needed to recognize one of the characteristics of the soul itself.

As I now write, years later, I can see clearly for the last blindfold fell, but the explanation for that rather cryptic remark must be held in abeyance. Without attempting to justify stupidity I now see that this was a classic example of true learning. There is really no excuse, I ought to have known. What is there which can project at such immense velocity?

'Light'

One of the characteristics of the soul is that it is Light. I had seen this light many times earlier – even at the age of eleven when I stood in the Pack Horse Yard and saw my future. At seventeen I had seen my young wild-haired person within a sphere of light and later seen my much older self within that sphere of light in Elaine's old kitchen. Following Simon's death I had seen the world about me lined in Light, seen this Light glow through the kindly loving people about me.

Light, indeed. One hundred and eighty-six thousand miles per second. But there was more to it than that, for this Light was an implosion of energy and the energy was an implosion of intelligence. It was not simply light per se; it was the carrier of all that could be known, all intelligence, for it was an infinitesimal portion of the MIND itself. Not subject to the limitations which governed matter.

But this soul, this Light, this Intelligence, could only be seen by the soul. It was not a physical object and because it could not be seen, was not subject to physical analysis such as matter was, it had been discarded as an aberration, having no substance in a scientific world. Was that concept strictly true? No, it was most surely not.

There was the brain to contend with and I thought of it often for I often saw now in the people I met just how much – or how little their brains were suffused with this Light which was the soul, the true mind, for in loving kindly persons it bled through the skin, through the actions and their tolerances. There were people who seemed to glow; by simply walking into a room they could charge the very atmosphere. Love. That was another characteristic of the soul. With a sense of shock I found I could add another characteristic: Joy. After leaving the Void I had known a Joy which was indescribable: Pure Joy such as is unobtainable in the physical world.

And the final characteristic emerged: Creation. Our souls were a miniscule, infinitesimally tiny reflection of the Infinite Void, the Infinite MIND and it was within that Void I had seen and known the site of all Creation. By extension we, the human race, manipulative because of the opposing finger and thumb could and did create on our own account, which was why we had left the caves millennia ago and reached the stars. The threnody was complete.

This was the human soul, but … but the brain itself, with its trillions of cells was the sieve through which information must pass and as light can be bent around a massive star, so the Light which was the soul could be bent if the cells of the brain were clogged.

When I had been confronted by that implacable, 'Who am I?' and been unable to answer, it was because I did not know I had a soul, although I had always been conscious of some unseen standard of perfection by which I measured my own behaviour and attitude and was externally found wanting. I had disliked myself for most of my adult life. Now I knew why. Pure I was not. I was trying but I didn't succeed very well. There were many impurities in my own brain, so it was no use my sitting on a moral fence admonishing all and sundry. Some of these impurities, clogged cells, I could recognize but there were also layers, which I did not. As I remarked earlier, this was the death of ego and it took an unconscionable time to die.

Laboriously and with painful slowness I could now make an inventory of the soul's characteristics:

Light

Love

Joy

Truth, which was absolute

Creation

All facets all combined into one meaning; that which motivated us, which propelled us, was Life. True Life. Inevitably, hundreds more considerations emerged and there were times when I wondered how my head could hold all this and why it didn't burst open or fall off.

So there were five characteristics which could be identified and they corresponded to the number of physical characteristics of sight, sound, smell, touch and taste. A finely tuned balance existed and in studying the researches which had been concentrated on the physical brain (a mysterious organ) it had been discovered that the right lobe was a kind of repository from which emerged – as they were described, the artistic emotions; love of music, of art, appreciation of beauty etc and of course it was abundantly clear that these appreciations were a direct result of the soul's emergence. All crafts, all creative abilities were a direct consequence of the soul's characteristics.

Now I remembered much, for when I sat on the wall as a child and told Elaine that this was 'not my home' I had been acutely conscious of looking down an immense tunnel, feeling somehow attached to the limitless splendour at the end and it had been on my right side. I recollected also that prior to seeing the majestic elephant in Emmie's little 'church' the waking consciousness had been on my left and the impenetrable darkness on my right. Indeed, there had been many times in my life when I had been conscious of a great benign darkness and it had always been to my right.

When one began to divide one could see the divisions, for the left lobe of the brain supplied all the instructions for the physical body. Ever more clearly I could see how the soul's characteristics be eliminated, for if you were to construct a 'think picture' and imagine what a human being would be if all the soul's characteristics were eliminated one could posit a physical human being in perfect physical health yet devoid of love, light, joy, truth or creation. The person would be functional only.

It is the soul's characteristics which makes us human, which makes us humane.

Inevitably, that statement gives rise to another thousand or so considerations but there I will stop for a while. Those are the core, the broad outlines. Inexorably the question to be posed is: 'Who and what am I?' Given another lifetime or two I could be more explicit.

It is with reluctance that I have written of the scene involving my husband and my daughters for my private existence is of no interest to anyone; therefore, let it be clear that the description was written for the sole reason of describing the fantastic speed of the other mind, the mind which moves when we sleep. Between my hearing my daughter leaving the bathroom and my reaching her before her foot reached the bottom step of the lower staircase, I had lived an episode which would have, in a physical sense, taken at least twenty minutes to complete. Indeed, it has taken me longer than twenty minutes to write. But the whole episode took place in an unimaginably tiny fraction of time and I could think of no better illustration than my own experience.

Chapter 17 – Moved to Reality

Following my stint in the salon during the hectic Christmas rush I was now redundant, but not for long as proceedings concerning the alterations to the property were now showing distinct signs of completion. Unearthing my blowlamp I began to strip the paintwork of the upper rooms, for all attractive reeding in the architraves had been buried under decades of thick brown varnish.

In early spring my daughter told me:

'Mum, I'm going to be married again and he's got his own house so I shan't need the flat after all. It's a very modern house and I don't care for it very much, but it'll do 'till we can get something better.'

With deep suspicion I said 'Are you sure about him?'

With certainty she replied 'Oh yes Mum, we've made it up and we're going to get married this year. There's no point in hanging about. Anyway, we've talked it over and you can have the flat. I don't think you'll get anything cheaper and it'll be big enough for you. If you don't mind my having the downstairs room at the back I'll pay for the interior jobs. D'you mind?'

Feeling rather trapped I said 'Well, I suppose it'll do. You're right in thinking I won't get anything cheaper because prices are going sky high in the property market.'

It all seemed like a fait accompli, but I was uneasy. There were obstacles that I could clearly see, but I was in the position of a beggar having no choice. There had been a residue of monies when I sold my house, but I had paid for a new roof on this ancient property, which had left a large hole in my finances. With a wedding pending that hole would increase and living as I did on capital simply meant that capital disappeared. There was no time now to 'try again' for although some interest had been generated to the extent that a well-known journalist and broadcaster tried to influence a well-known publisher to accept my writing, nothing had come of his intervention. In other quarters too some interest had been aroused, but I could not blame the non-takers for I knew in my bones I was not writing with the clarifications required. And the fault lay in me, I well knew it.

Any topic which remotely resembled the 'Paranormal' was a taboo subject, consigned to the realms of the improvable and therefore the province of the charlatan, the gullible, the poor unsophisticated native peoples who could not design hydrogen bombs, nerve gases or land mines and obscure ill-educated old persons such as myself. Categorized and labelled. Dismissed. The few, the very few less inhibited (and thus rendering themselves as suspiciously unstable) who dared to hint that there may be some foundation to such claims were regarded as being 'unsound' in judgment. One hostile opponent even announced publicly that 'he wouldn't believe it if it was proven' but as I am not in the business of dismantling egos I shall not disclose his name.

With no real anxiety, but rather a huge reproach at my own inadequacies I saw day by day that the final reckoning would arrive. I had now dwindling resources and would have to depart the world with as little fuss as possible. There was not time to 'try again' for I was up to my knees in plaster dust, nor was there any guarantee that I would write more clearly supposing I had either the time or the money.

It was very obvious how we learned because we learned when we slept. A little at a time, depending on how much we could individually cope with and to what use it could be put. Anyone who had a large capacity obtained a lot and we called them 'genius' and, of course, in due time the learning spread to other minds by reading etc.

During what I thought of as the 'big read' I had studied the researches that had been performed by those to whom this 'little death', as it was sometime known, held interest, even fascination. With this attitude I concurred, for my life had been changed irrevocably by what had happened during the times I spent in bed. Some surprising results had emerged; primarily that we all dreamed.

With a rather bald brevity I will describe some of what I learned. Subjects volunteered themselves as guinea pigs, students in the main, one of whom declared that he'd 'never dreamed in his life'. Electrodes were attached to the scalps of the subjects and connected to a machine which could register the patterns of the brain as the subjects slept. Quite surprisingly, when the subject who claimed never to have dreamed was roused from sleep in the middle of the night, he was able to tell vividly of what kind of dreaming he'd been living prior to being roused, yet could remember nothing of his dreams the following morning.

As the electrodes measured the brain patterns it was possible to analyze the patterns of waves into four categories of which but two will I use as illustration. One pattern was categorized as REM sleep, during which the subject's eyelids flickered and this occurred during the dreaming periods. The other was categorized as 'spindles' and was of very short duration. Using my own words, it was as if the brain went into 'over-drive' and for this curious phenomenon the researchers offered no explanation.

With no prevarication I write now that this is when the soul leaves the body. It cannot leave for long or the body would die; and because it is an implosion of energy, that energy can be stretched before becoming detached entirely. Evidence? I lived it, knew it and saw it.

Earlier I wrote of leaving my body, to float in a horizontal plane in my bedroom. I knew how to do this, I had done it thousands of times and it was so easy. But the prelude had been the moment my head rested on my pillow, for then the rocking sensation began, a rhythmic shaking which I knew was not my familiar and customary rhythm. This was different somehow, utterly painless, but not my conscious bodily rhythm.

Of course, I thought that my conscious mind had no control over this other mind, the reverse was the truth. This other mind was the dominating factor and it moved according to its own rhythm and in its own dimension of time. Being Light it could and did move at the speed of light, possibly faster, there was no method of measuring the velocity. Being Intelligent Light and a miniscule fraction of the MIND it could and did inform bodies, supply the bodies with new information.

Immediately prior to seeing the mind-which-lived-with-me-but-which-was-not-mine I had felt, for an instant, the fluttering, the different rhythm, but it became submerged in the awesome sight of the Intelligence which had directed my life. And I had known instantly that this mind was the one which had shown my conscious mind what that future would be.

As I write, the implications regarding the necessity for sleep extended in all directions. Puzzled researchers had attempted to discover why a perfectly healthy young body needs sleep, for it is possible to lie down and rest the body without unconsciousness. I had wondered about this apparent complexity when I was young. It was discovered (although human beings in general know it well) that if deprived of sleep, the conscious mind becomes disorientated, resulting in erratic disorder and if prolonged can result in death.

It is not the body which needs to sleep; it is the conscious mind which needs to be lulled into passivity. It is the soul, the other mind, which needs to depart and exist in its own dimension (which I can only describe as timelessness) and because it can and does move in future time it can and does impart information into the lulled conscious mind. It is the Sixth Sense. But it is Light, Love, Joy, Truth and Creation.

There is a popular belief extant in human beings who are wrestling with some problem, be it large or small and which no amount of conscious application will solve, that driven to the wall we say: 'I'll sleep on it.' Lo and behold we awaken to the solution. Nor is it the importance of the problem which is at issue, for it may be quite minor and trivial; but it happens and it happens to us frequently. Unequivocally, I write: It is the soul, the other mind, which injects into the lulled mind the solution. By this method Einstein knew the solution to his first thesis and he had struggled to find his solution for six weeks, then it arrived one morning after sleep.

Nor is his experience unique, for there are others on record, but as he was the genius of the century I have cited his experience. Overall, taking a worldview, one can see now how we, the human race, have exploded from the caves to the cosmos in an infinitesimal fraction of world time. Arrogantly, we supposed our brains to be superior in all aspects from all other living forms, able to manipulate the living earth. Yet those forms existed upon the earth without destroying their habitat, could we make an identical claim? All other living forms knew what they were, could we claim the same knowledge? Claim to know not 'who we are' but 'what we are'. Therein lay the true knowledge.

Yet there were still native peoples in the world whose innate knowledge permitted serene acceptance of sleep, accepting that a sleeping individual must not be brutally aroused for the soul had departed in this sleeping state and the thread which still linked the soul to the body must not be severed. But, of course, their brains were not suffused by untidy irrelevancies of a sophisticated nature.

'We once knew' I thought crossly, 'We once knew and we've forgotten. It's been buried beneath a morass of superficiality.' We're so sophisticated we've forgotten our innate knowledge. Regret the fact as I might – and often did – I lived in a physical world amongst a society so complex that regulations, shibboleths, social ethics and conventions had formed a carapace of impermeable material of granite like quality.

Finance, or rather the lack of it was bleakly gathering on my horizon and the spectre grew day by day. Had I lived on the other side of the world, the East, I could have set forth on the road, declaring myself to be on 'samadhi' and I would not have been supposed to be displaying strange behaviour. If I, an ageing woman followed this example I would be arrested for vagrancy, handed to some melting-eyed young social worker, examined for physical injury and recommended for psychiatric treatment.

To declare: 'I know the answers to the Paranormal' would have impelled this vernacular: 'This poor old biddy's lost her marbles'. With some justification, I thought wryly, for I knew, but I could not write cohesively as each time I began upon a topic, all other topics intruded, claiming attention. It was impossible to isolate anything with any great clarity, although certain aspects were beginning to form themselves into bare constructions. Interminably, the one question reared its head, 'Why me?'.

For reasons, which will soon be clear, I embark now upon a few details concerning my physical existence. Rising at the rear of the property was a thicket of riotous nature, sporting rose bay willow herb six feet high. This could be a garden and I intended to tame this over-sexed foliage. In the first instance I was generously given a little help to remove a ton or so of clay in which even rampant dandelions couldn't get a foothold, for my daughter and a kind neighbour laboured mightily at the project. Then I was alone, discovering decades of unspeakable rubbish, yet beneath was rich, friable soil. The whole slope fell quite naturally into two halves, removing much of the slope of the land. In the centre of the lower half of the garden I created a small lawn surrounded by flowerbeds.

I asked the builders: 'When you take that central wall out between the salon and the back room, will you save the stone for me?'

Cheerfully they replied, 'Course we will, love. What d'you want it for? Going to make yourself a hidey hole?'

'No' I said 'Can you see that wall on the right hand side, going up to the top corner where that old lilac is?'

'Yes, love. It looks as if it's had its day doesn't it? There isn't much of it left' they went on, 'd'you want us to rebuild it or something?' adding doubtfully, 'It isn't in the contract, but we'll do it if you want it on a separate contract.'

I returned simply, 'No, I'm not asking you to do it. I'm going to build it myself.'

The younger man said uncertainly, 'Have you ever built a wall, missus?' 'No,' said I, 'But I'm going to build this one.'

My daughter said dryly, 'If you cast my mother on a desert island she'd build herself a shelter and make some fishing lines. She'd survive.'

'Then she's not just a pretty face, eh?' the builder replied.

I thought: with a father like I had, chum, you were taught to survive. If I had a bomb in that lot I'd know how to defuse it. A survivor, yes, but I didn't believe I would survive this lot, for I was facing utter penury and had nothing left to sell. Even the flat couldn't be sold, for it comprised now a unit and no mortgage was possible for this was a flying freehold and money would not be available. In any case, I couldn't have bought another property anywhere as cheaply as this. It was as if I'd been backed into a corner. So I decided that although I'd have to leave it, I'd make it look as good as possible before the day of reckoning arrived and I would end my life. It seemed a pity, but I couldn't see any other choice. Stripped. In more ways than one ...

To the right and bordering the upper half of the garden was an old stone wall in reasonable condition which belonged to the adjacent property. It ended in the centre of my garden with a tall old privy, unused for years and although brick built these were old, well-fired bricks which had mellowed into a dark old rose colour. Obviously, I couldn't demolish the structure, so I decided to build my upper, broken down wall up to the brickwork.

Keeping their word, the builders piled the stone from the inner wall of the property and it was a delight to behold. Twenty-seven inches of cut stone, dense and of a gorgeous dove colour, not the local soft sandstone. Millstone grit. Being unable to get it through the back window they piled it upon the frontage and I carried as much as I could hold from there, through a passage and up to the top garden. It was laborious and backbreaking work, but there was no stopping.

From the builders I bought sand and cement and mixed the first binder. I cleared the aggressive young lilacs from about the parent tree and could stand now at the top of the slope. Below me lay the old foundations, deeply embedded. On this foundation I would build. Looking down to the brick wall I realized for the first time the enormity of the task, for I would have to build at an angle if the top of the wall were to be in any way horizontal. It was going to be a very big wall indeed. Could I do it? I would try.

It was July and the weather was almost perfect, bathing the scene before me into mellow gold. I picked up the first block of stone and as I bent to lay it I saw silvery outlines. Eerily, I had a sense of 'otherness', of being briefly, in another dimension. What was I about to do? Build a wall, what else? With almost no tools except my hands. In such conditions I began.

Spectators appeared from one source or another, all with identical comments:

'What on earth d'you think you're doing?'

'I'm building a wall,' I said and rather nastily, 'I'm not knitting a jumper.'

'Why aren't you letting the builders do it? They'd have it up in no time' the spectators asked.

I didn't reply with the truth, 'I can't afford to pay them' but simply reiterated, 'It's my wall and I'm going to build it.'

The spectators ended the conversation with, 'You'll kill yourself, you silly woman.'

I thought, 'That's exactly what I'm going to do when I've finished building' but I did not tell them so.

A typically male viewpoint, lofty and detached was: 'You've started off all wrong, Kathleen. Where's your line band? You'll never get it straight without one.'

I said 'I'm relying on my own eye to get it straight. Anyway, who's doing this, me or you?'

Every line of him expressed the male, with a superior, condescending attitude towards women in general. To him women were feckless, inferior in intellect, uncreative in talent and generally unable to function without male supervision. But to do him credit he brought a wheelbarrow and carried a lot of stone for me, but I wouldn't allow him to build. This was my wall and for some obscure reason I had to build it myself.

Betty arrived, clean and unchipped. She said, with the easy simplicity of sisters:

'You're daft, but I've known it for years and don't expect you'll ever not be daft. Nothing,' she added with conviction, 'nothing would ever persuade me to take on anything like that. But I've always been as idle as I could manage. Idleness suits me down to the ground.'

I returned, 'I've worked all my life and I don't ever expect to do anything else.'

'Well,' she went on with conviction, 'You'll kill yourself doing work like that. Building is a man's job, they have the muscles for it. Have you looked at yourself lately?'

I said 'I haven't had time.'

'Well,' she continued, 'you look as if you're going to break in half. You didn't have a lot of weight, but you're as thin as a rail.'

To some extent this was true, I had grown lean and hard. But I went on building nevertheless.

My daughter began, 'You do work that isn't necessary, Mum. It didn't need be that height. It isn't the Pyramids you're building. You could have built an ordinary wall like the one at the bottom. What in heaven's name's got into you? It's big now, but when you get to the brickwork it's going to be enormous. How are you going to reach up?'

I returned, 'I shall put a pair of oil cans down and lay a plank across.'

She said 'Then you'll have to stand on the plank. I could see you falling off it.'

I said with certainty, 'I won't fall off it.'

Yes, it was a big wall and I finished one Sunday morning. I stood then on my nicely growing turf and surveyed the finished project, bathed as it was in golden light. Rugged, irregular, it looked as if it had stood for a couple of centuries. There were gaps in it so that the wind could blow through, taking off some of the strain. No builder would have admitted to it for it was the product of a survivor, a jack-of-all-trades, but it was strong. This wall would endure. A lot.

As I stood in the sunshine I knew with strange exactitude what I had done: this was my life. The story of my life. Into it I had poured all those visions in the form of the great flagstones with which I had bound the twin courses and which did not now show themselves. Between those courses I had poured crushed hardcore, millions of tiny particles, each one represented a word of the millions I had read and the outer course glowed now, varnished in gold. It seemed strange, weird beyond belief to see my life thus represented, but it was true. No one could have built this for me, I had been obliged to do it myself, to live that life, two lives, twin courses bound by the huge flagstones of absolute truth which held my wall and my life, together.

Together the twin aspects emerged and I was too stupid to see them, identify them; I 'could not see the wood for the trees', for there was more to this than that which I was observing at the time.

With the last of my money I had bought a hundred aspirin and now owned two and a half pence, which would buy nothing. It was the time to take them. I had lived a strange double life, which was written in the wall, but I could not leave rubbish; so I gathered the household waste into a bag and went below to the garden to dump it in the dustbin, and it was as I held the dustbin lid that a new wall arose. Black, forbidding, impenetrable; it rose in towering menace, blotting out the glowing garden. It had a name and I knew it instantly: 'Pride.'

And this also was my possession, black overweening pride. It is said that a drowning man sees his life slide before his eyes in one immeasurable moment and I saw my life thus. Brash, arrogant self-confident: 'I can learn anything if I wish to. I can do anything with my hands if I wish to.'

On the flat facile surface of my social existence, my mother and my husband had known of this and fractured it passionlessly so that the spurious, grotesque mask which I wore in the physical world was a sham, a lie, one horrendous lie. For I had believed myself capable of anything and felt a contempt for those who could not learn, would not learn, were devoid of dexterity or facility of memory. I had been the actress on a stage and my part and dialogue had been written for me. Any other woman could have acted out the part.

What had held me together throughout my whole existence? It had been that other mind, the mind which had poured absolute truth into my uncomprehending conscious mind and supported me through those deaths and miseries; dark, benign, ever cushioning me, but a beacon, a standard which never dissolved as the brittle world about me with its artificial values decayed, its spurious integrities shattering into chaff.

What had I been given, been shown, had experienced? Truths. Truths, which were immutable and for which mankind struggled perpetually. If I took those aspirin my body would die and what then? A great yawning waste. What would I also destroy? All possibility that these truths would ever be shared. How could I, valueless, a grain of sand upon the earth, omit those truths? For what? Pride, my own unspeakable pride: 'I can manage. I can cope. Let the lesser beg and plead. I can cope with anything. Before I will beg I will die.' What did I matter? Nothing. In worldly terms I was nothing. And bereft of the mind-which-was-not-mine I would always have been nothing. I shrank into an infinitesimal atom-sized state of being as I learned my true value. If this implacable wall of pride was the barrier I would have to demolish it myself. I was so unimportant as to be utterly negligible, but the mind-which-was-not-my-own was of an importance which compounded the cosmos.

However I did it, however I bled, this wall of pride had to be demolished. In disgrace, in trepidation, I asked for help. Being almost sixty years old I was given help and by a very kindly man who, although I did not specify the topic of which I wrote, seemed telepathically to know that this was an important subject. Somehow he knew that I was not seeking to preserve my miserable person, but to preserve something of far wider value. In the interim I had to borrow. There followed the coldest winter for years in which I almost starved and almost froze, for the borrowed money had to be repaid. But I survived and that was all I needed to do.

Inexorably, the vision I had lived in which I had encountered my husband completed its truths, on my daughter's wedding day and with no word he rejected me with icy disdain. To that function I wore a new suit, coming by it quite unexpectedly and to which outfit my daughter contributed. As the details would embarrass living persons I will not write them. Suffice to say they were noted by living persons.

There will follow introductions now … My own ego was being dismantled, not in one fell swoop, but erased with painless (physically painless) erosion but mentally as if acid was dissolving my worldly view of myself. There were layers which lay in my brain that I did not know I possessed. Throughout the ages thinkers and philosophers had contested, in various forms: 'Know Thyself.' To this may be added, 'What does the thinking do for you?' Meet, in the following, a classic example of worldly ego.

Chapter 18 – Involvement

Good friends are a benison in one's life; the cream in the coffee, the patina on the furniture, and I was very lucky to have several such. One friend had erupted into my life who was the epitome of all that I normally avoided, for she was the froth on the beer; a tangible example of those who pursue worldly success (notoriety) and constant reinforcement of assurances that they are more talented, more perceptive, more thoroughly enchanting than any in their vicinity. All based, of course, on an inner insecurity, which was pathetic to behold. She had been on the stage, had been dislodged from the limelight and sought fruitlessly for the rest of her life for other stages, other admiring audiences.

My friend was aggressive, belligerent, seeking by sheer force of will, allied to a sophisticated fluency with words, to compel any with whom she came into contact to be impressed by the worldly view she owned of herself. As if reiteration of her talents could subject her audience to the self-worship she owned in abundance, thereby reinforcing that worship a hundredfold, seeking pathetically by such means an identity. For, of course, she dared not gaze upon her true identity which was actually identical to my own: Nothing.

Her body is now in desuetude, but when she was in it she had, of course, a name, so as she left issue I will not give it, but re-name her: Geraldine. At our first encounter she told my daughter and I that she was recovering from a nervous breakdown engineered by the abandonment of her by her second husband for another woman. Effortlessly I saw inside the real woman.

She told us passionately (it being impossible for her to issue any non-passionate words):

'I have a Sixth Sense. I know things and I could never persuade him that I knew. We used to have awful rows about it and he said I was mad. But sometimes I did know things, what we should be doing, places we ought to visit and stuff like that. He wouldn't have it at any price. He said I was dotty and it was all you could expect from a woman. No man would conduct himself by such idiocies. Men had created the world we lived in because they thought logically and could make things.'

And I said to him 'I can't tell you how I know but I just know and it's true.'

Then, without conscious volition, my mouth opened and I spoke words which I would never have dreamed of speaking to a complete stranger, words which did not originate in my own brain. As Geraldine listened in amazement I listened too, for they were not my words:

'It's like having another limb, another arm or leg which no one can see, but which you know exists. Because no one can see it but yourself you can't prove that it exists, it's so distressing. But it's always true and it's a truth you depend on more than any other. It makes you feel as if you'd be crippled for life if you lost it and you can't imagine how people who say it doesn't exist can operate at all. It makes you feel as if they are crippled, not knowing it exists.'

And I ended, with deep personal feeling, 'I know exactly how you feel, it's very difficult to live with someone like that.'

Stunned, she cried, 'No one's ever explained it like that to me before. That's it, that's it exactly. My God, it's just like that, like having another arm or leg. Kathleen, I can see it now. God, it's true. He said I was a fool because men could think objectively and I never quite knew what he meant, oh, it's so simple, isn't it? I ought to have known you ages ago, I could have told him then and explained it better.'

I thought, I've only just learned it myself, my dear and it's as big a surprise to me as it is to you, but I did not tell her so.

It is necessary to qualify the latter experience in chronological context, for my first encounter with Geraldine took place during the time when my husband and I had parted, but prior to my leaving the hairdressing business. During the hiatus and prior to the extraordinary visions I thought with 'Sixth Sense' but at the first encounter with Geraldine I did not know its identity.

The direct consequence of this first meeting evolved into some strange experiences. Firstly, she immediately conceived that I was some kind of Delphic oracle and even more strangely, where she was concerned I became one to a certain extent. There had been flashes of knowledge concerning what the fortunes of certain individuals were to be, but these were rare and I certainly did not suppose myself to be a clairvoyant medium of any kind. Yet where Geraldine was concerned I became so and she pursued me with vigour at any time when she had a problem she needed a solution to; even more strangely, I could 'see' where she was concerned. It developed into an odd relationship, hardly a friendship, more in nature of a support. A one-sided support, for Geraldine's extravagant activities were unconventional in the extreme.

I thought often: it isn't so much as my seeking this relationship as being unable to shake her off. She clung, demanding ... Insecure, constantly trying to force from me the adulation which she craved from the flat surface reality and which I withheld for I could see the infant within the woman, the bewildered child within the adult. More, I saw, one blazing day the woman she had been ... She was sitting beside me, pouring our her woes when I interrupted rudely:

'Geraldine, you have lived before and you were a nun. I can see you in the habit, black gowned and on your head is a big white coif with a huge forward bending brim, all starched as if you'd folded wings on your head. I can see beads around your wrist and hanging down on a chain.'

She gaped at me and then said wonderingly, 'I was a catholic, Kathleen. I am a lapsed catholic.'

I said 'You were a Catholic in an earlier life. You were a nun.'

And the difference between the two lives was so extreme as to be almost unbelievable, for this Geraldine needed men in her life as a desert pilgrim needed water. As I write I see her in the habit, but I do not know to which order it belonged. I have not troubled myself to conduct research on the order's origin or functions. Nor was this a surprising facet of Geraldine's present existence, for her life represented anomalies so varied as to make it appear as if she lived at opposite ends of a magnet; on the one hand demonstrating a wild generosity which was counter balanced by a greed so unpalatable as to make the flesh creep.

With this prime example of the nature of one of the two genders, I shall write now of a subject, which began to form into cohesive thought, following my first encounter with Geraldine and it was inspired by the preliminary conversation. As men and women are deemed to fall into two categories, so are their perceptions coloured by this division of the genders. Simply and neatly, there are twins:

'Objectivity and Subjectivity'

It is erroneously supposed that never the twain shall meet and each has been isolated from the other because men did not know who and what they were and women did not either. All had been confused by the apparent dichotomies which had been established millennia ago and had now been so firmly established in the psyche of each that it appeared to be such a rigid law that had permeated the DNA helix itself.

'I am a man, therefore ...' Men are the creative creatures, they produce artifacts, they create that which has previously not existed upon earth; works of art, buildings, tools, inventions ... I will elaborate no more, for the inventions of men are all around us in forms we understand and some we do not understand, but we accept the existence. Indubitably, they pride themselves upon their achievements, their capacity to create; their masculinity in that they are homogenously speaking larger in stature – a fact which makes them competitive in dozens of activities – and have invented titles and bonuses in order to visibly prove their status.

Of course, in many pursuits complex skills are necessary, this adaptable creature is adept at measurement, an integral necessity for invention. Added to this is the ability to focus their attention on to the subject in hand with great concentration. More pertinent is the question, 'Why do they do it?' And the hesitant reply, 'Well, men do these things. We're just built that way' is ineffectual, as is the often repeated contention, 'A man's gotta do what a man's gotta do' which is equally uninformative. Because if one does not know that which impels one, then one may as well whittle sticks. Or if one is content to simply accept the worldview of a man, the compilation of his habitat, nationhood, profession or job, his baggage and possessions, his idiosyncrasies, his physical stature or status, then the picture is incomplete. All the adjectives, nouns and pronouns simply mean that which is physically observable, but none of those descriptions will describe the energy which causes him to be functional. We know it is Life, but the crucial question is: 'What is Life?'

He may be one of the 'movers and shakers' of the world (for good or ill) and believe himself to be a whole unity, body and mind; but if he is able to love something more than his own person, then the question must be asked, 'What is this love, its nature, its substance?' Can it be subjected to the intense scrutiny, which men apply to investigation of the physical world, using the identical criteria with which they measure the infinitesimally small to astonishingly accurate tolerances? It is extremely doubtful if they supposed Love to be a concept or entity which could be scrutinized apart from the physical body for it appears to be an integral function of the body. Certainly it emerges as such, but it's actually not a 'thing' at all and contains no physical substance whatsoever. It is a feeling. And if the male is accused of harbouring 'feeling' in an even remotely scientific project, he is deemed to be 'unsound' and slightly suspect. This is particularly evident in a gathering of so-called world leaders where sombre decisions are being discussed (and frequently are concluded in irrational decisions).

Objectivity is the key. The ability to approach an undertaking passionlessly, permitting that which is perceived as distracting feeling to obscure or infiltrate the topic or subject which requires analysis. Chill objectivity.

So how is it possible to isolate 'feeling' from the subject, whatever the subject might be, without invoking the physical body and mind as being the repository of feeling? They appear to be indissolubly combined and regarding human activities which are so immensely varied I will not attempt to construct an inventory of them, they need to be combined; all feelings; for unless they are present one is left with chilly objectivity which is but one-half of that which ought to be a whole. There are two concepts to this equation: and subjectivity is the other half.

It would be possible and entirely unproductive, to pontificate endlessly on the characteristics of men, in an attempt to isolate the characteristics of the soul for the permutations are colossal. As colossal as the number of men upon the planet, all of whom are different from each other – despite similarities – each is unique. So taking the figure ten which is the number of characteristics which it is possible to unite into one single composite body, it is possible to isolate and thereby construct a picture.

Physical characteristics:	Life, the soul:
Sight	Joy
Sound	Light
Touch	Creation
Taste	Love
Smell	Absolute Truth

And all are filtered through the human brain, which is, of itself, an organ composed of trillions of cells, any of which may be suffused by any of the above characteristics and in a colossal number of permutations. Even the most miniscule preponderance of any can alter the whole balance, thereby causing crippling of the conscious mind. The average man is a fallacy, constructed by statisticians. No such animal exists. From the era of the ancient Greeks who produced startling thinkers and philosophers that have been accepted to the present day, all failed to make the connections which would answer the question which had haunted me as a young girl: 'What makes people tick?' and because the question had been considered objectively no final solution was ever formulated. Men looked outwardly, but the answers lay in the self. In knowing the self because it is insufficient to delegate oneself to the position of a disinterested observer; one is a participant in the human drama. Disinterested association, however plausible and erudite, tells but one half of the story.

Freud, obsessed by the supposition that the sexual urge lay at the core of human impulses and behaviour only chose one facet of the right hand column. There is more to creation (for that is what he isolated) than sex. This human animal owned an opposing finger and thumb, which gave him the ability to create on his own account, to create more than replicas of his own person.

Anyone who cares to make comparisons or to evaluate the right hand characteristics either in combination, or in varying degrees, bearing in mind there are countless degrees, may do so or not as he or she chooses, but it must be borne in mind that the five characteristics are filtered through the computer which is the human brain and if that brain is suffused in varying degrees of dogmatism, prejudice, hostility, spurious conventions, bigotry, etc then what emerges will be tainted in various forms.

For there is more, much more, to those five characteristics of Life and I will write them in due course. At this juncture I content myself with the following: I saw a tendril of the MIND suffuse this planet and knew then how life had imbued the planet. It was Pure Life, Pure Energy and Pure Intelligence.

Our first act following our entrance into the world and when our eyes focus upon the world in recognition, is to smile at it. Not because we can make invidious assessments as to whether our smile will produce a smile in return on a knock-for-knock basis. Not because we expect to gain any material benefit from smiling because our brains at the age of six weeks have no conception of reward or punishment for the bestowal of a smile. We just smile and it is the human physical expression of Joy. Cause and effect.

The latter is a subject on which much more could be written, but I attempt no thesis on any subject for there are too many subjects and I won't live long enough. It is simply one tiny aspect of the Whole, for it is the Whole I will expose, the core of being and I cannot write of all the myriad aspects of human beings; no one could. Throughout I tender that which emanated from the holy Geisha: 'Look the other way'.

As Edith Cavell was to say of patriotism: 'It is not enough', so I say of objectivity: 'It is not enough'. One must permit the emergence of subjectivity into one's deliberations and consequent actions, but to do so one must have a clear brain.

Geraldine was an entirely subjective person, relating all facets of her world into extracting benefits for herself. Her physical person was her world and she focused her attention on it just as a scientist would. So Geraldine, who was fully aware of owning a Sixth Sense, was a prime example of the futility of using subjectivity to focus her attention on the material, physical aspects of her person. Equally disastrous were the scientists who focussed their attention on that which was specious and fragile, ever changing; so that although their viewpoints were apparently diametric, they were actually identical. It is a commonplace phenomenon. The objective scientist denies the existence of the Sixth Sense because he cannot manipulate it, cannot subject it to measurement or exert upon it any physical control; and Geraldine who was fully aware of its existence, still used it to further her own physical desires and wants.

Such persons are not basically evil, but much distress can be and frequently is fomented by their inability to recognize themselves. We imagine ourselves to be a unity body and mind, but we are not; we have a trace, minutely in many, barely discernable in the evil, of the MIND within us. Remove a major part of the characteristics of the soul, the other mind and there is a crippling effect. It is as essential to include the subjective characteristics, as it is to understand the physical characteristics.

Poor unhappy Geraldine, who often 'knew', but owned no conception whatsoever as to how she 'knew' relied entirely upon her Sixth Sense and was dismissed as being a hysterical fool, unable to formulate her precognitive assessments objectively; yet maddeningly her predictions were often correct. But as her brain was almost occupied by self-interested motives, clogged by wounded pride, propelled by ambitions of a physical nature, that which did emerge of value was obliged to circumvent a monumental ego.

Chapter 19 – Dispensing

My doorbell had rung and when I opened the door a lady stood outside holding a magnificent bouquet.

She asked, 'Kathleen?'

Feeling rather perplexed I said 'Yes, but … I didn't order those.'

And I couldn't imagine anyone ordering such an array for me. She thrust the flowers towards me saying:

'I'm to tell you they're from Geraldine. She's sending them as a 'thank you' present' and she half turned as if to depart.

Perhaps I stuttered a little at the overwhelming generosity, then suddenly I did something quite out of character.

I said 'Would you like to come in for a cup of tea?'

And it wasn't an invitation one usually offers when someone delivers something at one's door. It's more customary to say 'thank you' and let the deliverer depart. But without knowing why, I had to bring the woman in.

She was neat and clean, in early middle age, but I got the strong impression that she was 'solitary' in some curious manner that I couldn't identify. Certainly she was not a very happy person, but I felt that it was a very self-contained unhappiness, that she needed help in some abstruse fashion but would not ever either admit to it or demand it. I made tea for her and the conversation we exchanged was so banal that I remember no word of it, merely an exchange of pleasantries, but as we finally sat facing each other she told me:

'I deliver for …' and she mentioned a well-known florist in the town, then went on, 'I'm a friend of Geraldine's and she asked for me specifically when she rang her order in. She said she wanted me to come and if you invited me in I was to come. I didn't know whether you would or not and if you hadn't I'd have just gone away again. But you did.'

And it was a question.

I replied simply, 'Something made me'.

'Yes,' she said, 'and I had to accept. Even if Geraldine hadn't told me to I'd still have come. I don't do this usually you know' she ended.

So I replied, 'No, I didn't think you did.'

And for a moment we just gazed at each other.

'She told me you can 'see' and you can, can't you?' then she said abruptly, 'I know you can, I can feel it.'

In a strange accord I said 'I'm not a medium in any strict sense of the word. I mean I don't sit around in purple velvet telling fortunes or anything like that. I don't really know what you'd call it.'

She said 'Well, it's not the only form of mediumship is it? I'm a bit doubtful of them anyway come to that. I used to be a spiritualist but I gave it up. There weren't to my taste really', then she added, 'You're seeing something now, aren't you? Something about me. What is it?'

I said slowly 'D'you really want to know? Are you sure you want me to tell you?'

'Yes' she replied, 'You can tell me anything. I shan't mind even if it's something not very nice. I wouldn't be offended. I don't think very much of myself anyway; I'm a very ordinary sort of person.'

I said slowly, 'What I'm seeing isn't at all ordinary and I've never seen anything like this in my life. I can see your soul and it's locked up inside a box. It's a rosebud, absolutely as perfect a bud as I've ever seen. But you've hidden it inside this box and the box itself looks as if it's made of something like lead or granite. It's as if you've wanted to protect this rose from all the world around you, for there are so many factors around you that would damage its petals if you let any in. So you've sealed it up, shut it away, but it's too lovely to be shut away like this.'

She said wonderingly 'That can't be me, I don't understand how you can think that.'

So I said 'I'm not thinking it, I'm looking at it.'

'Oh no' she protested, 'That isn't me at all. I'm just, just ordinary. I can work at some things, my dad was a chef and he taught me how to cook, but I haven't got diplomas or anything, because I'm not clever enough to really learn anything.'

Adamant now I said 'That is what I'm looking at. It's inside you and I didn't invent it, but that is your soul. The rosebud hasn't opened yet, you've shut it up, but it's there inside you.'

We parted very amicably in a curious disorder of disbelief which was also overlaid by a rather pathetic trust, for the only view she had of herself was the worldly view, but the worldly view was a spurious amalgam of physical descriptions, none of which described the true person. It was the other mind-which-lived-with-me-but-was-not-my-property which was seeing the rosebud, for of course physical eyes cannot see inside a physical form. This mind could see the subjective because it was the subjective, the other half of the whole.

As she prepared to depart she asked, 'May I come again?'

I answered quickly 'Of course, come when you like.'

And she did, frequently. That is how I met Lynette. It is her true name and she will not mind in the least my telling of the beginning, for over the years the rosebud opened its petals and was freed to bloom. There was to be an important consequence of this meeting which I will later describe, for it affected my life also.

I was lucky in that I had several special friends, comfortable as soft gloves, one of whom visited me on a regular basis. It was as we sat talking one evening that I suddenly saw: (knowing that she would dislike the use of her true name, I will re-name her Crystal, for she was possessed of a very clear perception concerning many worldly subjects). It must also be clear that on the subject which occupied my time and energy there was no collusion, not because she did not know of my interests for she well knew, but in some strange never-to-be-defined manner we did not discuss the many implications, yet in other respects we knew each other very intimately.

During this evening in question I suddenly said:

'I know what's the matter with me. I've been harbouring resentment for years.'

In considerable surprise Crystal said 'What a funny thing to say, Kathleen. I don't know anybody who's admitted to feeling resentment before. What made you think that?'

I answered 'I honestly don't know. I've just seen it and it's like dark sludge. It's horrible and I've had it for years.'

'What are you resentful about then?' Crystal asked.

'Do you know,' I said slowly, watching the sludge separate, 'I've resented my mother for pinning all her attention onto my younger sister and never seeming to find time for me. It's stupid, absolutely stupid, for I wasn't jealous of the young 'un because I loved her. It wasn't that I minded her getting the cream on the coffee, so to speak. It was because my mother wouldn't recognize that I had a brain and she cut me off at the knees because of it. I can see now why she did it, for I was bossy and self opinionated and she'd too much to do to be able to cope with it, so it was easier to just squash me and I've been resentful of it ever since.'

Crystal said 'Well, I suppose if we all put ourselves under that kind of microscope we'd all find something we didn't want to see. I know I would because my sister was a lot cleverer than I was and she sailed through university. Actually, I daren't lift that stone, for I don't think I'd like to know what I found underneath it.'

I continued, 'It wasn't just my mother, I resented my husband too. Everybody used to tell me how perceptive he was and a lot of his colleagues used to look to him for solutions, people with degrees and university training and I used to think I'm just the dogs body round here; my only function is to run the home and do everything for him, but I have a mind too, but nobody ever notices that. They think I'm just capable because I can cook and do jobs around the house, but I'm like a robot. You could train a cretin to do the washing up, but no man's ever given me credit for it except my father. But he didn't discriminate; he simply felt that as all human beings were born with brains it was up to them to use them. When I was very young I thought all men thought like he did and it was a crashing blow when I found they didn't.'

Crystal said 'I don't know whether I could admit to bearing resentment like that.'

I replied with utter certainty, 'I don't mind admitting it; I'm only too glad I've seen it. I think I've carried it around like a dead albatross for years.'

Later I began to wonder what other sludges were clogging my mind and brain. Yet none of it altered my growing perception of myself, for I seemed to be shrinking in a curious manner, shrinking into a nothingness, seeing myself as similar to a piece of old hosepipe I had in the garden and whose only function was to direct water in areas where it was needed, so that it wasn't the hosepipe which was of any value, it was the water and of course it was water which sustained life. Therefore my perceptions changed ... the death of ego continued ...

During this era there occurred one of the most strange events of my strange secondary existence. A vision, yet not a vision. As I lived it I knew some of its implications, but not all, for I lived for two weeks in a dual state and gazed in two dimensions. This continued throughout all my waking hours and although I had visitors during that time, I was preoccupied throughout their visits and I think they must have left quite quickly for I remember finding great difficulty in either chatting with them or listening to them, for that which I was seeing never subsided throughout my waking moments. There was also a strange physical side-effect, for although all was utterly painless I seemed to have difficulty in breathing and drew in air in great lung fulls, but slowly, as if each breath was some minor achievement.

It ought to have been disorientating, but was not. All day and every day I watched for two weeks, watched and learned. It began with a colossal pane of what we would physically describe as 'glass' except it wasn't glass. It was round, but I could not see the enormity of it for it was too huge to absorb its size and I was situated fractionally, barely fractionally to the right so that I could see each side and its transparency. Yet in some curious degree it was also opaque.

It was in space, an enormity of space, again too vast for description. The mirror which was not a mirror, had a name and the name was Death. To my left, at the extreme of perception was utter darkness, unrelieved of light and at no time did I gaze upon it directly for I knew that here lay Nothingness. I remembered the unbearable Nothingness, although the knowledge had lain within me from the time when I had entered it at ten years of age. It lay, inchoate at the perimeter of vision.

At the opposite perimeter of vision to my right, lay blinding light and again I could not and did not ever turn to look upon it, for I knew I would be blinded. It was too brilliant to be gazed upon, but it was also magnetic, it drew. Drew like a magnet.

This Light was drawing all that lay between the right and left of the Mirror which was Death. The limitless space before me was filled with human kind, billions of us and I watched the inexorable passage of human kind toward the seat of Creation, the antithesis of Nothingness.

All beings to the far left were but dimly, barely conscious of the Light. From their position it was an immense distance to the right and on those forward facing countenances barely the faintest glimmer was reflected in the faces. Yet all the perceivable immensity of faces were facing to the right, to the intense Glow. I knew that although they could not be seen, those people were floundering crazily, chaotically in intense darkness to the extreme left and I pitied them for I remembered but too well the insensate horror of being in a dimension outside of Creation, seeking in absolute desperation for some pinpoint of light, anything, anything whatsoever which would show that one was not alone, that some form of Creation existed. And I knew this to be the true meaning of Hell; it was a dimension unoccupied.

Nothingness. An absence of anything whatsoever which lay within Creation. A nameless, unutterable desolation of the mind. Not the ludicrous picture painted by the fanatics of a burning furnace consuming souls and overseen by a ludicrous overlord of evil. Hell is the dimension of utter separation from all that was ever created. And those who lived in this utter darkness had no companions, could know no one but their own souls. Nothingness means exactly that: Nothing whatsoever. It freezes me just to write of it, but I have known it; I write from direct experience.

As the thronging uncountable masses moved nearer and nearer to the Mirror-which-was-not-a-mirror, Death, all faced in the same direction and the glow on the faces deepened as they approached nearer and nearer. All moved inexorably toward the Mirror for there was no other direction possible for them to take. Then I noticed some of the faces which neared the Mirror and they assumed a greater glow, for I could see that to these the Mirror was not opaque; some could see, not fully, but could see more clearly that the vast glow before them existed. They were aware of it and not moving in either trepidation or ignorance or fear and the nearer to the Mirror they moved, the brighter the faces in the deepening glow of awareness.

I thought then of the dying and how often a brilliance is to be seen on dying faces. If they are lucid and can speak they become illumined with Light, unafraid and even joyous. They become perceptive and analyze those about them with great clarity. Many begin to distribute their worldly possessions, knowing they will not be required in the dimension to which they are moving. When one, during life, encounters this phenomenon it is a poignant experience and it happens to many who have struggled throughout their lives to amass more and more possessions, leaving those who watch the phenomenon in a curious state of awe.

I thought then of those who had been clinically pronounced as 'dead' and of how with the advent of new medical knowledge many had been retrieved from so-called 'death'. I thought of how they told of seeing wonders; wonders of colour, of white light, of seeing beauties which they attempted to describe, often incoherently, but with awe. And it was clear as crystal to see that the thinking mind does not die, for there were cases of minds looking down upon their recently vacated bodies and watching medics attempting to resuscitate those bodies, to persuade the life to return, often watching from a height and able later to describe the actions of the medical staff in their resuscitation attempts.

Clear now, with crystalline clarity: 'What dies? What lives?' It is the mind which lives on.

This is Arthur Koestler's 'Ghost in the Machine' and he and his wife ended their lives in despair, knowing there was 'something else' and being repudiated and rejected in humiliating fashion by scientists who denied the existence of the 'ghost in the machine' for they did not know themselves.

It is the 'ghost' which moves unhindered through time and space, for it is energy, intelligent energy and it is not inhibited within the energy which governs matter. Being no longer confined within the energy of time in which matter must exist, the energy which is the mind, moves in a different dimension of time. Cause and Effect.

The body is the machine and the power source, the energy, Life is the motivator. No matter how perfect that body may appear to be it is only a machine, virtually moribund unless the energy is present. Moreover, it is impossible to observe effects (the natural world and its living forms, ourselves included) without also positing a Cause. And the more is learned concerning the fantastic bewildering formations of living forms, the more it is impossible to contend that all the incredibly varied forms resulted from chaos, from chance formations of atoms.

'Ghost in the machine?' there is a ghost in every living form. It is Life. And Life, the Life which inhabits the myriad forms upon this planet, is an infinitely tiny extension of the MIND itself. There was the Cause and we are a few of the Effects.

Skeptical? Dismissive? Look the other way, for the other way is Nothingness and unintelligent Chaos from which anything may emerge given mega trillions of time and chance encounters of atoms, except that in Nothingness there are no atoms, for there is no Creation, nothing. Yet the more we learn of natural formations the more undeniable is that order, intelligence is present.

Thus I watched the unbelievably enormous panorama unfold, dazed with awe. For those who passed through the Mirror which was death still preserved the illusion of form, of shape and were retaining the appearance of form which they had borne prior to passing through the Mirror which was death. Ghosts, but with their intelligence intact except now they could see the immense Light, unblinkered by the clawing demands of the physical characteristics, unburdened by the insatiable demands of the physical bodies they had discarded. Still, they knew ...   For this was Life, living intelligent energy moving to the Creative Sources.

Two halves of the whole and I watched them pass.

The Visible and the Invisible.

And my perspectives shattered again into twin halves.

As the beings on the far right and approaching the Source were still visible, they had thinned numerically and I could only see them at the limit of vision. They were altering in perspective, becoming outlines now, dimly perceived shapes as they lost resemblance to human form for they were subsumed with Light, were being absorbed by the Intensity which I was unable to look upon directly; and the forms became incandescent with Light themselves and I knew they were being drawn in and completed their journey in ecstasy, to be submerged in Creation.

Chapter 20 – Trying to Solve an Enormous Jigsaw

During the following era I seemed to spend my life in thinking, watching how these visions amalgamated, formed into truths, altered perspectives; and each layer had to be scrutinized by comparison with all other layers, yet all layers fitted into the Whole. It was insufficient to write the chart:

>Life is:
>Love
>Joy
>Light
>Creation
>Absolute Truth

For other perspectives also needed to be written.

Life is Invisible. There is a cause and we are part of the Effect.

>It is Energy
>It is Intelligent
>It cannot be 'seen' by the conscious mind
>It can only be seen by the invisible mind
>It cannot die

What are we, when inside the form that is the body?

Matter and energy in combination.

Returning to the brain that I saw, all the energy was filtered through those trillions of cells and if those cells in any major number were coalesced into a morass, the light, the other mind could not penetrate. Then the brain as a whole could not conceive of the possibility of the existence of the other mind. It was deceived and thought of itself as a unified construction. Here then was an anomaly, for the form as a whole knew well that it must die. That was an absolute, a certainty.

With shock, I thought: When I saw that tall figure which was my still living father, tortured and in agony move towards me in the kitchen of the big house I thought it was Death which was moving towards me to enfold me, but I was wrong: It was Death which was holding him. We've got it all wrong. The truth is the reverse. It's pure Life we go to when we're not encumbered with a body. This we believe to be 'living' is a sort of death, but when the other mind is freed we can and we do, exist gloriously. We can and we do, exist in another dimension of time because we're not circumscribed to move and be in the energy of time in which matter must exist.

'Look the other way.'

It is this other mind which must be freed when the body sleeps and then the mind, the other mind, the soul moves freely in its own dimension of time. Not only that, this other mind is a dimension of Creation and I remembered the old shop in which those beings who used Light – being Light – to communicate with each other and produce wonders of Creation such as no words will describe, but which had melted my very bones with utter wonder and beauty.

Inevitably, the physical world intruded.

Lynette said: 'Kathleen, I've come to you as a last resort because I don't know anyone else who'll understand. I've tried talking to one or two, but none of them seem to realize what I'm saying. I'm in a sort of hell and I don't know how to describe it. There isn't anything which can be described. All I know is that I've reached the end and I want to die.'

I said 'I know love, I know where you've been, it's Nothingness and I've been there myself so I know how it feels.'

She said, in the limits of despair: 'Its just blackness. There's nothing there at all and I want to die. I think I shall kill myself and I won't feel as if I'll hurt anybody by doing it. I love my kids and I wouldn't hurt them for the world, but even they don't seem to matter, nothing does. So I've come to you.'

Anxiously I responded with 'I don't wonder you can't describe it because there's nothing there that can be described. Literally nothing. No hope, no love or light, no joy or anything which we know in life. But love, you'll come back.'

She said 'Is that true, do you believe it?'

I said with certainty, 'Oh yes. When you've lived in that pit there's only one way you can travel and it's up. And you're going to go up because you can't stay there. You're not a crab and you don't move sideways. I promise you love; you'll come out of it. Now, before you leave here, Lynette, you've something to do with your life. I can't say what it is at the moment, but you've something in your future.'

She asked pitifully, 'Do you really mean that, Kathleen?'

'Have I ever lied to you?' I said.

'No' she replied painfully.

But to all this there was a sequel and it changed both our lives. Lynette, painfully, timorously, was surviving. At each visit (two or three or more days a week) she unfurled a millimetre at a time. One afternoon we had sat chatting together when I noticed a darkness emanating from the wall to the left of what had originally been a fireplace in my small sitting room. Very quickly this darkness developed into a powerful irresistible Force. A Force of such intensity I found I could no longer speak, nor could she.

It was a Darkness that became tangible, similar to intense smoke but not physical smoke which causes the body to cough and choke. Yet weirdly it had the effect of immobilizing some of my natural physical processes and I began to breathe great lungfulls of air, conscious all the while that my natural locomotive abilities were being held in unopposable suspension. As accurately as I may describe it, it was as if the immense power of a cyclonic mass were to be held in stillness, yet still able to exert power over matter. I could no longer sit upright in my chair. Somehow, I had to sit on the floor and how I was to manage this I did not know. Millimetre by millimetre I slid rather than consciously moved, off the chair and finally reached the floor to lean against the chair.

Lynette lay in her chair and I was sure she was dead for her face had the marble-like pallor of a corpse. I could not help her, nor make any move towards her, but simply gaze at her. For more than two hours we sat, or rather lay, thus. I could see my clock and watched, bemused as the time ticked away.

Quite suddenly, the Force receded and Lynette said, stunned:

'Oh my God, Kathleen. What was that? What was it? I've never known such power in my life.'

At the question I now knew the answer 'Healing. It was healing.'

She said 'I thought you were dead. I saw you and I thought you were a corpse, you looked like a corpse. And I couldn't get to you to help because I couldn't move a limb. What on earth has happened here?'

I replied 'I don't know at this moment, but something happened that's important and there'll be consequences.'

She said 'Well, I can't imagine what you'll do next.'

In utter conviction I replied 'This isn't just me, my dear, it's for you too. You're going to be able to heal.'

Aghast, she denied 'Oh, no, not me. I couldn't do anything like that. You know me; I've a phobia a mile wide, I can't touch people and I can't bear anybody touching me. You're the only person who does ever give me a kiss and a hug. Everybody else knows to avoid me at all costs. Its only you, you bugger,' she said wryly, 'that never takes any notice of it. You just behave as if it isn't there and it's funny really, because from you I can take it, I don't mind. But as for healing anybody, that's out. I can't bear people to touch me.'

Smiling now I replied 'You haven't any choice in the matter, my love; you're going to heal people whether you believe it or not, so you might just as well get used to the idea.'

Lynette persisted 'Things like that don't happen to me. I know they happen to you, but not to me. I'm not like that.'

I said simply 'You are now. That was not my exclusive property. You were here and you're involved. It was for you too, so start thinking about it.'

Unconvinced, she departed, absorbed in thought, unable to adjust to that which she knew herself to be this utterly new concept, leaving me simply smiling, knowing well that this would change her life; knowing also that whatever errant misconceptions one owned concerning oneself were over-ridden by such Power. Power which one could not oppose, even if one wished to oppose it which was in itself unthinkable. This Power drew our life from us to a limited extent and replaced it with some of its own. It was a similar process to that which re-charges batteries.

Some weeks later Lynette announced: 'I think I'd like to learn, Kathleen. I don't mean sit for even an 'O' level, but learn something. Trouble is, I'm dim.'

'No, you're not' I said 'You're very intelligent. No one's ever bothered to see that you'd any training when you were young, but that doesn't mean you're stupid, because you're not.'

Lynette continued 'I've come to you to write a letter for me, so if that doesn't show I'm dim I don't know what does.'

I said 'All right then, get yourself enrolled in a class for utter beginners. If you start at the bottom you'll soon learn whether you're dim or not. Your trouble is that you haven't a rism of self-confidence in you. It's been suppressed all your life. The only roles you can ever see yourself in are the roles which the society around you has impressed upon you. They've been defined for you since you were a little girl but just as they inserted you into their slots, you accepted those slots as being you, but they're not you, you don't know who you are or what you're capable of, because that aspect's never been put to the test. So put it to the test and begin at the beginning.'

Lynette said hesitantly, 'Well, I suppose I could try that. Begin with the dunces like myself.'

I said sarcastically, 'Who knows? You might even find that c a t spells 'cat'.'

Lynette grinned, 'You are a bugger.'

'No doubt,' said I, 'but you've no ties now. Paul has gone and the children, so there's nothing to stop you climbing out of the conventional mould that the people who governed your early life poured you into. You've never seen yourself beyond the conventional titles: daughter, wife and mother and all those titles were devised and written by men several thousand years ago. It's been accepted ever since as holy writ, but it isn't holy writ. Just because the definitions were written by a miniscule minority of fanatics walled up into an isolated community doesn't mean that everything they wrote was true. It was only true according to their perceptions of truth, but if those truths were slanted in favour of the male perceptions it doesn't follow that what they wrote was absolute truth. They were biased and they were biased in favour of the male gender.'

She said 'I never looked at it like that.'

This was no one sided relationship for in analyzing her problems I also could analyze many others. Much had lain inside my own mind which required dissemination and clarification. I had known without knowing, seen without seeing. The very act of explaining the emerging facets and concepts to Lynette also formulated many long noticed discrepancies in the roles of the genders, so long defined and so ill-adjusted.

Lynette began to perceive:

'Yes, it's true. I had a picture of myself in my mind even when I was very young, because my mother favoured my younger brother simply because he was the boy, the male of the family and everything was adjusted around his needs and wants. The expectations for him were different from those for me. It was expected that I would work alongside my father and I didn't mind doing it because I loved him. It seemed to naturally fall into place that I would learn to cook because he was a chef, but now I think about it, no one ever asked me if that was what I wanted to do. It was just taken for granted.'

Then she burst out, 'I allowed it to happen didn't I? It never occurred to me to think any differently. I didn't go to college to get any formal training because I got my training simply by working with my dad,' then she added with some bitterness, 'but if I applied for a chef's job now I wouldn't get it because I don't have any formal education to prove that I can do it.'

I said 'But you'd like a paper to prove it, would't you? It's important to you now, isn't it?'

'Yes, it is' said Lynette 'But I'm dim. I don't even know now whether I could get a paper to prove anything.'

'Well,' said I, 'there's only one way to find out and that's by starting at the bottom.'

She went on 'Because I got married so young I just followed the stamp of 'wife'. I thought I should do what wives were supposed to do and I did that too. Then when I had a baby I saw myself as a mother and nothing else. By then it didn't occur to me to be anything else.'

I said 'so you simply observed the conventional written patterns.'

'Yes,' she said 'I did.'

I persisted 'But it's not enough now, is it?'

'No' Lynette reflected 'it's not enough. I'm not a chef any more. I'm not even a daughter any more, because our parents are dead. I'm not a wife any more and I'm not even a mother any more, except at a distance.'

I said 'But you're still here even if the labels have been stripped off. So who are you?'

'I don't bloody know' said Lynnette vehemently, 'You've pinned me into a corner.'

'No, I have not' I rejoined 'you've been dreadfully unhappy and you've come here for comfort and solace. And the only way I can see is through your soul, because my conscious mind doesn't know, it's not clever enough. But through it and by it I could see the real you, the real

'I' and I told you at the beginning what was inside you, that perfect rosebud and it's still there. It's that which needs to bloom.'

'God.' She said explosively, 'I'll do it. I'll enroll myself in the lowest class there is.'

'Good,' said I 'and you'll get a shock.'

Being transparently honest she admitted a few weeks later:

'The teacher took me on one side and said she couldn't understand why I was attending such a class. She said there was nothing wrong with my brain and I ought to aim at something much higher. So you were right, Kathleen and I had to admit it.'

And we smiled at each other.

As it is appropriate I will add at this juncture that she got a job and was quite proud of the fact.

I said 'Oh, that isn't it, you'll have something far more important offered.'

Of course, she didn't believe me, but her rise was rapid and she spent a portion of her life supervising a staff of more than four hundred people, together with numerous responsibilities, all of which she accomplished with rare acumen and ability. It wasn't all, but it was a beginning.

I thought: how much is being wasted in this country and the world as a whole simply because people had no conception of what possessed them. Academic abilities were but one half of the picture, in some cases barely that and the subjective was ignored or dismissed, yet it was the subjective which was now propelling Lynette and which was the key factor in her job. Nor is the story completed. As it brought her such wondering delight at the time, I tell of Lynette's glowing pride when she presented me with the copy of her first academic achievement. I have it yet.

The latter has not been written in order to either lend credence to the rising tide of feminism or to offer support of any such sect. The millennia of stultifying male domination inevitably ensured that such a rebellion would occur. On the contrary, it has been written to illustrate the power of the subjective. Had Lynette sought medical help following the devastating death of her husband, she would have in all probability been given soothing drugs, given counselling to poultice her wounds and more than likely have spent years of misery. It was the dark, filmy, opaque healing that cured her.

Chapter 21 – Attempting Explanations

At this juncture it is appropriate to render as nearly as I may, some descriptions as to what is meant by 'seeing'. During the 'big read' I had encountered a few tentative suggestions that this faculty may, in certain individuals, be an atavistic remnant of a faculty which was homogenous amongst prehistoric peoples; freely recognized and freely relied upon as it supplied them with reliable information which their limited physical senses could not supply. 'Seeing' led people to sources of food, informed them of which growing plants could be eaten with safety and which were poisonous. There had to be some source of information for the early tribes were nomadic and could not wander onto new territories and strip foliage ad lib or all would have died. It is a huge subject and I could write much on the whys and wherefores from a purely practical viewpoint. This is not a textbook and I shall desist from the practical aspects, concentrating upon the fact that the Life which propelled those early peoples, was and is, the Intelligent Energy. As their brains were not suffused by irrelevancies they could know by Life itself.

Amongst the tentative proposals was the proposition that early man owned a 'third eye' which was assumed to be the pineal gland in the centre of the forehead and it was this gland which supplied information and which ensured their survival. It was also theorized that mankind's increasingly creative powers had, over time, depleted this gland, for mankind had created other forms of communication, thereby rendering the gland partially obsolete and in some individuals it appeared to have become atrophied. Or was it? Or is it?

In a very personal sense I felt myself to be an anachronism for this area is where I 'saw'. It appeared inside and in the centre of my forehead and it was as if I owned a small television set on which truths appeared, scenes, knowledge which could not be even assessed at times, but it was always knowledge that no amount of conscious logic could deduce for it was knowledge of what was to occur in future time. By such means I saw, week-by-week, Lynette's future.

It was by such means that I saw my sister's death ten years before she died. I gazed at her body in horror, but in spite of my horror the truth would not be denied. This would be … Betty often twitted me in the language of siblings: dispassionate, critical in a manner which from others would be offensive, objective and disarming. She said with monotonous frequency:

'Your head is stuffed with a mass of totally irrelevant and totally useless information.'

Facts. Facts concerning many aspects of the physical world. But such irrelevancies were subsumed when I 'saw' for this knowledge superseded all the irrelevancies, obliterated them completely.

More than ten years ago I saw the scene concerning Betty. I would enter by her back door into her kitchen and the inner door which led to her living room would be closed. This door had a large glass panel of rather attractive design in relief so that only blurred images were visible through it. But I needed no blurred image for I could see to the immediate left that her stairs door was open and her broken body was lying on the ground at the foot of the stairs. It was then that I began the futile attempt to persuade her to sell the house and occupy a flat or bungalow.

It was an argument that continued for years, ending one day with her demanding:

'Kathleen, why are you always trying to get me out of here? This is my home and I love it, love being in this road. I've neighbours, people I can meet and talk to. The shops are only a stone's throw away and I like it. So why do you want me to move when I'm happy?'

I replied, 'I don't want to tell you. I don't want to talk about it.'

Betty persisted 'You're going to talk about it because I'm sick of hearing you mention it. Come on now, what is it?'

'Betty, I can't tell you.' I said miserably.

'You can tell me anything and I shan't mind whatever it is, but I can tell you now that whatever you may say I'm not leaving this house. I couldn't bear the hassle of moving and I wouldn't be happy now amongst a lot of strangers. So out with it' she said.

'It's not very nice,' I muttered.

'Nice or not, out with it and tell me' Betty ordered.

'Are you sure, are you absolutely sure you want to hear this?' I asked.

She said 'Stop prevaricating and tell me. I know there's some reason behind all this. I don't know what it is, but there's something and I want to know now.'

So I told her what I'd seen and she absorbed the information without the slightest regret or alarm, saying merely:

'Well, if that's how it's to happen, I'll be dead and I won't know anything about it. In any case, I'll be dead where I want to be dead, in this house and that won't make me sell up.'

For the time being the matter was left.

In retrospect I shudder at the fool I was to suppose that absolute truth could be circumvented in any possible manner by my personal physical intervention. Concerning the ramifications of the aspects of the invisibility of the soul's characteristics, the sheer uncountable number of signs as they emerged through bodies was too great for assessment.

A woman making a cake was using creativity in the same way that the genius Rembrandt used it to paint pictures and irrespective of the yawning value-gap which lay between the products, the basic premise was identical. Creation. It was useless to make endless inventories which illustrated the creations of mankind. Whilst the creations in many forms were superlatively beautiful, one needed to concentrate upon the impelling power that animated this errant living human form which was bent upon changing the aspects and fabrics of the planet which sustained it.

It could not be doubted that on the whole we were very impressed by our ability to create and some of the more spectacular preened themselves quite visibly with this proof of their creativity. Yet although I had been able to use my hands and mind quite freely in a general sense which caused many people to say somewhat enviously:

'Is there anything you can't do?' My small abilities had never impressed me in a way that truly mattered, for I had known them clearly for what they were: aids to survival, no more. I was able to function physically without creating anything very well, Jack-of-all-trades, master of none.

For months and even years, I squirreled hopelessly in this maze of creativity before the final answer burst in my head with explosive force and a thousand perplexities clarified like sugar dissolving in hot tea. It was Life itself which the artists in many fields were trying to express their admiration of and I knew then why men were so disposed toward vast artistic expression in so many fields: in painting, in composing music, in design, in architecture – the lists were endless and now I knew the reason which lay behind this vast outpouring.

What, primarily, is the criteria by which great art, great creative expressions are levied? The answer is beautifully simple: 'Does it live?'

Does it speak to one? Does a clear unamplified message conduct itself, perhaps over decades or centuries, to strike some individual with a pure clear clarion call 'This is Life speaking'. And if whatever it is and it may be a simple framed chair made by some obscure country carpenter, its message is direct and clear, it has beauty. For to create, one must allow the emergence of the soul into the creation. Anything less and sterile uniformity conceals the true nature of creation, stifling natural creativity. With and by such unnatural formations, designed solely for functional purposes and completed in many activities by robotic machines we have ourselves devised, we are gradually concealing our true natures. This is why creations which were formed by craftsmen from natural materials are so yearned for, so increasingly difficult to own or obtain; even if the objects in question are Chippendale inspired or emerged from the Leyden school of painters, or simple three legged stools, or a small girl's sampler. They live because a fraction of the soul's creativity inspired them.

Clear also, as to why men have been so predominant in the fields of artistic expressions and why such myths have arisen as to the inability of women to produce magnificent creations: it was, it is, quite simple, for women brought forth that which did Live and breathe and nothing which men could produce was a fraction as complex and beautiful. Women bore babies, new human beings who were brimming with life and chuckles.

Now more of Life's characteristics enter the fields of creation, for Love must enter also and Joy, for nothing which is beautiful can be created without those factors and in turn they inspire Love and Joy in the beholders, illuminating them with Light, inspiring them to declare, 'Oh, it lives', which is the supreme accolade.

Because one aspect immediately spawned dozens of other aspects I thought about the various art-forms in terms of substantiality and endurance, thinking that the making of music was undoubtedly the most wonderful for by its very nature it was insubstantial, ethereal; as one listens to one perfect note of music it is already melting, fading, for it cannot be sustained, has no quality of permanency, no material physical reality. Music is felt.

Pictures, frescoes, we labour to keep them intact, but they too are fragile and will succumb to erosion in time, however beautiful. Because it held perpetual interest for me I thought of all that I'd read of ancient

Egypt and the perplexity of archeologists who, in noting that the first purity of sculpture which emanated from the First and Second Dynasties was gradually eroded throughout the succeeding dynasties. Yet the treasures of ancient dynasties even of the later eras are stunning in magnificence, but the first were magical; even the two-dimensional photographs bleed their magic and I realized the reasons.

Early man, prior to the advent of writing, was attuned to the rhythms of the natural world and to his own. So often he had been portrayed as ignorant, brutish, communicating in grunts and unable to function by any other means than desperate fulfilment of physical need. It wasn't true. From the magnificent era when he ground the natural earth colours in order to draw upon the walls of caves he had been expressing what he thought of Life Itself. No one could draw those long lovely lines of teeming beasts unless one loved life, for that was what, even then, was being expressed. Those early sculptures of pregnant women which appeared to sophisticated eyes to be gross and crude, were simply expressions of his love for the new Life to be. Many theories have been proposed as to the promptings which compelled early man to burst forth into riotous creation, but I theorize not: it was Life Itself which spoke through the hands.

It was clear too why there had been a deterioration from sculpture of utter magic to the resplendent majestic expressions of later dynasties. It was beautifully simple: those first magical constructions were impelled by love of Life. The brains of those early peoples were uncluttered, unselfconscious; some would have seen departed souls as many throughout the ages of man had so seen them and thought them to be gods. As I had seen Elaine's father in his old home and he showed me his new home he impelled me into supposing him to be a god. Such 'seeing' was not the prerogative of any tribe or nation, it was homogenous and had always been so. Transference of adoration from a ghostly god to one who appeared to be god-like whilst in a body would have been an easy transition and people's beliefs were transcribed into superlative sculpture, for they were expressing in their creations adoration for what the soul could see.

Instantly I realized why the deterioration began: such supreme expressions of adoration became the object of later envy and greed and there commenced eras in which the physical was worshipped, not the spiritual. There was culmination in vast panels depicting the might and possessions of a Pharaoh with the irresistible power of a physical person. The magic had been transferred from the invisible to the visible. Of course, this opened entirely new vistas ...

As Shelley was later to say of the self-satisfied Rameses:

'I am Oszymandias, King of Kings, look on my works ye mighty and despair.'

Undoubtedly, the rot had set in. The purity had suffered a sea change. Man transferred his adoration of the soul, of pure life, to the physical aspect. Unfortunately, the style became fashionable and so it has continued. Even as I write. Particularly so now, in this era. But the mighty always topple. The physical decays. It is the energy which endures, for it does not decay. 'Look the other way'. Concentrating one's attention entirely upon one's physical person is disastrous, for the physical person will die and then what? What indeed ...

One joins the panorama on the other side of that Mirror which is Death. Thinking is a vortex, into which one may extend in apparently limitless upper regions, but one must always return to the central point of consciousness and there lies the immutable question: 'Who and what am I?' Discover answers to those questions and then one can learn, learn the true meaning of Life in its various aspects.

During this era I uncomfortably was obliged to exist, usually at odds with myself, knowing that some of my brain was clogged with matter I neither wanted nor required, but unable to isolate it or identify it, but it prevented me from writing that which I wanted to say.

A disproportionate amount of my time was taken up by the two classic examples of Geraldine, who knew well she owned a Sixth Sense, yet spent her energies on purely physical satisfactions; and Lynette who had a perfect rosebud, a symbol of a soul inside her and was learning slowly and painfully to release it, caring almost nothing about her physical person in the process. With such subjects constantly in my vicinity I had two classic examples of what could be and what ought not to be.

Geraldine had announced: 'I'm selling up and I'm going to live in Cornwall near my sister. She's a wonderful person, Kathleen and she's so wise and well balanced you wouldn't believe. She's a lot older than me and she's always taken care of me, more really than my mother did. With her I'll be all right. I can't cope with this lot any longer, so I'm clearing out and making a fresh start.'

I said quietly, 'You can't run from troubles you know, Geraldine. All you do is take them with you.'

'Oh, no.' she said confidently, 'Barbara will sort them out for me. I'll be all right when I can go to her.' and she paused, then continued, 'You see she's got a big family and most of 'em are around her. She's coped with them all and they're all my relatives, so I'll just be joining my own family. It'll be nice,' and she went on, 'You can rely on your own where you can't rely on acquaintances. I need people that I can rely on for I've met so many people who've lied to me that I can't trust them any more,' then she added hastily, 'not you, of course, I can always rely on you.'

I said rather dryly, 'Oh, thank you very much.'

She said 'Well, I don't always believe what you tell me about things which are going to happen to me, at least, I didn't used to, but it's happened so often that you've been absolutely right that I know you'll tell me the truth. Not many do' she added gloomily.

I said 'It isn't my conscious mind that sees the future, I told you that often enough.'

'Yes, I know. But if you weren't there I wouldn't know it, would I?' said Geraldine.

I thought: if you didn't prattle on about yourself you'd know more, my dear, but I didn't bother to say it for Geraldine was in full spate like an approaching tide and I was no Canute. In any event people with strong ambitions cannot be led, especially if those ambitions are directed towards physical satisfactions. There is free will and we all have to learn where to direct our energies. She was, for me, a learning process, a classic example of what-not-to-do. But she clung, for she could not frighten or coerce me, all her histrionics left me unscathed and well she knew it for she spent an inordinate amount of time in trying to convince me of her physical importance, but I saw always what she had been and she had been a nun.

Thus, in time, I met Barbara on what was their mutual stamping ground, Bodmin Moor. Certainly the healing process in my own person became charged upon Bodmin Moor and with startling results.

From Geraldine's descriptions of her sister Barbara, a picture could have established itself of a calm, detached person capable of dealing with all domestic disasters with supreme capabilities, unruffled and serene. I saw a dying, frayed creature at the end of her tether, unable to cope with her own problems, leave alone Geraldine's. Barbara, amongst many other previous illnesses, had the ever-present and mind-destroying Tinnitus and in consequence was an insomniac of staggering proportions.

As I sat beside Barbara that first evening I experienced the uncanny sensation of being inside another person and could see her past life as if a film was unrolling, saw too that she was dying by feet, not inches. Geraldine was none too pleased at my diverting attention from herself, but she concealed her chagrin as well as she was able, which did not amount to very much and was quite pleased when Barbara left for her own home, which was but a two minute journey.

As Geraldine had found employment she left early the following morning and at two in the afternoon I decided to visit Barbara.

Her husband said, in a state of perplexity: 'Come in, if you like, but I have to tell you she's still asleep. She fell asleep last night and she's never wakened. I've been in her bedroom and I can't understand it. She never sleeps at all until about six in the morning, but she's been sleeping for hours and I don't like to waken her.'

'Oh, don't even think of it,' said I, 'I can come back later to see her, but let her have her sleep out.'

And that was how it all began. There were to be some strange repercussions from that preliminary encounter. It appears to be superfluous to use the adjective 'strange' in any context, for the whole of my existence appeared to be one succession after another of strangeness and I can but offer that as each new strangeness appeared no rism of awe ever diminished as truths unfolded. I lived in a state of awe.

Following Barbara's long sleep she greeted me with:

'I don't know what you did, but it's miraculous. I couldn't believe it when Frank told me the time. I haven't slept so long since I was a child. How did you do it?'

I replied, 'I didn't do anything. I can't physically make anyone sleep other than boring them into unconsciousness perhaps.'

So I described to her the experience which Lynette and I had lived and ended,

'Healing is outside my physical provenance, so it must have gone straight into you.'

Startlingly, one evening, it so happened that Barbara and I were alone in her house. She was ironing at the time and I was doing nothing but watch her.

She said 'There's something I've been trying to do for six months now and I've tried very hard.'

I said simply 'You've been trying to get rid of self.' She put down the iron and gaped at me:

'How did you know that? I have not spoken to a living soul about this, not ever. I can't believe it. How could you know, Kathleen? How did you know that about me?'

I replied 'I just knew it. As you said it I saw it. Nobody's told me.'

She said with conviction, 'No one could have because I've never breathed this to anyone. I wouldn't have dared to for a start, for they'd have thought I was going dotty or something.'

I said 'It's all right love. I know exactly what you mean and what you're trying to find,' and then added, 'you're trying to find your own identity and it isn't simply being a mother to them all, or being a wife to Frank; you're trying to scrape off all physical wants and so far as I can see you'll have an easier passage than most because you've been on the giving end all your life. There hasn't been much talking where you're concerned.'

Barbara said with resignation, 'There's still a lot of self to be got rid of. I'm not perfect, far from it. I try to be good, but I'm far from succeeding.'

'I wouldn't worry about it too much, love, we're all in the same boat. You cannot be absolutely perfect in this sort of world and if you were you'd have no friends because you'd make everyone feel uncomfortable. It's only by recognizing your own shortcomings that you can sympathize and understand other people's problems,' said I.

Because I began to talk to Barbara concerning that which I had lived, I began also to think a lot and what I thought would be described as heretical; not that such a label bothered me, for it did not.

So I thought first about the art which did live. I thought about the jugglers of words, words which incised themselves over the millennia and of how they were incised into minds; for what actually were they, these curious statements carved into stone, impressed upon papyrus, leather or copper? They were thoughts which had been translated into and onto, physical substances, impressed onto physical minds. But how true were they? Or how deceptive? Were they the thoughts of single individuals who, having experienced visions themselves, were then able to transfer those visions onto some physical medium? Or were these writings a collective effort, the assumptions of a sect and a sect which devoted itself solely to writing? If so, how had they come by their information? First hand? Second or third hand? Were they told what to write? Ah, what a dangerous procedure that was, for storytellers embellish their tales with their own versions of events, colour their accounts with their own interpretive faculties. I thought of present day word merchants: one could lift one story from eight or ten newspapers and read an equal amount of varied versions of the one story, all slanted slightly differently from all others and one may choose any, but would any tell the absolute truth? For nothing less will do, if truth is to be told it must be absolute, uncoloured by even the smallest preferences, distorted by no person to whom one owes responsibilities. To relay absolute truth one must experience it oneself. Nothing less will serve.

But ancient writers lived together in sects, jealously guarding this curious art-form which appeared to be so innocuous, but which was, in fact, a deadly weapon, for it could be impressed onto minds. Words were thought, thoughts translated into words, then impressed onto some chosen medium and finally onto minds. Dangerous ...

Comparisons now, however long I scratched at this subject the more illusions emerged. Taking into consideration that I am, in my person, a practical, down-to-earth, very ordinary woman; existence for me had been no casual, airy fairy, lofty disregard of essentials, for if I had not paid my bills I would have been disgracefully prosecuted. No manna from heaven sustained me; I lived with the harsh economic facts; eat or go to jail or die. It was only in the final analysis when I prepared myself to die that I saw I was obliged to surrender my pride, for what I wanted to say was of greater importance.

Those early writers lived in enclaves and were supported because they were being paid to write. They did not exist in some word limbo, they existed because someone fed and housed them. In the case of the early Egyptians the current Pharaoh kept them and very comfortably too. That being the case, those writers were not about to incise a record of absolute truth concerning their Pharaoh, one does not bite the hand that supplies the milk and honey. One describes the Pharaoh as can be seen even now, three thousand years later, heaped with honours, supreme in majesty, representative of all that is powerful and a personage of total authority. To use the vernacular, they did not question, in stone, as to whether his parents were married or not. But the ordinary people who had not been admitted into the tiny minority of people who could read were simply told what to think and because this mysterious, powerful, art form was so apparently stable they accepted that which had been written.

Was it absolute truth? No, it was not. There were too many shades in it of self-interest. Too many directives from those who comprised the ruling bodies and who had to be placated. A partial truth is more dangerous than an absolute lie, for there is enough in it to deceive, to mislead. Women, of course, were excluded entirely from the art form's craft, it being considered that they could neither read nor write because it was the male of the species who was the creative character; and women were needed for performance of the chores which bored the males.

Symmetry existed in those early civilizations in that all worshipped a multiplicity of gods, in the Egyptian pantheon many were adjudged to be in animal form, but even minor city-states paid homage to a local god or goddess. It is unsurprising, for prehistoric man could 'see' and he saw ghosts, the apparitions of the departed. As such disembodied minds existed in a timeless dimension they could and they did impart information concerning future time and events which were to occur to individuals. Therefore it was quite natural for them to regard such apparitions as being god-like, having attained wisdom which was precluded from the physical conscious mind.

There evolved amongst the unruly tribes one who called themselves 'Jews' with the theory that but one God existed and this being was regarded as their exclusive property. They had had a history of enslavement, quarreled freely amongst themselves and laboured under a sense of injustice. There also evolved from the sect of those who could write, a series of laws designed to bring order and stability amongst their turbulent tribes. The laws were understandable if one considered the climate of the era and taking into account that they had undoubtedly suffered at the hands of the Egyptians. But those early scribes made one gross mistake and it was to endow their God with their own physical characteristics. Unable to physically exert revenge upon those who had enslaved and humiliated them, they endowed this being with negative qualities.

Revenge - their God would obtain it for them. A vast Judge who would punish transgressors by merciless banishment; repudiating the unworthy and condemning them to a fiery existence for eternity. So by degrees the twin concepts arose of a fiery hell supervised by a darkness of pure evil and a glorious heaven peopled by angelic beings, usually wearing ethereal wings, all confined by a golden railing with a watch keeper on the gate. In the centre was an omniscient being of male gender, mystical, yet capable of unlimited wrath.

Because it was so written, those strange incisions became to be regarded as holy writ and because this art form has this curious quality of permanence, there are many who still believe it, with variations, to be true. It is not true.

First and foremost one cannot postulate a concept which is deemed to be absolute Purity and then postulate that the Purity is also unalloyed evil. It is, by any form of logic, a contradiction in terms. Moreover it is blasphemous.

One cannot postulate a Being of infinite mercy, then insult that Being by praying for mercy, for in the begging one is implying that the Being is also merciless. To contend that this Being is a replica – of mysterious proportions and is also some form of matter is ludicrous, for all matter is subject to decay.

That which is not subject to decay is Energy. It is also Pure Intelligence, invisible to physical eyes. Visible only to the soul which is an infinitesimal extension of Itself. Then there was Purity.

Now I knew why I had been compelled into thinking about the nature of Purity, sifting and discarding all conceivable explanations as to how it could be truly described and finally isolating the fact that it had to be energy, for in all other contexts it was a descriptive adjective.

Being neither judge, jury nor executioner I am not awarding blame or reproach to the ancient Jews, for belief in gods was homogenous throughout the world and still is, however bizarre some of the interpretations appear to be. But the true answers lie within: 'Who and what am I' and to find those answers one must pare off the accumulated detritus of millennia. It is not easy. At the time I knew all this I still could not write it coherently because there was a barrier in my own mind and that which filtered through was like pieces of unconnected film.

Undoubtedly, one must separate physical characteristics and isolate their functions. Actually, it was a simple procedure: they existed to permit the body to function, no more no less; but anyone who rushes to save another body which is in danger of being killed or maimed can override the natural physical characteristics and there is a glimpse of the other mind. What one cannot do is to attribute the physical functions and reactions to danger, or feelings of the need for revenge on those who have offended the physical body to the other mind, for they are incompatible and negative.

All in all the ensuing theories which came to be accepted as facts were built upon a false premise, therefore the ethical beliefs which developed from the premise were inevitably misconstructions. To the conscious mind they appeared to be rational and logical. Man was created in their God's Image and it didn't occur to them that it simply wasn't possible to create one vast image which was also physical. The traces of the Eternal were to be found in the other mind, the energy, Life Itself …

But it all appeared to be feasible for it satisfied the physical instinct to retaliate when the physical body is misused or attacked.

Inevitably, when one of their own number was to declare (or so it is supposed) that one should love one's enemies however badly those enemies mistreated one, it was a proposal that was the very antithesis of all their composite beliefs. It ended all their social and ethical structure, so they repudiated the man and did it by the use of one of the prevalent punishments of the era which was bloody in the extreme. To ostracize Jews for a couple of millennia is unacceptable, for if a self-declared prophet were to arrive upon the world scene which is now prevalent and was poor as a crow, with no financial support, he would obtain short shrift in all important spheres. The media would rend him and no gilt encrusted pulpit would receive him. If those remarks sound like cynicism I offer no apology; they are simply fair assessments based upon the fact that I live in the world together with everyone else and only a complete cretin could fail to notice that many social attitudes could benefit from a good spring cleaning.

To perpetuate the myth that the God the Jews invented is at once malicious or a wreaker of vengeance is an untenable theory and one I repudiate totally. The MIND I was so privileged to know is utter Purity and to beg for mercy is a blasphemy, a direct insult, one which I find intolerable, for the direct implication is unmistakable: you believe that MIND to be merciless.

It is we ourselves who, by clogging our brains with self satisfactions, self triumphs, all of which relate directly to our physical persons, cripple ourselves mercilessly, for we direct our attention to that which is subject to decay and will not endure. Moreover, no one can intercede on our behalf, or be bribed to intercede, for no one can communicate directly with this MIND. It is too vast for human comprehension, for although I was permitted to enter and to see IT – as I do every day of my life, I still cannot describe IT for there are no words which will describe IT. Simply to see IT and know that IT exists fills me with an awe that never diminishes.

Therefore, I accept from no man, nor from any visible source, the insistence that they are able to convey what they believe to be 'God's message' for they are, as am I, no more than one atom in the Universe.

Nor will I accept any contention that without the intervention of those who publicly claim to be 'God's representatives' and thereby self-constituted interpreters of 'God's Will', are able to relay instructions as if they were on professional speaking terms with a MIND which their limited conceptions cannot encompass. Such arrogant claims are puerile, as false as the premises on which they were originally based.

Exhortations and instructions based upon false ethics are not only futile, they are dangerous. Let those who proclaim them learn the true meaning of 'Purity' and one learns not by accruing, but by shedding; by scraping off the detritus within one's own brain.

God is not a male being; God is a MIND and within that MIND male and female genders were conceived, as was every living form on this planet.

Chapter 22 – Healing

Healing is a subject which is attracting more and more interest and inevitably, more and more opposition from certain quarters. The manner in which Healing operates is regarded (apart from one or two experiments conducted in what are claimed to be within scientific parameters) as improvable, mysterious and therefore suspect. Those who benefit from Healing very naturally believe in it implicitly.

It is not my intention to dissect scientific or non-scientific attitudes, but rather to relate my own experiences in this field, together with the repercussions which followed the day on which Lynette and I were suffused by healing.

Having earlier seen and disposed of a well of resentment I had carried about for years I still hid behind a wall of cynicism and could 'play to the gallery' fairly amusingly. My temper had improved, but it still flashed out on occasion. I had become more tolerant of foibles; this was very necessary as I had so many of my own to contend with. In short, I found some people did not inspire love and I did not love easily or indiscriminately.

Lynette, on the other hand, was so suffused with love that she loved all with whom she came into contact, some of whom behaved disgracefully towards her. In short, she melded with healing as cream flows into coffee; for carrying no baggage apart from the curious phobia which repelled physical contact she simply became a masseur and natural healer.

Needless to add, she eventually entered into a training schedule and emerged with qualifications and great distinction.

I marvelled at the transformation in Lynette for her whole life had been changed. Unable to touch or be touched, she now 'touched' with as little self-consciousness as she breathed. Her life had been transformed.

I tell of this, my secondary existence, without prevarication, warts and all and I also tell that this enormity of healing power was, at times, too much for me because I did not know how to handle it. I learned that I could not heal my nearest and dearest, because my own ambitions, feelings, intruded.

In most cases the healing was concentrated in the palms of my hands within a very distinct area, but not always so, for very often it was concentrated in my feet also. It could and sometimes did, spread throughout my body to the extent that I felt as if every cell (trillions of them) was an individual powerhouse. Comically, I often wondered at such times that if I held a light bulb in my hand it would light up spontaneously. It was hot without heat, hot without burning. When I saw that open brain I had seen how the individual cells lit up with the suffusion of the soul, the other mind. In healing the procedure was exactly the same, but it now emanated physically.

To each person I told: 'It is not me who does this. I take no money for it because it is not mine to sell. It comes from another source; therefore if you want to thank anyone, then you must thank the Source, not I. My only function is to pass it on.'

There was no possible rism of doubt, not then, not now, as to the Source: this was from the MIND. No other source could or does exert such immeasurable power. It was a concentration of Pure Life, Intelligent Life that produced this heat which was not heat, this invisible glow which was being transmitted. Life to life, from Pure Life.

Other strange effects materialized when this glow appeared, for as soon as my hands touched the person in question I could see inside the body, see the bones which were out of alignment, see the darkness of disorder where no disorder should be. It seemed perfectly natural, although in worldly terms it was impossible; one would need a machine to see inside a body. It was the 'ghost in the machine' that saw. Having no formal medical training whatsoever, it was my hands that saw and they moved as if with a life of their own. I never knew simply by a touch of the hands what the problems were, but as they touched I could then see the problem in my head. It was as if a weird form of communication was immediately set in motion.

During the times when healing was in progress there always appeared in me a curious side phenomenon and I was anxious to reassure people that they need not worry. Very regularly I would heave with great uncontrollable sobbing sighs. Eventually I realized that the erosion of pain, or whatever the trouble might have been, emerged backwards, so to speak, through myself. For of course I did not do any personal weeping, but the effect was fairly uncomfortable to behold for others, yet it gave me no distress.

There were many aspects to be considered concerning this healing power, I never knew what would happen, or even if anything would happen at all, for it really was nothing to do with me, I was just a piece of hosepipe through which energy flowed. But there were some extraordinary results, some almost instantaneous healings, some more prolonged. And some which were rejected out of hand by bigotry and prejudice – although the latter were very few. Overall, I knew nothing until physical contact was made, for as I said earlier, I had no medical training. Come to that I had little education in any field of a formal nature, but at least I was spared the prejudices which appear to be a concomitant of formal academia.

There had been an evening in Barbara's house when I had been completely suffused with healing power and slid to the floor, heaving with great gasping breaths barely able to speak. I believe Frank thought I was having some sort of fit. Yet my conscious mind was quite lucid and knew quite clearly that the house was being charged with energy.

Later I told Barbara, 'You can heal.'

'Never,' she said firmly, 'I could never do that.'

Equally firmly I said 'Oh yes you will. You mightn't believe it now, but you will. This isn't my prerogative, it's for everybody and it spreads. Everybody has this power if only they knew it.'

'I wouldn't call you a liar, me dear, but I have to say I doubt it. It isn't in me, I'm not like that' said Barbara

'You don't really know what you're like. Anyway, I'm not going to argue with you, because it'll happen whatever you think. You'll see' I vowed.

Barbara said uncertainly 'well, it must be marvellous to have it and I have to say I'd like to be able to heal, but I truly can't imagine myself ever being able to do it.'

I replied, 'Do you know, love, we haven't even begun to tap our reserves; we have immense access to power we haven't even dreamed of yet. It just needs passing on and that's all I do. Look at yourself, you think you're just a wife and mother and you think that's all you are, but it's not. For goodness' sake, you roused yourself to learn three languages and I can't remember my French. Is that stupid?'

Barbara replied uncertainly, 'Well, I was a lot younger then.'

My final comments were 'it makes no difference. Anyway, it'll happen and you won't have any choice in the matter. I've never had any choice in any matter. If I'd had any choice I don't suppose I'd have wanted to live those deaths before they happened, but I did. Of course, the compensations have been enormous, beyond belief, but it hasn't been easy and I've wished a thousand times it had happened to someone else, someone who could have told it better.'

Some time passed, but Cornwall stayed very vividly in mind. It had not been merely the visiting of a friend. A conviction that more was to occur stayed fixedly in my head, but I could not imagine any what, how or why.

Geraldine said over the telephone 'I have to tell you quickly, Kathleen, that I've just come from the doctor's and I've got cancer of the liver. There's no hope, it's a death sentence. I don't want you to fret about me, because I'm not afraid of dying, you know that.'

Almost immediately I was given a first class train ticket for any destination by an old friend of my daughter's. Her husband had obtained the ticket by some fluke and handed it on saying, 'Give this to Kathleen'. These were an astonishing series of coincidences one may suppose, but I did not believe so.

In unaccustomed luxury I sat in the train at Leeds station and saw. I 'Saw' in amazed disbelief a word that hung in huge white letters:

'Miracle'

Whatever context could this be? Certainly, it was nothing to do with me, for I was not the kind of person who had anything whatsoever to do with miracles. Come to that, I didn't really believe in miracles anyway. It would be in some other context.

Then, superimposed upon the blazing word, I saw Barbara, the tired harassed woman I had first known and as I watched I saw a new Barbara move easily out of the top of the old Barbara's head. The true Barbara, the real woman, not the frayed lady that the world saw, but the real person, the 'ghost in the machine'. And this Barbara was as different from the old as it was possible to be. Erect, assured, confident and serene, she left me in awe at the transformation.

By English distances the journey to Bodmin was lengthy, but throughout the whole of it those visions never altered by one whit and I saw them for the duration of the journey. Barbara I could understand, Miracle I could not.

They were all staying in a large rambling house of great lineage with a lovely, tangible atmosphere.

Geraldine was dying, unmistakably and with none of the explosive hysteria and hyperbole which had characterized her life. Like an automaton now, I moved without conscious thought or intention, merely saying,

'Do you know love, you could do with a massage', knowing full well that I was not competent to massage anyone. Yet it all seemed to be perfectly natural and as impersonal as handing out cups of tea. Yet there is no doubt that she relaxed utterly, so much so that when the professional masseur arrived, whose function was ordained as part of the medical service, she said in astonishment:

'You don't need me here. It's all been done.'

'Yes,' said Geraldine, 'my friend's done it.'

'Oh, is she a professional too? She must be to get you like this. All my patients are locked in tension.'

'No,' said Geraldine, 'she's a healer.'

The lady left without protest, although obviously puzzled, but she departed saying,

'Well, it's obvious you don't need me and I've plenty more to see to, so I'll leave you with her. She seems to know what she's doing.'

In that she could not have been more wrong, for I had not the slightest idea what I was doing, I just appeared to be propelled.

On the evening of my arrival I had told Barbara,

'You are going to change and it's dramatic. You're going to change into a very confident character, very powerful. Events won't control you, you are going to control events.'

She replied, 'I don't believe it. I just get carried along, I always have. I just simply go on when anything erupts round me.'

'I know' I said 'You've been dragged behind other people's plans. But it'll stop and it'll stop very soon, certainly before I go home. It's beginning now.'

She said with utter weariness, 'I'd like to believe that, but I can't. I've been giving in for years and I can't change now.'

'Barbara' I said 'I saw you when I sat in Leeds station and I tell you now that a Barbara is coming out of you, that you've never suspected was there.'

To cut a long story short the transformation occurred whilst I was there. From being a passive weary spectator she became a powerful, confident creature, one of the movers-and-shakers.

A few days passed and Geraldine said she felt a little better, more than a little, to be accurate. Then came the evening when we were all sitting together in the best sitting room with two other visitors. The men were lawn mowing and it was a big undertaking so we were uninterrupted.

Suddenly, Geraldine burst out in one of her old furies:

'You know something, Kathleen, you know something about me and you're keeping it to yourself. I think it's rotten of you, I thought you were my friend and you could tell me anything. For God's sake,' she went on bitterly, 'I've told you things about myself I haven't told a living soul. But you're keeping something from me now and I've a right to know what it is.'

Barbara said warningly, 'Geraldine, don't. This is not the time to get yourself all worked up.'

Geraldine flashed, 'It's all right for you, she's told you what she saw concerning you, but there's something concerning me and I've a right to know. I want to be told as well.'

Then she turned to me and went on in fury, 'If you can't tell a dying woman who the hell can you tell? I'm not a fool, I know this is a killer so out with it, you owe me that.'

So when I explained that I had seen one word in brilliant white light: 'Miracle', but even then none of us were any the wiser, but everyone was very silent thereafter and we dispersed quietly. I was more perplexed than they for I could not associate any kind of miracle with so ordinary a person as myself; they were in the province of prophets, holy creatures, good people, mystics and in none of those categories was a place for me. Nor, come to that, did I want such a category. The evangelical rather repelled me in fact. What was I then? A person of no image whatsoever. A nothing and I recognized that fact very clearly.

During the following morning Barbara and I were alone and she said:

'I daren't tell her, but the medical people have given her until September.'

Instantly the words emerged and I said 'No, three weeks'.

'Oh, my God, Kathleen, so soon?' gasped Barbara.

Solemnly I said 'Yes, I'm afraid so and it'll be fairly quick.'

It was late July and the weather was lovely. After a brief lunch I suddenly said to Geraldine who was now up and dressed:

'I think you could do with another massage.'

'All right, it sounds like a good idea. I have to say I feel better after it' Geraldine replied.

Just the three of us were in the house, so Barbara and I got her comfortably settled on the big refectory-type table in the kitchen and facing the windows. Suddenly I noticed a hollow in her back and said

'Geraldine, have you ever been shot?' for it was an indentation which resembled a bullet hole with no puckering of the surrounding flesh.

Startled she said 'Of course not. Who'd ever shoot me?'

Without thinking I laid my right hand over the indentation and got a shock which made my brain reel, for as I lifted my hand I saw the cancer emerge from her body in one great lump larger than a tennis ball, but it was not round, it was the shape and colour of a beehive and utterly foul to boot. I must have cried out for Barbara came running out of the laundry room:

'Kathleen, what is it love? What's matter? Has something happened? Are you all right?'

Barely able to speak without stammering I told them what I'd seen.

In the air about I could see miniscule black specks all active, all vile and I remembered no more of that afternoon, except that the miracle had happened, but it was none of my doing. I'd only been used.

Prior to my return I told Geraldine, 'You need washing out, love. You could do with a whole new blood supply.'

She said uncertainly, 'There's no possibility of it, is there? If I went and asked for one they'd want to know why and if I told them they wouldn't believe a word of it.'

'No,' said I, 'I'm afraid they wouldn't. Well, you'll just have to eat all the blood purifying foods and try to do the best for yourself. Medical people wouldn't believe you and they wouldn't believe me, but it's gone, Geraldine.'

So I wrote her a kind of diet sheet, listing all the foods I knew of which would purify the blood, but I was uneasy ... I knew Geraldine and knew how perverse she could be. Would she eat them?

But she lived and the medical staff became perplexed. She should have been dead, but she bloomed and they could not understand this. In November of that year she came to stay with me and sparkled.

The following January she visited her consultant to be given an opinion of the X-rays that had been taken.

He said in confusion: 'I have to tell you that I don't understand this at all. Your liver shows new tissue and there is no cancer left.'

Geraldine unselfconsciously told him, 'Oh a friend of mine took it out. She's a healer.'

Then disaster struck in February, for Barbara was called away to a tragic event concerning one of her own family, leaving Frank in bed with a virulent strain of influenza. Geraldine was obliged to nurse him and she succumbed to the virus. The news was relayed to me that she was dying and I went to see her, knowing when I did that there was now no hope.

I said 'You haven't eaten the stuff I told you about, have you?'

She replied wearily, 'No, Kathleen, I haven't.' then she added with complete honesty, 'I've been perverse all my life. It's my own fault.'

So it was left and she died shortly after I returned to my home.

At least, her body died, but Geraldine did not. Much later I was to read of the truly appalling effects which materialize prior to death by liver failure. One of the MacMillan nurses told Barbara:

'She had no resistance to the 'flu virus.'

On hearing this I thought, 'the healing works when the instructions which go with it are obeyed. But they're not my instructions because I don't know anything consciously; the instructions come with the packaging so to speak, but if people choose to ignore them there is nothing I can do. After all, we have free will, we can accept or reject as we choose.'

It may appear as if I am absolving myself, or diminishing the value of healing, but that is not so, for I was to encounter one or two instances in which the knowledge arrived with the healing and was ignored, so when this happened I stopped. It was too precious to waste upon the wilful or the arrogant. I treated this power with awe all the time, awarding to it my total belief in its sacredness and was myself willing to subvert any ambition of my own in order to pass it on and expected those who received it to regard it also as sacred.

This is not an inventory of healing; therefore I shall continue in another vein, although much happened of a miraculous nature to many people. In one respect those who could actually feel the healing power spoke of it as having something akin to 'pins and needles' except that there was none of the distress which that condition causes. Some felt heat, but not a heat that burned. Some simply were cured instantaneously without feeling anything whatsoever. Gradually, I began to notice more and more that the power knew exactly what to do and when and how.

Because I could not say:

'This is the work of the MIND Itself' I said almost nothing but, 'Don't thank me, award your gratitude to that from which it comes.'

The principal was there. I could know it, recognize it, abide by it freely, but I couldn't see its extensions.

Chapter 23 – Attempts to Clarify

As time progressed my list of the other Mind's characteristics increased and I now add a few to the original list. Let it be clear that all the inferences which inevitably stem from the cores would take a couple of thousand years to write and I will eventually make some comparisons of the more prominent as they affect our lives. So the heading 'Matter' may be taken as meaning the human body, irrespective of gender and I realized the following:

MATTER		ENERGY LIFE	
Sight Sound Smell Touch Taste	Combine to allow the body to function and protect itself.	Joy Light Love Creation Truth	All combine to emit Life given a perfect state of physical being and an unclogged brain, devoid of self-admiration and ambition.
There must be added			
Physical Visible Negative	Unless the attributes in the next column are added, the final item is a combination of negativity and death.	Non-Physical Invisible Positive Intelligence	Therefore energy but a propellant – Life, the energy
Death		Life	
Subject to decay		Cannot be destroyed	

Juggle them all at will in any countless numbers of permutations; the answers yield the identical results. All is filtered through the twin lobes of the brain. If, therefore, the brain cells are solidified accumulation of attention to the left hand column's distinctions, there will be a diminution of the right hand column's positivities. In short, if you spent all your life bestowing your attention upon your physical body, attempting also to procure for that which is physical all the physical luxuries which it is believed will enhance the body in power and stature, you are 'backing the wrong horse' because the physical is impermanent. You will decay and then what? What, indeed?

Science has imposed its criteria by omitting from its investigations the right hand column's characteristics.

Now I add a further pair:

Objectivity and Subjectivity.

And there is where all the problems begin.

Physical matter, including bodies and stars, have been investigated to the nth degree by wholly objective scrutiny, focusing attention on one half of the whole and neglecting to suppose that it was the energy that required analysis, but it could not be investigated because it was invisible.

To simplify to the core: a corpse may have had an astounding number of brain cells, but if one removes Life from it, it is useless. But the energy which powered that brain does not die. Yet, we all must sleep; primate or peasant; the obscenely rich and the abjectly poor; all must sleep and that is when the souls departs to exist in another dimension.

I add now:

TIME	TIMELESSNESS
The dimension in which matter exists, the visible.	The dimension in which energy exists, invisible.

It must be accepted at the outset that what is to follow is not inspired by either resentment or malice; I illustrate simply that which is obvious. Governments (few of whom are to be trusted, many of which are composed of the power-crazy) have funded Science in general by truly horrendous amounts of finance. The said governments perhaps blinded and awed by the so-called majestic brains of scientists, have funded research and development in the optimistic hope that the scientists could, or would, discover some outstanding secret of Nature which the said government could and would use to further their own power-hungry status. It is Science in general which has held the real 'clout' and in the wielding of it they have isolated themselves from the greater mass of humanity, some with condescension, some with thinly veiled contempt for those who could not read their algebraic language, myself included. But I point out that humanity in general does not require any known language in order to communicate, for the energy which is living intelligence can and does, communicate in its own time, its own space. It can communicate over distance without the use of binary language.

That Science in general has repudiated many of the formal Church's doctrines is understandable, for many doctrines are based upon false premises, myths and legends; adhered to because the written constitutions coalesced into equally isolated hierarchies, all of whose powerful officers engaged themselves in consolidating their personal status and positions. It is ironic that the 'clout' of Science is the antithesis of the 'clout' of Churches; yet the real truths lay between the poles, lay in people. For not all the weighty pronouncements from either of the poles could, or did eradicate the innate knowledge of Life, the atavistic sense which first propelled men to draw upon the walls of their caves, to impose upon those walls that which they loved and admired: Life Itself. There were no schools of art or teachers. Pictures erupted without benefit of history, for here was where the history began.

Again, it is ironic that Science, delving into the atom's interior, should cause many physicists to rather despondently turn away from the postulated array of quarks, admitting that the single building block of matter could not be isolated. At the other end of the pole the Churches also continued to portray that which could not be proven and some continued to reinforce their theories with the dread spectre of eternal punishment and banishment from a God that was also a postulate, equally improvable and invisible.

Blazingly, none looked within themselves. None asked the vital, the only necessary questions: 'Who and what am I?' For it was within those twin postulates that the answer lay. But to even begin to understand one has to be willing to clear the conscious mind of all descriptions which relate to the physical person. One must eradicate all conceptions which are visible and which only describe the physical worldly honours. It is not easy to voluntarily take a hammer to the shell and discard the fragile shards of what one imagines to be one's status. I had little problem in consciously shedding for I owned no status to begin with; I simply lived two lives and they ran concurrently except for the fact that I lived much of my physical existence knowing what my future existence would be.

So by Science on the one hand and the church on the other, I was the joker in the pack, except living in such conditions was no joke, it was for real. Writing, writing and defeated by logistics for I could not write an equation that would describe the events I had lived and known. Yet it was during this period that something stole into my mind, crept in from heaven knew where, nor can I tell either when or how. Usually, new perspectives erupted in my head with the force of a bomb, but this seemed to slide into consciousness like a spreading dye and when it formulated I realized that it was a factor that had been clogging my brain for years. Quite nastily:

Ambition

I had wanted to rise prominently and declare: 'I know all the answers to what we call the Supernatural' and so vindicate myself in some unpleasant manner. Then I saw how ludicrous it was, for I couldn't write lucidly of that which I had lived. Something of a catharsis, but even when I rid myself of that I still couldn't write exactly for I was bogged down in comparisons and the permutations within the comparisons were horrendous to behold, impossible to calculate. Many times, in utter despair, I wished myself dead, blaming no one but myself for ineptitude. Yet somehow hauling myself out of the abyss to re-write, to re-think. Very obviously it didn't behove me to chide anyone else for fumbling after the natural truths and rendering only partial explanations, for I had seen the Whole Truth in one fell swoop and I saw the mind-which-lived-with-me-but-which-was-not-mine, my property and I still could not describe it lucidly, for I was trying to describe the Invisible, Energy imploded into unimaginable power, unimaginable Intelligence. Only words as tools and they were hopelessly inadequate. In some ways I was in worse straits than the men who drew on cave walls, for they had natural talent and I had very little talent. They made their feelings visible, but I was using black-on-white words to express life and the difference lay in the brains. Mine was clogged.

There came the day when I was sitting in my armchair and the perspectives changed once more. I did not know it at the time, but from then on the horizons were to widen and the nature of the visions encompassed not only my mundane existence, but more extensive fields.

Electron microscopes had produced a blurry image of an atom. I well knew the theories that described the nature and appearance of the surrounding electrons for they could be waves or particles. Much empty space surrounded the atom's nucleus and I knew by now the reason why apparitions could move so freely through what to the physical would have been an insoluble barrier. For the mind, in the form of the erstwhile body, was energy, so there were no insuperable difficulties as the living energy could pass freely through matter. Matter, being itself an illusion, was composed mainly of empty space. Consequently, living energy moved through space and this explained why ghosts moved through solid walls, for the walls were not, are not, solid.

Suddenly, I 'saw' and knew immediately that I was seeing an electron. It hung before me in an illuminated space, ovoid in appearance and it was spinning so rapidly that the outline was blurred. It resembled what used to be known as 'tops' on a spinning jenny and I had once seen one of these immensely long machines in action. The threads spun to fill the tops which spun at a rapid rate, filling with thread as they did so. As I can think of no better analogy, that example must suffice. Of course, this whirling electron moved at a far greater rate of spin.

As I watched I saw the thing unfurl itself into a long wavy banner, yet at no time did the banner itself, gauzy as it now was, ever disintegrate. When the electron unfurled itself to its limit, it simply rolled itself into its previous appearance, an ovoid top, without, of course, an engaging spindle.

It may sound very simple, but it was anything but simple, for unmistakably the thing knew what it was doing. The furling and unfurling had been quite deliberate, not in any respect a fortuitous occurrence; so although it may appear ludicrous to contend that an electron was and is, purposeful I can only say, in absolute truth, that it was purposeful, not in any respect an accidental procedure.

With this realization a thousand other considerations clamoured for attention. Electrons surrounded all the atoms within the Universe, even the simple hydrogen had one and the more the atomic scale increased the more electrons were allocated to each different substance.

The atomic table itself was a miracle of orderliness. No such orderliness could be attributed to chance formation, so once again I thought of the American 'numbers racket': if one were to declare that the structure of the atomic table had been formed by chance encounter then one was in the big league of numbers and the permutations were colossal.

To paraphrase Einstein, 'The most surprising thing about the Universe is that we can understand it.' Of course, it was designed by a MIND so vast I couldn't describe it and as this planet was subsumed by that tiny tendril which had partially left the MIND to infuse Life in it, there was no wonder we could attain some limited knowledge of how the Universe was composed and why the atomic table was a miracle of orderliness.

But there was even more to it than that, for I began to realize why mankind, throughout its history had held belief, irrespective of how the beliefs were constituted, or in what manner they evinced themselves. The belief had always existed that some unidentifiable Being or Mind existed which the physical characteristics could not identify, but the soul could know for it had originated from the same Source.

More profoundly still, I realized that a trace of the MIND was in matter also. The whole Universe was an expression of the MIND itself. We lived within it, we existed within it and I looked at the alternative; it was:

Nothingness - Outside of Creation. We lived within Creation.

Therefore, it was crystal clear as to how and why mankind had always postulated that another concept, vast and accredited with vast perception existed, for we existed within the MIND and all that was visible and observable was created from and by, the MIND, therefore containing a trace of the Ultimate Intelligence within the visible. It was and is, perfectly easy to see the visible Universe as being logical and intelligent in formation, any fool could see it as such by simply comparing that which was visible and removing intelligence from it, then considering what the visible Universe would be without the MIND's order. The answer, of course, was chaos. For the atomic table to have formed by chance, by the random collisions of particles, one would have to postulate formation by chance and that would involve a time scale longer than the estimated time of the original formation. Two concepts remained: Purposeful and Purposeless. No contest exists. We live within an Intelligent, purposeful Universe.

Staggered, my conscious mind reeled at the conclusions I was seeing, for these findings stretched from the microcosm to the macrocosm. So many implications ... I could not write them all ...

Therefore, I simply write that we exist, as does the Universe, as matter which is visible, within extensions of the MIND. Is the visible logical, understandable; or is it chaotic and the result of chance formation? There exists no doubt. We exist in a Universe which is an extension of the MIND and to discover this truth one need only consider the alternative which is chaos. The principle is exactly the same as the discovery of time as an energy in which matter exists, for if one removes the concept of time/energy from matter, a frozen Universe would be the result. In exactly the identical formula, if intelligence is removed from the visible, chaos will result.

It is not a matter simply of discovery concerning the visible, it is what would be if intelligence were removed and the atomic table would be in disorder.

Cursing myself on almost a daily basis for ineptitude I felt that somewhere in all these answers was a formula if only I could isolate it and with all else I had seen it would be exquisitely simple.

Chapter 24 – The Impossible Made Valid

Specifically now in chronological order, my sister Betty began to be ill. Sometime earlier she had been thrown in the air by a hit-and-run driver and I had taken her from hospital to nurse. On the deceptive flat surface of reality Betty appeared to recover and function, but I felt in my bones that overall her body had suffered long term damage. Indeed, in the interim she called on me with increasing frequency for aid and as I had travelling to do, it was not easy to reach her or return to my own home.

Almost two years later my daughter came rushing up the stairs calling:

'Mum, I've had a phone call from Auntie Betty's neighbours. They say her light is on downstairs but they can't make her hear them and she doesn't answer the phone, or come to the door. They're very worried.'

Knowing exactly what had happened I said, 'Ring back and tell them to call the police.'

My daughter answered 'They've sent for the police, Mum, but they want you to know. I'll call a taxi for you.'

It was a rush, for I was in the midst of Betty's washing, but it had to be left and I changed hurriedly into outdoor clothes. I knew as surely as I breathed what had happened and what lay at the foot of those frightful stairs.

Betty lived in a fairly short terrace of stone-built houses, the fronts of which all had small gardens facing the road. Behind the houses was a paved communal space.

At the back of Betty's house was a small group of women, two of whom I recognized as her nearest neighbours. All began excitedly to talk but I was in no mood for chatter and pushed my way through the back door which had obviously been forced. Very quickly indeed a pretty young WPC came into the kitchen, closing the inner door and said firmly:

'Who are you, madam?'

I gasped 'I'm Betty's sister. Stand aside please, I want to see her.'

She said, placing herself against the door, 'No, I'm afraid not. My colleague is there, but you can't go in.'

Angrily I said 'You have no authority whatsoever to prevent me. I am her nearest living relative and I demand to see her.'

'She's had rather a bad fall and I'm afraid you can't go in yet. Come with me' and so saying she somehow persuaded me back to the knot of women, saying to them,

'Could you make this lady a cup of tea, please?'

Several offered, but I stood, trembling from head to foot, unable to assimilate that which I had known ten years earlier to be true.

I said 'I tried to get her out ...'

To my astonishment her two nearest neighbours began in unison:

'Yes, we know. She told us both a couple of years ago what you'd said would happen. And it's happened ... oh dear, it's happened. Come on, love and have some tea.'

Aghast I said 'She actually told you what I'd said?'

In unison they replied 'Yes, she did. She said you'd tried to get her to sell up and she said she wouldn't move for all the tea in China. She told us that you'd walk in that back door and find ... and find ...'

And her great confidante said gently, 'Come with me love and I'll make us some tea.'

Like someone poleaxed I followed her and was sitting on her sofa when the WPC returned. She asked me for identification and address, then enquired the name of Betty's doctor which I gave. Unable to comply with any more with regulations I said:

'Don't prevaricate with me. Tell me, is my sister dead?'

The WPC replied gently 'Yes, I'm afraid so.'

I persisted with 'Then I want to see her.'

She returned with 'No, I'm afraid you can't. She's had rather a bad fall and it's better that you don't until ...'

I thought wildly: 'What am I asking questions for? I know, I've known for years... She's lying there smashed up like a rag doll, oh my God.'

It may be supposed by a disinterested observer that I behaved like an arrant fool; that knowing the truth I ought to have come to terms with it and remained unshaken. Icy with horror I shook like a leaf, for I never got 'used to it' for feeling cannot be eliminated from my person and I hope it never is. As siblings we had argued and often been cross with each other, but we had loved each other and that cannot be, must not be eliminated from any relationship. The manner in which she died seemed peculiarly horrible and still affects me to the extent that I would never willingly enter that road again.

It seemed odd for the Coroner's office to issue sympathetic statements, but such arrived with the rider that they were pleased to inform me that no official identification was required of me as that had been given by her doctor and that they were pleased not to have to call on me as she had suffered rather badly by falling. It was also confirmed that she had died before falling. It should have consoled me, but it did not. I knew in my bones that she had known a moment of utter terror before she fell.

On the day of her funeral my family, her friends and I gathered in the anterooms, then suddenly, without warning, she occupied me and I moved into the arms of my dear son-in-law weeping uncontrollably. All were astonished at a reaction none had expected of me, the non-screamer, the non-hysterical. It was not hysteria, it was deep unutterable grief and it was Betty's anguish I wept.

Why, then, have I written at some length concerning this very personal tragedy? For one purpose only and it is this: in a kind of public statement it had been said by scientists that only if a death could be foretold would the claim of precognition be given serious consideration. Let them consider this. I certainly did not tell of the nature of Betty's death to her neighbours, she told them herself. Proof you wish? There is proof. But I also add that I do not personally care a whit whether it is believed or not, for I do not cherish the opinions of people who can only claim to know their own identities by presenting lists of personal achievements, for such lists blinker, blind the absolute truth with facile titles.

It had been a long hard winter and the demands on my time and energy had been great. For the first time in years I had managed to save a little money and decided to take a holiday at my own expense, for the first time in years. There was no doubt as to the destination, I had to go to Crete, go alone and try to find what lay inside my head like dark lava.

When need arises the means arrive to fulfil the need and with no trouble I got an apartment in a very nice hotel within reasonable walking distance of a large village and with miles of beach on which to walk. Privacy I needed and privacy I received, rising each morning to see the sun and sea, miles of open country, mountains and below me the most glorious garden which invaded me with beauty. So I walked and walked for the greater part of every day. I walked and thought and met some fascinating people of several races who, unburdened by my stiff English upbringing were unafraid to greet me and tell of their lives and interests.

All in all, it was right to go to Crete for I too was cured of something, but it all happened in silence in my own head and I told no one of this. In any case it was Invisible.

Chapter 25 – What Lives, What Dies?

It was a day in summer in the year of 1996 and I write now in strict chronological detail, for much was to occur.

I had an extraordinary vision and even more extraordinarily I knew throughout that it was a vision I was living. It was as if my whole mind was there, so that some of it I was able to analyze as it was happening. It seemed as if I was somehow suspended in a domain of time and I felt 'yonderly'.

It commenced by my finding myself in a cellar and to the left of my vision were three or four stone steps, very clean. Within my perimeter of vision I could see the cellar walls and they were brilliantly, spotlessly white, yet I knew that this transformation had only recently been the result of a very thorough cleansing, but it was not paint that had been applied to what I knew were old stonewalls beneath the white covering.

Quite clearly I thought: By Jove, someone's worked hard on this place, I never saw walls so perfectly white and certainly not cellar walls. There was a brief moment when it became puzzling as to who or what had managed to clean this cellar so thoroughly and apply this thick coating of white brilliance, but I couldn't solve the mystery, so I turned my attention again to what I could see. There was a companion here, slightly behind me and to my left, but at no time did she say anything, yet she seemed very familiar and I felt I knew her well, was comfortable with her.

It was obvious that I had to climb those few steps, perhaps four or five, in order to get out of the cellar and there was never any doubt that I had to climb them for at the top was a kind of door, but rather a barrier and it had to be negotiated before I could get outside. Into what? I didn't know, only that there was a route and it must be followed. In the angle formed by the side of the steps and the facing wall to the right was a kind of huge table which was also an integral part of the cellar itself. On it was half of the largest brown earthenware bowl I had ever seen and instantly I knew what it represented;

This was Matter. Earthenware. The earth, a representation of the earth. Matter of which the earth was created and I recognized this instantly, thinking: Yes, that's very appropriate, but the other half is energy and continued to climb the steps. When I reached the barrier everything began to whirl at a tremendous rate, so that I could not see any of the passing scenes in detail for they passed with such rapidity it was like seeing a kaleidoscope running at a furious rate without being able to absorb any one picture in it. Time. It was time passing although there was no way of estimating any length of time, but it was the dimension in which the physical existed, in which matter existed, I knew that for certain.

With no sense of transition we were through and my companion remained just behind me, still offering no comment. It was a lovely scene, a vast expanse of lawn in which people were sitting about in small groups, but not in any sense was there crowding. This land was a peninsula and it was obvious it fell away to a valley on the left. On the opposite side was also lovely land, mown and green, in very good condition. Beyond the vistas lay the sea, blue and dreaming in the bright sunshine. To my right was my house and it was huge. I could only see a part of it for it lay at the perimeter of my vision, yet I knew it to be prominent on this headland. Yet strangely, it was not mine in the sense of ownership or possession. Rather as if I were some kind of rather inadequate custodian. Being essentially practical, the domesticity came to the fore and I remarked to my companion:

'As all these people have chosen to visit, the least we can do is offer them some tea and I'll see if I can scrounge some biscuits from somewhere.'

As she gave no reply I thought: it looks as if you'll have to sort it out for yourself, but you can't let them go away without even a drink. Then it dawned on me that we hadn't enough milk in the place and I seemed to wander about in a futile manner trying to get someone to get some milk from somewhere, but there was no response at all. I thought: well, if you can't get any help you'll just have to find some yourself. I wonder if I'll be able to carry enough for everybody. It was rather a problem, because I didn't know if I could haul enough, but I'd just have to try.

So I set off alone to my left, covering quite a lot of this extensive lawn which sloped downwards a little until I reached a spot where I could see the valley bottom. A road ran up the opposite hill and to my utter amazement I saw the Golden Coach of England appear at the top of the hill, drawn by the famous eight greys. It rolled comfortably down the hill to the valley road and melted, literally dissolved into mist. Then I knew, with absolute certainly, that this symbol of sovereignty was going to disappear. Not with violence or active intervention, but simply melt into time and it was a very sobering thought. Still, there was nothing I could do about it, or even wanted to do. It had been powerful in its own era, but that era was ending. And I thought: all monoliths topple. Man keeps on erecting them because he won't learn from history, but they all topple in the end because nothing we create is permanent or durable.

Somehow, in the interim, I had made arrangements for milk to be delivered and returned to the house.

My companion was waiting and I asked: 'Would you like to look round for a bit?'

She didn't reply, she simply assented, so we went in. Some people from the lawn were pottering about in a wide corridor to our left, so I led her to the right and we passed an open door leading to a vast exquisite room which had been newly refurbished. My companion gazed inside with enchantment as I explained:

'Yes, it's all been done out, it needed refurbishing.' Then I added, 'This is only one room, you know, there are lots more ... they go on and on ...' and I turned to my right, to the future, dissolving into the mists of future time, yet knowing that this was permanency, not the illusionary impermanence symbolized by the Golden Coach, but a reality which would endure, would go on and on ...

Then I awakened. Stunned. A new reality. A different reality. A future reality. And I had to climb those steps before I could leave the cellar. The Monarchy is going to fade into oblivion. How, I didn't know, but something was going to happen which would effect a change. Now I knew the meaning of the house. For years I had dreamed of huge houses, all of which were mine, but not mine. All had needed refurbishment and I could remember those dreams well. But this, this was different from any dream. This was a future reality. I felt disorientated, as if I had been caught up in some enormous event over which I had no control, but was an active participant. There was meaning here which I could see but dimly, yet none of it was random or chance happening; it was all part of a greater reality with no particle anywhere of the fortuitous.

So I talked of it, telling Lynette what I had seen and telling Barbara also. Some weeks passed, not many and although I cannot pinpoint any date, for I do not spend my time watching calendars, a great explosion occurred in my head. It was as if a bomb had exploded causing not the smallest pain or injury, but yet if felt as if the world itself had shattered.

There was another Universe.

A Universe of Energy.

Invisible to all physical matter, bodies.

But this Universe was the true reality.

It was the Universe of matter that was the illusion.

'Look the other way'.

I thought helplessly: we've got it all the wrong way round. We believe this to be living because we occupy a body, but it is true Life, Pure Life we depart to. We are our own ghosts and the body is the machine. Like all machines it breaks down. But the knowing ghost does not, for there is the intelligence.

Dazed by the vistas I could see the twin Universes stretch out before me and realized that the twinning commenced in one's own person, in the twin lobes of the brain; left hand, right hand; the visible and the invisible; the comparisons went on and on …

But overall there was a slight disparity, a ratio that I had noticed again and again throughout the 'big read' and which I had not understood. It had surfaced in the Paul Dirac numbers, surfaced in several more theses of which I had kept no note for bibliography, yet it existed. Murray, some years ago, had compiled a survey in order to establish beliefs in the general public as to whether belief in the 'Supernatural' was prevalent and there the approximate ratio of beliefs surfaced once more. The ratio is sixty, forty which together comprise a Whole. Now I realized the nature of the discrepancy, for it is within energy that matter emerges. From the invisible emerges the visible. And from the invisible emerges intelligence.

From the matter crushing accelerators particles appeared, particles born of energy and there was a natural law which was perplexingly revealed also; two particles in collision always spin off with a right handed left handed spin. Purposeful, purposeless? Creation or Chaos? Natural law? Then in what MIND was the law devised? I thought: one cannot have it both ways, one either admits to intelligence in the visible Universe or one posits chaos. If what one reveals by one's investigations (such as the atomic table) is order, then one must posit that the order cannot have been so by chance formation.

As I am not writing a text book I shall cease making such

comparisons, let those who have elected themselves as investigators of matter and with many disastrous results (the hydrogen bomb, for one) allow that an Intelligence greater than can be visualized, had imposed this order. Chance cannot be admitted. We live within a created Universe and I saw and knew the Source, the MIND. I see it all my days.

Stupefied with wonder I now saw the true meanings of this twinning process and I decided that I must now re-write. My part in all this was so unimportant as to be utterly negligible. So in the September month of that same year I wrote myself out of it in the main and it became a kind of tract. Facts, I thought, facts are what is required. Who would want to know anything about me? If I can present some solid evidence it is that which will be accepted.

Somewhere in my life there was always an example of futility, or something I had lived, known, recognized and by actual experience could later relate to. Just such an experience now repeated itself. Briefly and offering no names, I tell of a time when I first began to write and following those incredible visions which occurred after the decision was made.

Two well-educated people, man and wife, knew me at the time and they seemed unduly interested as to why I had abandoned my share in our small business in order to write. They wanted to know: What was the subject? What was so important that I would sacrifice my only visible means of support in order to write of the subject?

I had no desire to tell them anything, but the husband worried at the topic until I at last succumbed and told them of those visions. His first reaction was explosive:

'A bloody woman! A bloody woman, of all people. It's damned unfair. A man sweats all his life looking for answers and a bloody woman walks up, just like that and learns 'em.'

Hurt, I tried to point out that there had been a huge penalty, for I had lived the deaths of my sons and my father prior to those deaths. However he was extremely aggravated by this learning, believing it to be the prerogative of men as it had been for more than five millennia. Yet in spite of the male advantages none had produced any explanation as to how the Paranormal evinced itself. Such reaction was not peculiar to him, for an identical reaction could be expected from a much wider spectrum of males. They had created the civilizations and women played inferior roles. It was unnecessary for the latter to think on large important subjects for they were inclined to hysteria and incapable of forming balanced logical judgments. Men thought objectively for they were only too conscious of their own identities which had been compiled by the early writers with what they believed to be great accuracy.

It may be supposed at this juncture that I seek to promote or support the age-old 'battle of the sexes' but anyone who reads these words must disabuse themselves from the idea, for it is not true. I sought only to show the nature and being of the subjective, its meanings and attributes; that which is mysterious and which cannot be subjected to scrutiny by mechanical means. If bodies, either male or female dismiss or cripple themselves by the repudiation of such attributes, they become damaged and the effects spread.

This man's opinion of me was extremely low in the academic sense and as I had no great opinion of myself, knowing well that I had had no formal training in any discipline but by actual living, I felt inferior and unable to adjust my behaviour to the invisible standard which I knew existed.

Finally, but privately aghast, I allowed myself to be overridden when he took my writings and re-wrote them. When I held the finished manuscript in my hands I then knew what it contained without ever requiring to read it. Quite conclusively, he wrote me out of it.

Years later, during that September month, I did exactly the same. Throughout the whole of those years of writing I had taken advice from those who I believed were more qualified than I and followed such advice thinking and loathing the 'I'. I believed myself to be incompetent and a fool. So I had written in what I hoped was a lucid academic manner, knowing as I did that I was no academic.

Immediately prior to the Christmas period of that year I offered the manuscript to the Spiritualists' Union, thinking that as I had once been healed by the ordinary people who sat in Emmie's room, at least I could extend my gratitude in this manner. At least, I decided, they may be able to make use of this knowledge, for they had a very bad press over the years and I had admired their courage in adhering to their beliefs in spite of quite savage calumny.

During that year I had a sharp vision which shattered me. Before me was a small group of people in what appeared to be a quite beautiful location. As they stood in a loosely knit circle my eye was drawn to a tall dark haired young man who I felt was very good looking but as I couldn't see his face I could only feel that he was somehow familiar to me. The group had obviously been deciding to go somewhere and they began to move off which meant that the tall young man still had his back toward me. But a slight fair youth detached himself from the group and spoke to me directly, full face.

He said 'Mum, we are your sons. That,' and he indicated the dark haired young man, 'is Simon and I am Andrew. You have forgotten us.'

There was no time to protest in anguish:

'Oh, darling, I have never forgotten either of you, I just daren't remember.'

For then I awoke and wept. I ought to have wept much earlier. A coward, for when I remembered them I remembered the agony too and it had been unbearable.

Chapter 26 – More Amazements

Barbara rang: 'Kathleen, would you like to come for a holiday around Easter? ------- is coming down and he says he'll bring you in his car?'

'Yes,' I said 'I'd love to see you again. It seems ages since we had a get-together? Are you sure he won't mind?'

'No.' she replied, 'He says he doesn't mind a bit. I've already asked him. So you'll come?'

I answered 'Yes, thank you, I will'

So it was arranged. Rather vaguely I wondered what would happen when I got to Cornwall. Something usually did when I was in Barbara's company for any length of time and Cornwall itself seemed to produce some quite extraordinary reactions in me.

However, nothing mysterious happened at all, for the family at large were in a ferment and I spent the greater part of the time on the outskirts, giving unwanted advice and helping to decorate the house.

Before leaving Cornwall I asked Barbara:

'We haven't had much time together and you look tired out. Would you fancy coming to me sometime in the summer?'

She said fervently, 'There's nothing I'd like better.'

'Right then' I said 'we'll settle on a time.'

But there had been time to describe that long unusual vision which described the dissolving of the Golden Coach and I had said somberly:

'It's going to end, that era. I don't know how or when, but there's an end coming. And you'll be with me, for it was you in the vision.'

It was a large prophesy, important in worldly terms, but I knew no more detail than that. And Barbara would be my companion when it happened, or at least at the outset of the actual affair, for some of the spectators were already in place ... To elucidate upon that rather cryptic remark I must remove the following explanation out of chronological order and return to the beginning of the year 1997.

I had decided it was time to sever relationships with the Spiritualists, as I did not join formal creeds. Lynette called and I told her of this, adding:

'I think I'll have to stop going. I'm so uncomfortable I don't know what to do with myself and I shan't go again.'

She cried out in real alarm, 'Oh, you mustn't, you mustn't give up, you've got to go.'

In some surprise at the sudden vehement outburst I said:

'Why on earth shouldn't I give up?'

Lynette replied 'You went to the place years ago, you told me you'd been and you gave up I know but you mustn't stop, you've got to go on going. You've something to do there.'

I said 'I'm not really wanted there. I said that I was on fire with healing and I was given to understand that it was because I'm a rank amateur and that if I wanted to heal I'd have to take a long probationary course. If you think I'm going to sit for some exam you're mistaken. It's supposed to be that you have to learn to handle it, but I can no more handle this than I can fly. It just is and I've no more jurisdiction over it than I have over the sun rising. No way,' I went on, 'no way. I'm giving up.'

Just as positively Lynette argued 'And I'm telling you, you can't, you mustn't. You've something to do there and it's very important. I don't know what it is, so it's no good you asking me, but Kathleen, you have to go. Promise me. Anyway, I'm not going until you promise.'

I replied, grinning, 'I wonder if it was a good idea to encourage you to get yourself some training, you've turned into one of these bossy women and you think you can dangle your qualifications at me just to make me feel inadequate' and we laughed together.

Having given my promise I kept it and sat through another evening of discomfort. The Spiritualists have a very pleasant ritual which permits some time after the service for an interlude in which tea, coffee and biscuits are served in another room and people may sit about chatting. As I walked to the top table with my coffee I noticed a lady sitting by herself, but I did not take the seat directly opposite, but rather to one side. Yet even as I approached I could feel the melancholia which emanated from her in waves.

She began to talk, mere introductory phrases, but I couldn't stand the preparatory chat and said:

'You're very unhappy, aren't you?'

She replied, 'Yes, I am. I, we, I, have a lot of trouble.'

'Yes' I said 'I know.'

A flood was unleashed and she told me of her daughter who had developed a serious problem which I will describe as a 'nervous breakdown' without being more explicit. Unfortunately, such problems are too widespread in our society, but I will not embark upon the whys and wherefores for when one cuts to the bone it usually means that an individual is deeply unhappy. By this time I was chary of telling anyone that I could heal, or to be truthful, could pass on healing, for at no time did I ever regard it as my property. But in this case … At last, tentatively, I said:

'I can pass on healing.'

She said 'Would you? Would you really? I'd give anything, anything at all to get her better.'

So I told her the conditions:

'I make no guarantees of any cure, for I never knew what the outcome would be and the only guarantee possible was that it never harmed anyone. No money must be offered, for healing was not mine to sell.'

If she found those terms acceptable I would try. So a deal was struck, for the lady was snatching at straws by then and the problem had continued for some months without any apparent hope that it would improve.

Fervent with hope she accepted the above conditions, but I well knew that the lady herself needed healing (but of a physical nature), so as she did not mention herself I remained silent on the subject. At the time agreed both mother and daughter arrived and when I saw the daughter I saw a person from whom all but essential life had departed. For a second I felt great alarm, what could bring this attractive young person back? Healing did. In an amazingly short time she reverted to what I knew to be her natural effervescent bubbly nature. This was Lynn.

Halfway through the first meeting I said:

'It's Mum's turn now.' and they looked at me in surprise.

Mum's name was Bessie. Bessie sat, bewildered:

'But I didn't ask for … I didn't say, I didn't think …'

Taking her hand I said 'But you do have trouble, don't you? Your legs ache and they're making mine ache. It's gone on for years hasn't it?'

She said 'For ten years at least. They ache all the time. I've more or less got used to it.' I said 'Well, I don't know if it'll do anything, but I don't mind trying if you don't mind allowing me?'

A blow-by-blow account I will not write, but there is one circumstance which needs, I believe, to be written and it is that I saw a bone in one of her legs bent up at an angle from the knee and that was the seat of her troubles. To spare this leg she had used the other leg, which resulted in both legs being painful and swollen. The swelling couldn't be seen for she always wore rather baggy pants. Later Bessie told me that she had been born with one leg bent upward at the knee. Anyhow, the upshot was that Lynn was cured and Bessie freed of pain. They were startled, but not so startled as I, for I never get 'used to it'. It is always a source of perpetual awe to me. Never, but never can it be taken for granted, nor can one ever claim personal triumph, for that would be despicable. All one can do is to pass it on; it is no one's personal property.

There is always a tendency for certain people to gravitate and this occurred the Sunday following my first meeting with Bessie, for our group of two became enlarged by a man and wife couple and although the conversation became quite general I noticed their clothes which were outstandingly good and very formal, but appropriate for them. Usually, I could not later say what clothes are being worn by anyone, but there was something about their clothes that held my attention. I discovered later they had all been made by the lady who was a trained tailor of remarkable talent. A retired teacher of her craft.

On the following Sunday evening we again congregated at the top table with our coffees and it chanced that I sat opposite the husband. Again, the conversation was generalized and I cannot remember a word of it. But I saw inside the head of this man and what I saw frightened me out of my wits. A darkness, pitch black which lay beneath and tapered like a vile river down to the back of his neck. This man was dying and if something was not done quite quickly it would be too late. A few months, no more...

Bessie must have said how much better she and Lynne were feeling, for the couple seemed to know that I could pass on this Power.

One day, as they passed by our property they offered me a lift and uncharacteristically I invited them to have coffee with me. In truth, I couldn't wait to put my hands on his head. Between my seeing inside his head all conventional proprieties seemed to disappear, so whether I had asked his permission or not I cannot say. All that is clear is that I did so and watched, in total awe, a large beehive shaped mass of vile substance emerged from his scalp. Knowing it had not all emerged I suggested they return later, which they did and the rest of the disgusting mass emerged also.

A month later I was told that he had been declared an official invalid, that he had a cyst upon his brain, that no surgeon would dare to penetrate his skull and that nothing further could be done for him. He also admitted his life had been a rarified hell and that as he walked his dog one morning the thought had entered his mind that he was dying, but of this he had told no one.

Later, I told Lynette what had happened and she said cheerfully, without reservation:

'I told you so. I told you, you hadn't to give up going.' I concluded 'All right, Mrs Know all, you've got full brownie points. So don't rub it in.'

This interlude has been described for one purpose only, for this is not an account of 'people-who-had-been-healed', the implications relate to the strange vision during which I saw the Golden Coach of Britain. These were the group of people for whom I needed milk, because each time they came I always, of course, offered them drinks of coffee. It was all beginning to form itself into the truths I had seen a year earlier.

Barbara arrived for her holiday with me, composed, with her air of control so different from the crushed Barbara I had first known. To Barbara herself I vented some of my life-long frustrations. It was unforgivable and I knew it. Some people (of whom she had been one) seemed to regard me as some kind of latter-day oracle, some kind of special person and I knew with certainty I was no such thing. 'Of the earth, earthy', was a true description of myself. As ordinary as the butter and bread which was my staple diet. What I wanted recognition of was the facts that I had learned concerning Supernatural events which I knew to be absolute truths and of which I had spent all I owned in trying to prove. Moreover, I had received no help from those who had been helped by this absolute truth, for having received it they had kept very quiet about it thereafter. It was the taboo subject, the improvable, the even-now suspect subject and those who had received actual physical help did not advertise the fact for fear of being thought foolish. I, on the other hand, had no 'clout' in any direction and if I wrote that which I knew to be true the consensus of opinion was and I well knew it: 'The poor old bat has lost her marbles'. So the upshot had been that while there were many who had been on the receiving end and been very glad to receive, no one anywhere was willing to stick a head above the sand and give me public support. I was on my own and I did not know where to turn. Only one Source could help me and it was to this Source that I appealed.

I said 'If these truths are to be known the ball is in my court. I can't sell myself because I don't think I'm worth anything.'

If it could be called 'praying' then that is what it was. Poor Barbara was on the receiving end of all that frustration but at least she saw me as I was, a bit of old hosepipe through which energy flowed.

At last she said quietly: 'I've always known there were two of you. When you first walked into my house I saw a little girl and I always wanted to put my arms round her, comfort her and cuddle her. But just behind you was a tall dark figure, a man. I never saw his face but I knew this man was with you all the time.'

I replied bitterly, 'I've always known someone was there and I was just being used. Emmie was right, even though I always denied it she said I was a medium and that's what I've been. We all are, Barbara, I looked it up in my old Webster's: Bodies which move in space and time. That's us, the whole human race, but we've built ourselves such a complex physical world that we don't know who we are now. We've so many labels from birth to death we don't even know our own identities. If you get down to the core you can see we're just matter and energy and the matter's going to decay, but the mind doesn't. Oh, Barbara, it's so clear, it crystal clear, but there isn't a physicist anywhere who'd give me the time of day. I'm uneducated and I don't move in the right circles. I can see it all so clearly, I can't write it properly, but it's nobody's fault but my own. Oh my God, it's all in my head and I can't get it out. Why me? Why didn't he occupy someone else, someone who can get her thoughts into order, someone with training and someone behind to push her? Why the hell me?'

Barbara said quietly, 'It wouldn't have happened to anybody like that because they'd have been considering their own position in life all the time.'

I said 'I have no position. But it's so simple, Barbara, if you can't move matter into future time what can move? What does move? It moves for everybody. If you only get a mere premonition it's a signal that you know of something that's going to happen, so it isn't that we can't know the future, it's the only dimension we can live in.'

It would have been more appropriate for her to spare herself this outburst and hit me over the head, for that is where the barriers lay and I couldn't see what was under my very nose, so it was actually useless to rage thus at social blindness for I was one of the blind too.

    Then the world erupted.

Chapter 28 – A Conclusion Shaped

It was early Sunday morning and the telephone rang. I rushed to answer, for Barbara was sleeping and although it wasn't likely that she would be disturbed through the thick stone wall, I wasn't taking any chances. My younger daughter said:

'Mum, how are you? How's Barbara?'

I said 'Oh, we're all right love.'

She asked 'Mum, have you heard the news?'

Startled I asked 'No, what news?'

Amazed she said 'You're sure you haven't heard?'

Wondering if some huge natural disaster had occurred I said:

'What news are you talking about?'

She replied simply, sombrely, 'Princess Diana is dead'.

I knew instant grief. How could this beautiful young woman be dead. She was rich, the centre of attraction around the world, yet the object of great pity, for her grief was visible, unconcealed, in direct contravention of the accumulated conventions of British society which demanded chilly repudiation of subjective emotions.

My daughter and I talked for a little then I turned on the television set and we terminated the conversation, such as it was. Together with millions around the globe I was dumbfounded by what I was learning and the implications were staggering in a personal sense, for pity and awe fought now for supremacy in my mind.

Primarily, the Golden Coach (symbol of sovereignty) that I had watched a year earlier had dissolved into mist. I had not seen the cause of the dissolution but now Diana was dead the implications were astonishing... She had loved, not wisely, but too well. Too well for convention. Yet Love was the lynchpin, the glue which bound living species; so the insult and repudiation of Love lay in the jurisdiction of convention. Ergo, there was something seriously wrong with convention and very many were its victims.

I had described that vision to Barbara and she was here, staying with me. When she appeared I told her the news baldly, brutally so; and she, the dignified, capable, confident recipient of her family's woes burst into immediate tears, as did millions of others; and she wept for a week, murmuring, at times:

'If anyone had told me that I would weep like this for someone I never met, never knew, I would call them a liar; but I cannot stop, Kathleen.'

Each time I replied, 'Don't mind me, my dear, cry all you want, it's better out than in. If it ever reaches the stage when we can't weep for a stranger we might as well pack it all in, for life wouldn't be worth living.'

Then I began to think and the following emerged.

Primarily I thought of this land and its history and together with all the important histories ever recorded. It was bloody and vicious, a saga of successive conquerors with bestial appetites and devoid of scruples. Power. Of course, what else could it be? From the infant wrestling of small schoolboys in a playground to the monstrous wars that decimated millions, the males fought for supremacy. What could cause the dissolution of the one world-renowned physical, visible – only too visible – representation of power and majesty? Love would be the dismantler of that which had held the ultimate prominence in this land.

Now it was as if my mind detached itself. I saw over the previous millennia of visible physical symbols of sovereignty. I saw the Pharoahic dynasties, three millennia of which had fallen to dust. When, I thought will we ever learn the true values? What is brittle and fragile and what is enduring? It was easily traceable throughout the ages, the Roman Empire had crumbled beneath its own weight, so had the Minoan, the Chinese; all the monoliths toppled because they were built upon false foundations, specious beliefs from the time when we had lost our true beliefs, knowledge of ourselves.

I thought of the mere thousand years of British monarchy and saw the futility of its origins. How impressive it had all seemed, yet the foundations were brittle as chaff and chaff is dispersed, would now be dispersed by the Invisible: Love. What pageantry had devolved from the early bloody shambles of those who had fought mercilessly and without scruple for the crown?

Those who had deemed themselves to be the ruling bodies of Britain had evolved into the hierarchies that wielded the power: the Church, the Law, the armed Forces, the State in the form of Parliament and at the top the Crown. All meshed into Power, the visible trappings of power and the robes and accoutrements which were designed to define their various status. It was very good theatre, supported as it was by the resplendent trappings, very impressive indeed and it impressed many who were not even British. No wonder the British were such good actors and actresses, they had had plenty of practice. In combination it impressed the world, but people can be easily deceived by the flat surface of reality, except the flat surface reality is only that and no more, beneath that exterior is the interior and the exterior is subject to change and decay, however impressively the visible is presented, but below is the invisible and that is not subject to decay.

It was in all their interests, these hierarchies, to support each other to the hilt and they did so with enthusiasm, for in the final analysis they could call upon the Church to threaten malcontents and dissenters with various descriptions of eternal hell. For a long time it all worked well. John Osbourne was to name it collectively as the 'Establishment' for; of course, those at the summit of the various branches were drawn from a minority of families. It was from these families that those at the summit were drawn. And it was from these families that the ethical and social doctrines were established. As Nancy Mitford was to define: these characteristics described the 'U'[1] from the 'non-u'. So because these definitions were the crème de la crème on the surface of British social usages and ethics, they filtered down through the multi-layered cake which comprised the nation; they were presented to the world as British values.

Two hundred years ago I would have been either stoned to death or burned at the stake, for the Life I had lived, the secondary existence, fitted into none of the acceptable categories that defined the social and ethical climate.

Yet I was living it and I had no choice in the matter. Well I knew that this threnody ran through all the written beliefs of five thousand years and had originated in our ancestors of pre-history.

Chastened, I watched a thousand years of accumulated protocol demolished, without public violence, subsumed by the short loving life of a loving woman. Chastened even more by the realization that I had lived this truth a year earlier, not the mechanisms which would be involved, but the result which was to follow. The artificial protocol would succumb to the Invisible.

The unnatural façade that had accumulated over the centuries collapsed in an outpouring of public grief. It is doubtful if people

---

[1] 'U' means upper class and 'non-u' means all the rest.

actually knew why they grieved, but this death, so tragic, demolished the illusion that the British were stoic, not given to public display of grief. They wept openly and freely without reserve, rich and poor, classless, sophisticates, for Love had been publicly rejected, but it was stronger than the physical illusion of a thousand years of power.

During the time she spent with me I had told Barbara of an earlier and wonderful experience I had lived and realized later that I had shown her, in that corridor of my vision, that which had been refurbished, but I knew there were still steps to climb out of the white cellar and I did not know who would clean that cellar or when. If I hadn't been such a fool I would have seen it all in its true context, but I did not and there being no excuse I offer none.

My younger daughter said 'I need a holiday badly. David can't go anywhere, he's too busy, but I've told him I'm going and taking the young 'un. Would you like to come with us, mum?'

I said, with no enthusiasm 'Well, I'm not sure. Where were you thinking of going?'

'I thought Greece' she replied, 'I know you like Greece and I do, so what about it?'

'I can't think there'll be much vacant now in the holiday line, they'll all be booked up.'

'Well, we can go and ask for nothing. They do have late vacancies. Let's go on Saturday afternoon.'

Very reluctantly I agreed, whilst rather hoping that nothing would be vacant. In that I was disillusioned, for a vacancy was on offer for a place in Crete. I didn't want to go to Crete, I'd been to Crete and although I'd enjoyed it very much I have an odd belief that one ought not to return to a place one had enjoyed, for it always seemed rather inferior and unsatisfactory the second time around. As it seemed churlish to say I wouldn't go, we did in fact go there.

And I seemed to split apart. Weirdly, I could see it happening with a part of my mind and was totally unable to stop myself. It felt as if I'd been invaded by some mischievous vulgar imp of devilry which was using me to speak and some of the words I said surprised those who listened as much as I myself was surprised to see them emerge. Burn as I do with embarrassment at the recollection of some of the words I said I shall write but one example and this was in reply to a sexual proposition from a drunken bank manager who could have been my son:

'One would have to be a masochist to wish to open a seventy year old grave.'

It was all-disgusting and I was very glad to leave the place. Then truth, at last, dawned and I realized that yes, I had had to go to Crete and live this unpleasant experience. Spring-cleaning was required and it began. That cellar was in my own head. My own person, own brain and there followed a most extraordinary four days. Twinning with a vengeance. The whole experience was exactly like having a vision, but this was do-it-yourself and it was the other mind which did the cleansing for one cannot wash out the muck of years out of one's own brain, with any physical scrubbing.

Brilliantly clear now I gazed about this symbolic cellar and found to my surprise that the rear, which I had not seen in the vision, was a bathroom. Water; of course, water the conductor of electricity was the conductor of light. There was a hand basin and over it a mirror screwed to the wall. As every millimetre needed cleansing I lifted it down, cleaned the inside of the threads of the screws and the holes which had held them. Performed the same with the hand basin fittings and when those were spotless, cleaner than new, I turned my attention to the walls. It was a terrible job, for I sluiced and scrubbed those walls until the stone appeared and then sluiced and scrubbed until the stone looked as if it had been newly hewn. But it was my other mind that did the cleansing.

Whatever I was doing in my physical existence this cleansing continued. On the second day I scrubbed a hole in the hand basin wall and an ugly dark sludge poured in from the world outside. As there seemed to be no way of washing clean this gusher I decided to plug it and actually watched my own ghost hold something like a nozzle and pour into that hole a concentrated white material which at last filled the hole like an impenetrable plug.

Recollection is clear; I remember watching and wondering what this white substance was which was like no substance I had ever known and I realize now that it was a concentration of light so imploded that it had actually taken on the appearance of thick white paint, except no paint was ever like this.

It was not a large room, but on the facing wall, the one which extended to the steps and to the right of which was the enormous bowl representing the earth, was the bath. So all that had to be cleaned and hosed and scrubbed. As each of the four walls was cleansed I watched my own ghost, my other-mind-which-was-not-my-mind spray the whiteness densely over the whole area.

When the vision first occurred I had wondered who and how this brilliant whiteness had cleansed and coated old stone to such an impenetrable surface. Now I knew. Those walls were sealed with that which was impenetrable, sealed thickly, permitting none of the sour sludge outside to enter. Now I could leave, climb the two remaining steps and go forth.

When I emerged I knew what the barriers in my mind had been and it was ludicrous: I had been trying to PROVE those truths and they did not require any stupid proofs, they could stand alone without any intervention from me.

What a crass fool I had been, how could anyone be so stupid? All those wasted years pathetically making inventories to show the dualities: writing of endless comparisons to show how and in what aspects, the other mind emerged. My own feeble appraisals of my person viewed in the light of social requirements, social demands; trying to impress with an erudition which I never owned; feeling that if I could make a strong enough case then someone, somewhere, would grasp these truths for I had lived those truths. Of course my brain had needed cleansing for although I had known for a long time that I was nothing, of no more physical value than a length of old hosepipe, that hosepipe had to be clean on the inner side, for one cannot pour clean water through a clogged ducting.

I thought then of my pathetic attempts to write, of my absorption with those who purported to be academics and held diplomas to prove the fact, what of they? Their very physical proofs of status were blinkers, society's reward for truths which were only partial and almost all misleading. Did I have to appease such people? No, I did not. Nor would I. Suppose my syntax was not up to snuff? Suppose I ended my sentences with a preposition, what of it? To no one had I ever pretended to be that which I well knew I was not, a scholar. But, by God, I thought, I have lived and lived through the whole gaunt of human emotions. I will write again and when I do it will be warts and all and me speaking but emptied now of all attempts to impress by a scholarship I don't own. I lived truths which were Absolute, this has never been a theoretical exercise dreamed up by a scholar who can only investigate truths lived by others, my life has been blood and tears and the peak of a wonder beyond ecstasy or rapture.

This is another wall, a wall of words. My old stonewall is still in the garden, rugged, built without line bands, but men have climbed it and it has taken their weight. What will this wall hold? Ah, that is the future time, the only dimension in which it is possible to function whilst we are imprisoned within our bodies.

There, for all to see, is the Subjective, the other half of the Whole and the great earthenware bowl, the Earth, is matter, but it was the Subjective, the other mind that cleansed the cellar, the Invisible, the all-powerful.

Proof? Oh no. Now I am under no obligation to offer other than that which I have written. The onus is now transferred to those who believe that they are the sum total of their physical characteristics, to conclude that which I have written as untrue. The Subjective has been suppressed, used for squalid purposes, been allocated inferior roles for millennia and I intend now to show its true status.

A victim I had been of what passed for conventional thought. Flat surface ethics, all contrived to present contrived and facile beliefs. The golden Diana's official family were all victims of the identical erroneous façade; had been compelled to exist within a tightly woven blanket compounded by the powerful hierarchies which depended for their continuance upon brutally calculated definitions which actually imposed a kind of slavery upon the victims. She had lost her life. I had nothing to lose for I owned no status. If it was supposed that I was a cretinous fool it was of no consequence; and the obligation to offer proof began to diminish.

It all evolved into an era of intensive thought, although for years I had done little else but think. Now, of course, the perspectives had changed dramatically, causing all the thinking, analyzing and conclusions to alter: no new phenomenon, for it had been happening for years. Each time I had written some new perspective had arisen which both modified and added to the earlier perspectives. Like a gaffed salmon I had wriggled upon the hooks of convention and my husband's directive:

'Prove it. Prove your Sixth Sense to be true.'

Like a fool I had tried to prove it and when I lived the answers, the answers were so comprehensive that I had tried to write the questions which the answers clarified; and, of course, it had been an impossible task from the outset for they were so extensive. But. As ever, a but …

Now there was no obligation to prove anything to anyone and if the findings I had lived remained unread and unheard I had given everything of myself to write them; if that was insufficient it would not be that I had not made the attempt.

Uncannily I spent my days hung in space, so to speak, seeing always now the vast Benign Darkness filled with indescribable Glory and equally indescribable Intelligence; and wishing I could traverse the vast distance which lay between, knowing well that I could not. Wishing that I could be extracted from the turmoil, for it seemed as if my head had been scraped clean and I often thought wryly: 'This truly is like having a hole in the head'.

Enlightenment? Yes, but it had also had its penalties for I could see the idiocies which humankind had fabricated and presented as irrefutable truths which in many cases had simply constructed platforms for the enhancement of the individual to mount and declare his self importance, yet knowing nothing of the energy which really made us 'tick'. I could see the futilities which arose from such posturing and remembered Shakespeare's words:

'All the world's a stage and men and women only players …'

But this was not a play; this was reality, for there were now weapons which could destroy billions, injure all living species and render the living planet grotesque and sterile by misuse of the Creative characteristic.

So much … So many aspects … Where and how did it all go wrong? At what point in history were women relegated to the slave mentality when both genders were necessary for creation? I thought of the Minoan frescoes in Heraklion which depicted happy unselfconscious women taking part freely in the social existence of the era. I compared those Greek women to the subdued and artificial figures of my youth, northern women who were a tough, unsentimental breed, having worked in the same trade as the men, subservient to their church decrees and with roles minutely specified in all aspects of social existence.

Very seriously I wondered if men also were not victims, propelled by their genes which demanded they should be competitive amid other males, obliged to prove their fitness to breed by continually fighting for the privilege. Times when I wanted to howl aloud, 'But we are human beings. We are more than the sum of our physical appetites'. Then I subsided again; despairingly realizing that no matter in which avenue I gazed the same implacable question remained:

'Who am I?'

And until we could reply to the question we would flounder on, creating havoc for ourselves. Round and round went the arguments in my head, even allowing for the fact that in seeing that Immensity of Intelligence day by day and knowing myself to be no more than one electron volt by comparison, thereby precluding any rism of self-importance, something still impelled me to write. All flat surface considerations evolved into irrefutable flat surface logic:

'You are a totally obscure, ill-educated, female, old and clout-less. You have lived a strange secondary existence, so what? Many people have strange experiences. What makes you think yours are any different from theirs? What makes you outlandishly suppose that you have anything to write which will make even the slightest differences to anyone, leave alone to several more?'

Thus it continued. A war between the physical and visible and the invisible energy.

There was more; I had lived through repudiation, hostility which was at times virulent, been dismissed as futile if not actually insane, so why did I not simply roll over, so to speak and die gracefully? In truth, I very nearly did, for I became ill unto death as the saying goes and had it not been that I was too ill to make decisions for myself I would certainly have died.

Expectably, I saw ...

At the time I was listening to a visitor, but was hearing little of her rather childish diatribe for I was seeing, in minute detail a sword made of piercing light and it made me afraid by its virulence for it seemed to portend something dreadful although I could not imagine its significance. On the following day I knew I had contracted some truly awful illness, then days passed of which I have no recollection. Later, inevitably, I saw again; three monstrous insects of unnamable species, but which I knew had injured me irreparably. So it proved. I will not elaborate.

From this I learned to be more charitable to the physically injured. A new era began. Some time passed. But during this era a resolve hardened into steel. Many of the former arguments (with myself) became resolved; many of the former reservations concerning the flat surface social and ethical climates and the truths I had lived battled no longer. Nothing now would prevent me from writing these truths; if I were to lose my life it was of no consequence. None of my former ambitions existed and strangely I arrived again at the fulcrum which had existed when I first decided to write: if I failed it would not be because that which I had seen, lived and known was untrue, but because I was incompetent to describe them. And the provision still exists.

Chapter 29 – Losing Conventions

According to the ethical standards of flat surface reality all new discoveries are only of value if practical use can be made of them. Admittedly, many discoveries of value began by pure abstract thought (and the latter is a subject of great interest in itself, but not one I shall pursue here) which then emerged into practical use of a physical nature. Being female I benefit from the use of vacuum cleaners and spin dryers, for instance. Therefore it may be justifiably asked what possible use is it to know of the nature and functions of the trace of the MIND within us? Too many of these writings may appear to be a frivolity. To others, the somewhat deranged ramblings of a disordered mind. There are those who would declare them to be a fallacy from beginning to end and those who support ancient teachings will no doubt wish me great ills – and possibly attempt to inflict them … There will be some who declare they have never experienced a precognitive event in their lives, that when we are dead we are dead etc.

The above is known as the Devil's Advocacy and I have touched on such because I have, by flat surface standards, lived the life of a practical housewife and am not exactly naïve concerning western opinions which are based upon hierarchical values which must be protected in case the hierarchy is toppled. It is the identical tenet Benjamin Franklin used when he was moved to say that 'we must hang together or we will hang separately.'

It is with no expectation of replies that I write the following questions and quite naturally there is no compulsion to offer any replies, but … if whomsoever reads these words does reflect for a moment or two, he or she might discover some surprises. For even the most mundane of lives are punctuated by small oddities in the fabric of existence. They are not subjected to intensive analysis, nor rigorous scrutiny for they appear to be so, well ordinary. We expect them to happen now and then even if they do not quite fit, so to speak. Most certainly if we throw a ball in the air we know it will fall to the ground and Newton discovered why it fell. We have a kind of in-built sense of the classical laws which govern physical events. It is when some small event occurs which does not concur with this in-built expectation that we are a little startled; we may not look for reasons and we may believe that reasons do not exist. What we do not do is to forget our precognitive experience, for it never completely disappears and if we hear someone relate a similar experience, our own returns very vividly.

What then is the limiting factor concerning these oddities, supposing one experiences a definite premonition as to the outcome of a proposed event which may be entirely different from an outcome one might reasonably expect to happen given the information already available. Considering the plans already made for the event with all the apparently valid reasons why it must follow a certain course, even allowing perhaps for the possibility that the plans must be subject to amendments of some kind, why the premonition that the outcome is going to be drastically different from all the quite logical preparations. If, then, the outcome proves to reflect one's original misgivings then what factor can be called upon which justified the misgivings?

Does one murmur feebly, 'I felt something was wrong...?' That will earn one a reputation for deficiency of mind.

One might volunteer, 'Well, we put it through the computer and the computer said the plans were all right.'

Such is the belief in the computer's wisdom that the accusation will follow that the machine was not properly fed: rubbish in, rubbish out ...

Oh the fragility of the tenuous feeling and how irritating to the purely practical. How on earth is one to rely upon such errant assumptions? They are not logical ... Oh dear. What kind of fool bases knowledge upon something so abstract, so invisible, so tenuous and improvable as feelings?

Let there be an end to supposition: deal now in physical facts. It is known amongst the physicists that a material, physical experiment can be altered by the presence of an observer and that phenomenon is on record. Not an observer who is willing the outcome, or the alteration of what has been logically predicted of the outcome, for it was expected that the predicted outcome would be the predictable result and the experiment was to confirm the logical result. But something very strange intervened when the observer was physically present during the experiment for the result underwent a change, arousing much consternation. The very fact of his being there was upsetting the logic, upsetting the experiment.

So what was the intervening factor? Something was there indisputably. But what? It could not be seen. It could not be scrutinized by any of the apparatus at the physicist's disposal. It defied logic.

Of course, it depends upon what one supposes is the only possible form of logic which is available to human beings.

If one were to enquire of the physicists, 'Who and what are you?' one would no doubt be inundated with descriptions of their academic achievements, their status and their position in the pecking order of the community, possibly their hobbies, passions, interests; if married, descriptions of their wives and children, their publications and possibly their overall ambitions. Of one thing one may be sure, the lists would be long and detailed and relate to their physical persons. Watching a very famous physicist on a television programme I heard him reply to the question of belief in spiritual matters:

'I don't bother with such things' and it was evident that he was no ogre, but a very kind, intelligent and altogether charming individual. But ... And the buts increased in importance.

Could he or his colleagues offer physical explanations as to why experiments were altered when a human body was present and not so when the watcher was absent? Could he or they tell me how I could live three deaths before those deaths occurred? But they physically happened.

The explanations are simple and lucid: the physicists have concentrated their attention on the physical, on the material, the visible and those are but one half of the equation. Heisenberg's 'Principle of Uncertainty' was more valid than he suspected. To know, one must consider the Whole and not confine oneself to scrutiny and analysis of one half of the Whole. Consider matter and energy.

All the watcher needed to ask was the simple question, 'What is there in me which could alter the physical experiment. But the trouble has been that the energy was not thought to be any more than a force-in-itself and owned no visible characteristics.

Although it can in no way be pleaded that extenuating circumstances could be offered as excuse for the physicists to omit to consider that energy was and is the important factor, for if one of their number had displayed public interest for, or belief in Supernatural topics he would have speedily lost all credibility amongst his peers. It might be acceptable to insist on the belief in a God if one is of the calibre of an Einstein, for he was protected by his genius and the matter could be absorbed as being an idiosyncrasy; but for Science in general it would not further anyone's career to declare a belief in the physically improvable. Rubbish. Sweep it under the carpet and that is what has happened. Another big But … It has not gone away, has it?

The whole sorry argument has been based upon Science's own criteria and that has been that for a fact to be true and to physically be true it must stand the test of being repeatable. It was laughable in a world which changes microsecond-by-microsecond; hilariously disastrous. There was a second definition also which read that if a medium could accurately predict a death then Science just might review the situation.

As to the situation regarding the repeatability of the experiment which is altered by the simple fact of being physically observed, a quiet veil has been drawn over this discomfort and there are others. I did a great deal of reading and observed some anomalies.

Why, it may be asked, have I written these words concerning Science? Sour grapes, perhaps? A rather unpleasant revenge because women do not receive the honours which many who have accolades heaped upon them refuse simply because of their gender? Whomsoever reads these words is free to put any interpretation he or she chooses as to my motives. My intention is simple: I wish it to be known that a MIND exists. No more, no less. And Science is an area that has a great deal of clout. Politicians court the scientists in the hope that the latter will produce fantastic results that can be marketed on behalf of the nation, thereby reflecting favourably upon the politicians themselves; and favour to the latter is as cream to a cat. Consequently, Science is courted – never with quite all the finances they believe should be awarded, but enormous sums nevertheless. Curiosity is only appeased by vast expenditure and only for a very limited period, because it never dies. A great deal could be written concerning that aspect also, but I will desist. This is not a sociological treatise.

Only one question remains: is the scientist producing that which is positive or that which is negative? Only he can reply. Of course, should he design to reply at all he may say that what results from his findings are not his responsibility and that if his researches are used negatively then no blame can be attached to him which immediately betrays the fact that:

a) he does not understand human nature;

b) he does not understand himself.

None of us can 'opt out'; we are all responsible for our actions and inactions.

Medical Science progresses at a bewildering rate of knots and I shall make no attempts to either describe the findings, or comment upon the value of the findings. One aspect only will be the topic and it is one which is so perplexing that a television crew composed a documentary film on the subject which several million people must have seen. The real significance was that the facts were presented, but no comprehensive answers were supplied. In total it represented an anomaly similar to the throwing of a ball into the air and discovering that Newton's law had been somehow deflected, so that instead of falling it kept on moving. No rocket fuel was or is involved in the perplexity. All participants were either medical staff, doctors and nurses and a few were patients who were very ill indeed.

It is generally accepted that after very few minutes a seriously ill patient displaying no apparent signs of life is in danger of being described as 'brain dead'. In such situations the medical staff work frantically to restore life to a body which is showing no life on the monitors. They have many procedures to follow and aid them, but they work very hard indeed for the time in which they can work is limited. Sometimes they are successful and the body in question is resuscitated. Dead and then alive once more.

To the amazement of medical staff some of the patients to whom such experiences had occurred began to describe the scenes involving their resuscitation with great accuracy. They spoke of watching their bodies being worked upon although their bodies appeared to be dead and they did so from another location in the room, from above and near the ceiling. Moreover, their descriptions were later confirmed by the medical staff. So what had really happened?

Obviously, the staff could not see the watching minds for they were invisible to the physical minds, yet they existed. Existed as ghosts. Existed in another dimension of space and time which can only be occupied by living intelligent energy. It is that simple.

Now I invoke a patient who was a living person, but as I cannot identify him for obvious reasons I shall name him 'Tom'. Let it be clear that I do not know if he is alive or dead as I write these words.

My first introduction to Tom took place at a small party given by a friend of my husband and the male contingent all knew each other well for all were interested in their all consuming hobby and as I believed this hobby to be rather infantile I was prepared to be rather bored during the conversations. How the conversation with Tom began I cannot say, but as it progressed I discovered him to be a highly intelligent individual, well read, much travelled, very articulate and possessed of a dry and penetrating wit. Certainly, I found his sense of humour very refreshing, which was possibly made more surprising given the intense passion of the males for their hobby.

At one point I said 'I'm rather surprised to find you're a member of this gang of fanatics'.

Tom replied, 'Well, certain aspects interest me, but I can't say I'm passionate about it and I don't go to the meetings very often. But I've known ____ for a long time in other directions and I didn't suppose a party would consist solely of comparing notes about the hobby.'

During the conversation we discovered a mutual interest in history and he told me of some fascinating finds in Nottingham. Overall it made for a pleasant evening although I had expected to experience the kind of moderate rigor mortis which usually afflicted me when in the company of such fanatics.

A short time later I met the party's host and he said that Tom liked me very much. As I had laughed at Tom's jokes it was not so surprising, for one is endeared to anyone of either sex who can share a sense of humour. As time went on I think I met Tom on three similar occasions, always at someone's house and in a company of people. Someone told me just how intelligent Tom was and how in his own field was quite famous. But there the matter ended; Tom was a friend of other friends of my husband.

Perhaps two or three years later my husband said:

'____ and I are going to the hospital tonight. Tom is very, very ill and there doesn't seem to be much hope for him'.

I said 'Oh, I'm sorry to hear that. Yes, you ought to go and visit'.

And so they did, twice. As there seemed increasingly no hope to be entertained I expected the next news would be that they were attending Tom's funeral, but eventually – after some weeks – my husband said that Tom had been taken home, so I presumed there had been a complete recovery.

Six months went by, then one day the telephone rang and a voice said:

'Kathleen?' I replied 'Yes, speaking.'

The voice continued, 'This is Tom.'

Very surprised indeed I murmured the usual platitudes, wondering why he had rung me; I was merely an acquaintance, certainly had not visited him when he was ill and I hardly knew him. As all the implications were flashing through my mind astonishment predominated, but then I began to listen.

Tom said 'You know I've been in hospital?'

So I said 'Yes.'

He went on rapidly 'I nearly died and I was clinically dead for two minutes. I could see my body lying on the table, they were doing all sorts of things to it and it was all hateful. Kathleen, I have to tell you all this because you are the only person I know who will understand what I'm saying. I've wanted to ring you for months but I wasn't well enough. Kathleen, when I was out of my body a tall entity was in front of me; I think it was a man, but it was all dark; I couldn't distinguish any features but it said over and over again, 'Come with me' and I said to it, 'Like hell I will, I'm going back' and I did, I went back into my body. You do understand don't you Kathleen?'

In sadness I replied 'Yes, Tom, I know what you're saying' and after a few commonplace remarks the conversation ended.

But I had a lot to consider now. In the few times we had met there was never a time when we had discussed any matter which related to any Supernatural topic. We had spoken of history, archaeology, old houses, the countryside, all interesting and widely ranging subjects, but never any relating to my precognitive experiences. Indeed, at that time I had never even told my sister that I knew my sons would die; for me this was the forbidden area and most certainly I did not want strangers or near-strangers treading over it. So how had he known that I would understand? Why, out of all his important interests and activities, having acquaintanceships in many, had he told me? On the flat surface of what we choose to call 'reality' there was no way he could have known, but there are other avenues of knowledge and they are invisible. Telepathic exchanges conducted in silence.

About two years later there was a sequel: I was walking along the main street of the town when my sleeve was gripped. Slightly annoyed at the intrusion I turned to face a tallish man, quite heavily built but with a ravaged face.

He said 'Kathleen, love, don't you know me any more?'

For an embarrassing moment I did not, then was profuse in apologies. There followed the customary platitudes and enquiries as to his health etc, then having appeased the social conventions I was glad to leave, for the unspoken undercurrent was choking me. He was ill, very ill indeed and I wanted to cry:

'Tom, you should have gone with whoever came to meet you. You are never going to be well or happy again in this world. Tom, I am so sorry, so very sorry'.

Convention forbade it and I obeyed convention, sadly. As I continued my journey I remembered something my mother and the old ones used to say, uninhibited as they were in the rock bottom of realities, in spite of their churches' directives: Yonderly, Tom looked yonderly. He had experienced a foot in two worlds and was torn upon a fulcrum, existing wholly in neither. Telepathy had existed between Tom and me, but always silent.

It is tempting, at this juncture to pontificate upon the credence or values which exist in flat surface society, but I will resist for I must continue along my chosen avenue, or what is truthfully the avenue along which I have been pushed. Often reluctantly I might add, for this had been a thorny pathway. It is not that many other aspects of these topics could not be written, for the ramifications of all those experiences extend continuously, therefore I must be circumspect and economical.

It may be supposed that the instance earlier described concerning the distortion of an observed experiment and the fact of Tom's experience bear little relationship to each other. The circumstances were wholly different and the locations many miles apart, yet one aspect was identical for both. It was the ghost in the physicist that was intervening in the experiment and the ghost in Tom which left and met another ghost. The very word 'ghost' has collected about itself much acrimony; there are those who declare them to be a figment of disordered imaginations, as well as those who see them on a regular basis. Many with a religious bent use the word 'spirit' and imply that it is a very precious commodity. It can, of course, be used as depicting a bright, sparkly individual, one who animates whatever group he or she happens to be part of; and naturally it has a counterpart such as dispirited, spiritless which are the negative responses. So we actually know the meaning of the spirit without ever analyzing just what we mean when we use such words as adjectives or pronouns. Why then should the word 'ghost' arouse such controversy? Is it because so many are described as headless nuns, or evil entities?

Philosophical discussions have long belaboured this question. Arthur Koestler did not see the final answer when he wrote (after much experience and deep reflection) 'The Ghost in the Machine' and he was so near, so very near the truth. He believed that in a human being lay a ghost, an added element, another sense and a sense which did not die. For this belief he was ostracized by the scientific community and he and his wife committed suicide in the end. His death was sad, very sad. Let it be clear that if I decided to end my sojourn it would not be because I was disbelieved by the insensitive. Having no status to uphold I shall write of what I lived.

For the true answer lay in understanding the nature and characteristics of life itself: energy and an energy which does not die and cannot be killed. A mind, and a mind which is the intelligence. A mind which the body must surrender when we sleep or it will die and sleep is common to the whole of the human race. There is the 'Ghost in the Machine' for our physical persons are dependent not only on food and water but on what we believe to be our sanity (although there are individuals who apparently suffer a lack of that commodity).

Life is the spirit and to those of a religious bent it has another name: the soul. Did we ever know who and what we were? Matter and energy devoid of self-supporting images? Oh, yes, early man well knew; if he had been stupid, seeking only to promote his view of himself as rich, beautiful, successful and important he would not have known of the invisible something else. As it was he had to seek his food and shelter by his own wit and skill, but when he created that which had not previously existed he carved an inscription which has been discovered all over the planet.

The circle is the shape of the natural world, of the stars and of the Universe. In Valetta's museum are some of the first sculptures depicting heavily pregnant females, ugly as sin to our eyes, but thought beautiful for they represented life, new life and therein lay belief in beauty. There is much speculation concerning our origins and prehistoric man and there is a popular belief that he was little more than a brute beast. He was intelligent for if he had not been so he would not have survived. So where did the prompting come from? When changes are made one must inevitably postulate a Source. All he learned to create sprang from new knowledge; no teacher existed, no books of reference, no historical experiences. One cannot invoke the trial and error theory when the question of gathering fruits or growing plants were concerned, for errors of that nature would have decimated whole tribes. So what led them? Can it be defined as instinct, for if it is so defined one must also define the nature of instinct and it cannot be defined because it is invisible? Knowledge undoubtedly, but none of the physical senses can touch, smell, taste, hear or see it. So what is it? Life, of course; intelligent energy, but invisible.

Much that occurred to human beings during the prehistoric eras is either lost or ill defined, but it seems fairly certain that protocivilisations grew and flourished. During those formative years human beings very naturally operated in groups, for therein lay help and protection; and as the groups increased in size there would inevitably be one. perhaps more than one, who was more sensitive than the rest; one who could 'see'. They were Shamans. Native peoples throughout the planet have always had them, sometimes called the 'wise ones', sometimes 'witch doctors', but always acknowledged to be necessary and valuable and regretfully it must be accepted that some took advantage of the fact. In 'seeing' they could see ghosts, entities in apparently human form, but possessed of the ability to transcend the limitations posed for the physical body so confined in time and space. Predictably, if information could be obtained from those who were not so confined such information was extremely valuable and the Shaman was regarded as being very valuable as an interpreter. There is always a 'But' ….

Apparitions were identified as being dead people who, having transcended the time and space confinement and having attained a mysterious magical power, were then, over time, adjudged to be gods and goddesses. Appearing to resemble human beings, (which they did) but human creatures nevertheless, it was inevitable that they were awarded human physical characteristics also. In consequence whole pantheons of gods and goddesses appeared and in many different states and nations. There was War, Love, Retribution, to name but a few and there is no doubt that they received much attention to the extent that temples were built in their honour. If a human being wanted some advantage for him or herself what more natural than to plead with some magical being to intervene? Craving love one could offer prayers to Venus. Offer sacrifice if necessary in some form or another because human beings expect some reward for their labours, so it was only fitting that these Supernatural beings would expect identical attention.

We might smile condescendingly at the apparent misapprehensions of those peoples, but I have to admit freely that when I saw the figures of White Light I not only knew them to be transcendingly beautiful, but also transcendingly true. Of course, there was more; there was a Source.

For centuries, for millennia, such beliefs were accepted regarding the Supernatural beings; even comparatively tiny city states such as Petra had their own localized deity. Disparate tribal factions coalesced into small nations, then even bigger nations; and as the numbers increased, as the creative faculties developed so, pro rata, did the opportunities for mayhem increase and barbarism increased accordingly. There was little or no moderating factor to subdue the warring tribes and nations. Men fought, for the rewards were rich. The early creations were of unsurpassed beauty, so if land could be taken so could all the spoils be taken too; and as they had gods with even greater human characteristics, equally capable of mayhem on a vast scale the law of 'might is right' flourished over the near, the middle and the far east.

Egypt was a lure, a beacon; its desert lands fed by the magical Nile, a land spilling over with bounty; its riches compelling nomadic tribes to serve its people. Over time the stage was set for confrontation on a global scale and not simply for the era, but for the millennia which were to follow.

Chapter 30 – Looking Back

Of all the arts writing is the most durable and evocative, even surpassing the impact of the Great Pyramids of Giza. Writing is the art of transposing sounds into words and words are the result of thoughts; but the problem with thoughts is that they are invisible. But if the thoughts are even slightly off balance how true will the words be that emerge? To what extent, for instance, will the thoughts be in relation to the social ethics and the local environment of the writer when he or she decides to inscribe the thoughts for posterity? Will they be influenced or distorted by either the ethical climate or the nature of the nation or tribe? Can they ever be wholly objective? Will what is finally written be absolute truth? Or will the words inscribed as truths be deflected in the smallest instance by the physical, ethical and social situation in which the writer must exist? Disinterested they are not.

There are a large number of questions but are there any suitable replies? Being of an essentially practical nature I began with the inscriptions purporting to describe the Pharaohs of Egypt who were believed to be gods. They depicted their enemies as barbarous killers and as bestiality in various forms was practiced, it was accepted as being quite normal behaviour. There was an applied condition however, for on the death of a Pharaoh a kind of kangaroo court was held during which his heart was weighed in order to establish his purity. There was a second condition also which governed the scribes' descriptions of Pharaohs: he it was who paid them, provided them and their families with houses and sustenance, so what they wrote was not from disinterested altruism. Hackneyed as it is: one does not bite the hand which feeds one. A skeptic draws his or her own conclusions.

There is more: the art of writing was confined to a very tiny minority of people and the secrets were guarded on a father-to-son basis. As it held this curiously permanent quality it was accepted as being true, but was it all true?

Only partially and the partial element makes the whole very suspect. If any present day equivalents are necessary one need only ask oneself just how much truth lies within present day reporting of current affairs.

Returning to history and that which emerges from two millennia ago reveals powerful warring factions. Great and powerful nations were competing for supremacy. All with their pantheon of gods and goddesses skirmishing, flirting, loving and hating just as in the counterparts on earth, but with the additional faculty of intervening in human physical affairs if they so chose. So to encourage fortunate intervention they attracted much attention, much homage, many sacrifices. Thus the scene.

But there was upon that scene another rather less powerful contender consisting of a number of disparate tribes who had also invented their own form of writing (again performed by a tiny minority) and commensurate with the preceding centuries' habits had given themselves a name: Jews. Having been enslaved they had suffered much from the Egyptian rulers and slavery beneath that rule was not an existence to be desired. Their escape was concurrent with the island of Thera exploding, thereby causing a tsunami which in turn gave them passage over the Red Sea and to which they attributed the said deliverance to their (and here lay the remarkable clause) their own defined god. This was a monotheistic god. No surrounding here of female deities distracting the processes of divine authority. The god of the Jews was male.

Regarding the rest of the prevalent beliefs they conformed to the history that this awesome deity would intervene on their behalf and inflict retribution of a comprehensive nature on their enemies. As the males did the fighting their god was inevitably of the same gender.

Predictably, they endowed their god with human characteristics. Nor could they hardly be blamed for doing so for similar beliefs were symptomatic of the previous eras, all of which awarded top status to the male. Imposed further on this scenario was a carefully constructed set of laws, many of which began with 'Thou shalt not' and implicit in the instructions were veiled threats as to what would be the fate of the malcontents who disobeyed. These were harsh lands, breeding harsh penalties. The god of the Jews was depicted as owning a dual nature: at once all-forgiving and at the same time wrathful and terrible in anger, reflecting with accuracy the people of the era, not only themselves. They were all victims of social schizophrenia.

One cannot describe perfection and endow it with the negative. It is a contradiction in terms. But it was held to be logical, truth. And truth which was slanted from the outset.

But the repercussions have been so extensive it is as if an ocean had engulfed a whole continent, for there are those who still believe this to be true. Men were describing themselves. They had been misled by apparitions, by ghosts and deduced that men were created in the identical physical image. Nor was that supposition the truth. But it was all a scenario which appealed for it appeared to be logical in human terms: what more satisfying than worshipping a god who looked like a human being but was omnipotent into the bargain? This permitted a dialogue to be conducted, not on quite a one-to-one basis, but satisfyingly cosy in that one could conduct a conversation with such a being. One could even interpret the will of this omnipotent being to some extent and given sufficient social importance in their own right. And there were many who did just that. What is more surprisingly alarming is that many still do just that. But I do not believe their interpretations, except in one respect.

Greek influence was waning although the clarity of their thinkers was undiminished as was the peerless beauty of their sculptures. Predictably another race arose to claim domination and authority over all it could subdue and by whatever means were available. Scruples were not on the agendas. It is doubtful if they were even recognized and most surely when the intention was to conquer, the methods employed were simple and succinct: kill the opposition.

There is no cut-off date when one huge power begins to slide and another ascends; there is always a blurring, an interim period between one set of conquerors and the next. I take up this potted history at the time when the Romans had conquered the Jews and occupied Jerusalem, that blood-soaked city which was then a citadel of anguish and nothing has changed. It is my personal belief that it ought to be vacated in order that Nature be allowed to heal the wounds. That is an inflammatory statement and there will be others …

There seems to be little doubt that one of the Jews advocated that they all should love each other, Jesus by name and a Jew, hailed as a prophet then as now. Disentangling all that has been written of this man would be akin to counting grains of sand upon some large beach. The social climate of the time was one of furious hysteria and my practical knowledge of people and their utterances compels that unless what is happening is recorded there and then by totally objective scribes, then as the writings accumulate so does the possibility that some of the versions will be either slanted conclusions, or suspect in accuracy. Having actual experience of the inability of witnesses to render an accurate statement as to the relating of a personally observed crime, I am not so sanguine as to find absolute truths in the myths and legends which have arisen in the millennia following Jesus's death. It is fairly certain that he was nailed to a cross for that was but one of the bestial punishments of the era. It is also fairly certain that he claimed to be the son of the Jewish god and inextricably bound within that claim was the belief that god was a man.

God is a MIND and within that MIND were the genders created. From that time on the Jews have been villified and let no one suppose that I am taking up the cudgels on their behalf; they are able and willing to do their own fighting. But it is essential to understand what the prevalent social climate consisted of at the time.

It was an inscribed belief that their god was male. An inscribed belief that this omnipotent male could and would punish dissenters and malefactors. So when one of their own advocated that they should love their oppressors such advocacy was the antithesis of their beliefs; was destroying the foundations of their nationhood. The simple exhortation was true, for love is the fulcrum upon which humanity must rest but the Jews had been enslaved too often, they wanted revenge and hoped their god would exact for them that which they were physically unable to obtain by their own efforts.

The repercussions have been enormous, are still being experienced, still being fought about and fought for but when the original premise is faulty then the errors multiply extensively. We live with them as I write.

With no remorse that I am writing heresies and expect attack, I will not retract, for I saw that MIND and it is pure intelligence, neither male nor female; but the Creator of the necessary twin genders.

There followed a long period described now as the 'Dark Ages' probably because no race had taken up the mantle of the foregone empires and impressive history is at its most explicit when there is a dictator to describe. It must not be supposed however that nothing of note was occurring for another empire was in the making. Having lost their empire the Romans were creating a second empire, albeit on very different lines and aims. Certainly it was more subtle and did not require vast armies to supply. It was, in effect, a very different kind of slavery. They repudiated their pantheon of gods and goddesses in favor of the Jew who had advocated love. And the Catholic church was born.

Having already much experience in empire building and the

allocation of power and titles to be allotted within the hierarchy, a similar structure arose with an added advantage. Where previously the aim had been to establish physical authority, they now could establish spiritual authority and a devastating authority it proved to be. For although men required no great persuasion to fight (they had been doing so for centuries) and prove themselves to be brave warriors, thereby enhancing their status amongst their fellows, it was a different kettle of fish when the choice was between belief and non-belief in a prophet, because for the latter one could be promised hell-fire in perpetuity.

Imbalance between an omnipotent god and rejection by this god was neatly redressed by the fabrication of another powerful individual, the Devil, together with descriptions of a goat-like man-like being of infinite cunning and an enormous capacity for inflicting punishment infinitum. A twin, no less. Heaven and hell. Each domain bore its complement of assistants in various roles and of varying status: the Egyptian habit of weighing the head of Pharaoh was abandoned in favour of a gate-keeper, St Michael, who duly inscribed the aspirations and histories of applicants at the gates (large and golden, of course) and submitted them to their god for approval or disapproval; and if the latter, one was dispatched to the other end for an eternity of burning. It was all very comprehensively portrayed and artists enthusiastically produced vast paintings to reinforce the beliefs. There was even a token amelioration added by the belief that as the Jew was a god his mother must be unblemished purity also. It was not a great deal in favour of the female, but it was something, for all the rest of the cast were male. What else? It has always been thus.

Heresy indeed. Will I be shot? It is of no consequence.

As such theories awakened an echo which appeared to be satisfying regarding crime and punishment; cause and effect; they attracted adherents by the millions, for such innately human characteristics could be understood by humans: an eye for an eye, a tooth for a tooth; very satisfying to those who desired revenge but could not physically obtain it. But underlying all the glittering apparatus lay one uneasy fact; one could be refused entry in the final analysis, for this god could be merciless. A neat solution was established and a very profitable one: one could pay for forgiveness of one's sins whilst still in a physical body and the church appointed people on the staff who would grant forgiveness for a fee.

As a business enterprise it has never been equalled. But none of them ever understood the MIND. None had ever understood that the MIND was not a male being, but a Pure Intelligence which had conceived the necessity of creating male and female genders in order that creation could flourish and continue.

Time passed and the Catholic church held immense power, dominating many states and nations. Those who opposed their harsh and merciless dictates were suppressed with the customary bestiality of centuries past; the Cathars of France being such victims were burned for their temerity. Roman rule tolerated no opposition and in the name of Love they suppressed it.

I turn my attention now to a period of English history but first must briefly state that several races had ravaged this quite small island and conquerors had impressed upon it their own particular beliefs, always with violence. Gentle persuasion is not a characteristic of conquerors. At the time of which I write (approximately the beginning of the last millennia) England had been seized by a Norman, together with his cohorts. They believed themselves to be of greatly superior quality and had formulated a society which I will name as upper crust; it being a society which held the reigns of power, spiritual and secular. As the original conqueror, William had cleverly ordered a comprehensive study of the whole land and he had allocated large sections of it to his assistants. Of course, even a large chunk is insufficient to the greedy and as most of them were very greedy they plotted and jockeyed for even better authority. Kingship was at stake and many and varied were the machinations of their descendents in pursuit of this prize.

During the previous millennia few women emerge as being of historical significance: the Egyptian Queen Hatshepsut, Cleopatra, Joan of Arc in France and the English Boadicea. None lived to any great age, impinging as they did upon male preserves and not then to be tolerated.

Superseding the Plantagenet reigns there appeared upon the English throne by the savage customary mayhem, a new King, Henry Tudor by name, overweening by nature, self consciously aware of the great power he wielded and resembling (from his portrait) a self-satisfied pig, if such a description could be applied to very intelligent animals. During his quest Henry committed an outstanding act of defiance: he defied the Pope and changed the course of English social and spiritual history, creating thereby a Protestant church, the official Church of England.

Chapter 31 – Reprisals

Vast amounts have been written concerning Henry VIII's momentus decision to repudiate the immense power wielded by the Roman church and I do not propose to add to the weight except in this respect; although the power to administer had changed dramatically, the underlying beliefs in the writings of those ancient Jewish scribes had not, they were still extant. God was a man and the commandments remained unchallenged, but the proposal that the mother of the man who was declared to be the son of the Jewish god and awarded spiritual status, was now repudiated. It was a popish device and women were not accorded any measure of power at any level, so the thesis was abandoned. In retrospect it is ironic that following Henry VIII's abortive attempts to beget a son, he was succeeded by a woman, Elizabeth the first, thereby changing the course of history.

As the theories of heaven and hell were so well established (and very useful in establishing order amongst the populace) they were retained together with fitting punishments of a gory nature for malcontents and dissenters. The ancient Jewish commandments suffered no diminution of authority, they were far too useful when writing newer and more specific laws. Convince a man that he would burn in an eternal hell if he were to disobey the laws of the land was a very convincing argument. As full of holes as a sieve in practice, but as the powerful hierarchies decreed that such beliefs emanated from the Christian god they served to establish order and confined the unruly. It is rather uncanny how many still accept these beliefs.

How often have I heard in my lifetime the words, 'May god forgive me?' Always, inevitably, rises that ancient and erroneous belief that god is a man and that man is made in identical image, therefore all the many negatives practiced by human beings are a reflection of this interpretation of god. Purity is unalloyed, it is the thing-in-itself. Invisible, of course.

Protestantism arose. There was little about it that was pure, but it spawned several of the narrow minded thunderers from deliberately simple pulpits, many of whom were fanatics and bent on eradicating all suggestion of luxuries, of pomp, of ceremonial practices. All visible accoutrements were simplified to the extent that only apparel commensurate with concealing nudity was permitted. These were lean times and predictably doomed to extinction for the English, although lacking the creative talents of Greece, of Rome, of the Egyptian empires, had one great love and talent: they produced pageantry of great splendour and writers of great perspicacity. One supported the other and as this powerful upper crust liked to display their power (it being a visible reinforcement of their authority) they obliged with enthusiasm in both the secular field and the spiritual field. Ceremonial occasions brought forth velvet, brocades, furs and jewels, eliciting awe and reinforcing the multi layered cake which was English society.

Fashions cause the pendulum which governs social ethics to swing, but throughout that English history one ethic did not change: there was to be no diminution of the man who believed himself to be the son of the Jewish god with powers of divination, of precognition and all contenders in this mysterious field were dispatched with the customary brutality. All such practices were deemed to be pagan which caused the very word to assume a whole contingent of unpleasant connotations. Only the Jewish man who uttered predictions was permitted to voice them. There was a cut off point; prediction was his sole prerogative and all others were consigned as witches, instruments of the Devil and deemed to be evil. Only three centuries ago I would have been burned or stoned to death, it is that simple.

But the powerful church, despite its authority, could not and did not eradicate that which the prehistoric peoples had known so clearly, but having constructed an edifice so rich in possibilities they were not about to allow it to be questioned or doubted, so if by using the tool of evil witchcraft to describe the precognitive and describe the forbidden subject then it was so used. Scruples did not enter into it. It was vigorously promoted that only by way of accepting Jesus that one had any hope of entering heaven: accept his declarations or burn. A but. As ever a but ...

In this case a very significant qualification indeed: he had, there is no doubt, adjured people to love each other, for it was by loving that a loving god could be recognized. Not because of him as a person, but simply because he had recognized that the Jewish god was a loving god. There is a subtle difference in emphasis and it applied to a far wider field than the Jews occupied, this was a world view and he was by no means the only person to detect this strange invisible quality. In the wider field it did not matter who said that love was the crucial element for it extended to all peoples, all races. David Attenborough discovered to his charming amazement that even a mother spider loved her young....

By the establishment of hierarchies and the mechanisms whereby they could function to the best possible advantage in what purported to be unassailable power, England assembled an extensive empire of the Monarchy, the Church, the Army, the Navy, two houses of Government which, in combination, were a considerable force. But another hierarchy, young and pushy, self confident and possessed of unshakeable curiosity was rearing a questioning head. Its appetites were gargantuan: this was Science and a gobbler of traditions. It was not at first realized just how this new ravenous infant was potentially dangerous to the smug hierarchies, for Newton had proposed his theory of gravity and it had proved to be of great interest, quite fascinating, explaining as it did why a ball fell to the ground when thrown in the air.

Not quite so interesting when Darwin, after much consideration and with trepidation announced that we were descended from the apes. Definitely not interesting, for this was bone cutting stuff and it raised a furore amongst the upper layers of society. How dare he suggest so appalling a theory amongst those who believed themselves to be the Master race? It must be supposed that they had been taught history when young, but it is evident that they had never learned that monoliths topple.

As a theory Darwin's proposal had some foundation in that animals do indeed adapt to new conditions. But he missed a fundamental truth: in order to adapt, to learn, one must possess intelligence. One must know when changes in attitude are required for survival. There are so many disparate species, so many differing forms of life. So what was the only common factor?

It was, it is, Life Itself. Living intelligent energy which had proposed the changes from the outset.

But, of course, given the social climate of the era which believed the animal kingdom to be brute beasts and nothing more; believed that the servant classes to be little better, were not about to conclude that animals were prompted by anything more than instinct. But no attempt was made to define instinct either in people or animals. It could not be defined, it was invisible.

So by the common, if unwritten consent of the hierarchies, including that fast growing infant called Science, all reference to

Supernatural experiences was not only forbidden, but any seeking to increase his or her income by a little fortune telling on the side were subject to fining by the Law. Predictably, it had lain underground for centuries, yet none of the so powerful hierarchies had ever succeeded in obliterating it in spite of the clout they wielded. It was designated as a refuge for the gullible, a market for the charlatans and forbidden absolutely in social circles, or as a tool in government. Any who indulged in Supernatural effects of whatever nature were adjudged to be suspect in intelligence and unsound in competence. No viable objective decision could be constructed by such mysterious improvable tactics.

In any case the Victorians needed no outside help for the world they were creating was a physical world, one of machines and artifacts. Imaginations could and did run riot, as invention followed invention in an apparently in exhaustive torrent. Even the most insignificant human activity spawned a tool of some description, even such a one as to propel a lady's bum into her carriage. That such inventions were farcical was irrelevant; it aided society and the latter needed feeding.

Science was no longer in the latter years a squalling infant, but a gigantic avid creature, intent on unravelling the secrets of the physical world of Matter. Matter could be deduced from its actions upon other forms of Matter and by use of varying energies to propel them. All conclusive information could be described in writing and masses of it evolved.

Amid all the profundities which were being revealed, all Supernatural events were as repudiated by Science as the earlier fanatical hot gospellers had repudiated slothful luxuries; although each, if questioned, would have furiously denied any connections whatsoever. But all were adamant in their beliefs even if the subjects appeared to be the antithesis of each other. They did not agree, but their responses to disagreement were strangely identical which should not cause surprise for all were males, who angered easily, often with little provocation, but especially if they were not one hundred per cent certain of their facts. Even the tiniest doubt could undermine.

It might have been supposed that in all this welter of new discoveries there would have been some amalgamation between the new Scientific discoveries and the ancient Supernatural beliefs, but it was not so. Science reigned, at least on the surface, but the beliefs of the previous ages remained and are growing. Denial could not kill them.

Suppression of belief in the Supernatural did not succeed, no matter how socially unacceptable. The powerful hierarchies forbade its existence and denied its existence. Why so? Because it was older, was imprinted into the very flesh bone and blood of human kind.

It was life. Living intelligent energy bearing a minute trace of the MIND from which it sprang and all futile attempts to suppress it would inevitably fail.

So why did women in far greater number believe in Supernatural experiences? Very simply, they had been suppressed for five thousand years, treated frequently as being of inferior mental status because they had not built bridges and temples, had not invented the thousands of artifacts in general use; yet even so they had this uncanny ability to sort the wheat from the chaff without ever being able to describe the processes by which they made their deductions. There were lightening appraisals, A to Z in one breath, where men deduced throughout the alphabet and could trace a course in writing which they called 'logical thinking'. It is unsurprising that neither could understand the thought processes of the other and naturally this was a source of irritation to both, sometime violently so. More: the roles of women had been defined for them millennia ago and the male strength had made physically certain of this confirmation, for if any of the weaker creatures protested she could always be chastised, beaten into submission. Many were. Many still are.

Stirrings were beginning at the beginning of the new explosive century, the twentieth as time was dated. Very few bubbles arose to disturb the creamy layer of complacency which capped the extraordinary layer of the whole of English society. To any foreigner it must have appeared to be an insoluble puzzle and one which only the English themselves could decipher and which strangely they understood as if by a kind of osmosis. In short, all knew their place in this multi layered structure, so that when the meagre bubbles of dissension arose from women they were regarded by a mixture of emotions: amusement, scorn, opposition and a kind of tolerant amusement in that they had a point in wanting the vote, believed they should be allowed authority over their own finances but it must not be allowed to get out of hand and if necessary they would be restrained. The Law was the Law; everyone knew the status of women, it had been defined millennia ago and there was no valid reason why this Law should be deflected.

Consequently the Suffragettes were given a very hard time as their protests were not confined to verbal opposition, they had the impertinence to physically defy the Law, chained themselves to railings and the like.

Of course the female protests against millennia of near slavery were simply a taste, a forerunner of what was to come; but traditions which had solidified are not easy to dismember. With the inevitability of sunrise war began. It never actually ended; there was always a war in progress somewhere in the world, but this was memorable, spectacularly vile; an obscenity which eroded faiths and shattered beliefs. When men were compelled to build bridges using the corpses of their fellows in order to ferry the guns over rivers, many began to question the existence of the god they had been taught to believe was merciful and loving. (The description concerning bridge building just described was told to me by my father who fought for almost the whole of that war.)

Erosion had begun in ancient faiths, ancient teachings. What would emerge? Predictably, achingly so, another war began and the means by which men killed each other became more and more sophisticated, ensuring the deaths of countless millions. Accident of gender was not a consideration; women learned to fight. Subtly, as dark water swirls below that which appears to be clear, a newer, a different phenomenon was gathering momentum for women were beginning to realize potentials which had lain fallow for millennia. Intelligence. Ignored, dismissed, but never annihilated …

The Second World War was a catharsis.

Chapter 32 – Challenge

It was patently obvious now that it was impossible to re-cork the bottle in which had been confined the moral, spiritual and decorous values which had, on the deceptive flat surface of physical reality, been the self assured stability of England. It had always been a façade; the English talent for words and acting had deceived many nations. It was with some surprise that other nations discovered that the thousand years it had taken to amass the view they had of the English should crumble so quickly to reveal what? They could be as immoral sexually as a Tangier brothel owner and as impertinent of the Law as a stone age tree dweller. As repudiators of Church dictates as any of the former 'native' peoples they had hitherto attempted to wean from their natural beliefs, no matter how bizarre. The English entered the so-called swinging sixties with astonishing verve and aplomb.

Out came the women; the millennia-old repudiations discarded with their hemlines. They too had learned to fight and were learning rapidly that their minds, so long repressed, were as agile as quicksilver; they could learn and learn quickly; learn to do jobs which had hitherto been regarded as male provinces. It was as if that long repressed intelligence had been given greater impetus by the very fact that it had been so long held in suspension.

From the male viewpoint this was an extraordinary phenomenon and bewildered many. Men had been deceived by five millennia of dominance, of what appeared to be the natural ordering of society. They disregarded the fact that it was they themselves who had defined the roles; but after five millennia it was confusing to find what they had believed the natural order to be, could be so quickly dismantled. A man was the head of the household and his wife held second place. In matters which needed logical and objective assessment regarding the children, it was he who made the decisions, infinitum. How could such illogical creatures as women be expected to arrive at logical conclusions? The truth was, of course, that neither knew how each other's minds operated and the battles of the sexes grew accordingly, becoming ever more heated.

Gently, but painfully the Churches slid into near oblivion. It was no longer possible to exhort people who had cleared bloody parts of other people from piles of debris to 'Love thy neighbour'. Insistence upon a loving and merciful god was repudiated by many who had seen sadistic bestialities practiced on young and old and fighting men and women. Many said that no god could exist who allowed such atrocities to happen.

And the squalling infant which was Science was now grown, appetites unslaked, into a towering monster which dominated all the once so powerful hierarchies. It had established itself, proven itself; it had discovered the means by which all life could be annihilated and the planet rendered sterile. What more proof could be needed to enforce the fact that the material physical world could be unravelled, that the minds of Science superseded all other minds? Here was proof. As ever, a but ...

A strange phenomenon was emerging, rather too vague for identification for it was hydra headed, difficult to analyze and it was strangely pervasive. Very loosely, for it emerged in very different and unexpected avenues, it began to be named with the collective noun: the Supernatural. And the problem was that it could not be confined within one or two or even quite a number of lines of investigation, nor any visible field of matter, nor to any particular group of people. Its very elusiveness roused passions for it could not be pinned to a slide, or held in the hand, or tasted or smelled or seen. It was elusive, but it kept emerging in the most unlikely places and conditions.

By this time the British Parliament had decided to rescind the law regarding mediums. Belief in and consultation of sources of precognitive faculties had produced an astonishing interest in the subject as a whole. Newspapers hired seers, astrologists and the like to provide daily or weekly information as to what the future would hold for persons born within a specified time and many – perhaps furtively – read them. Television programmes began to appear depicting some inexplicable incident or other, but none apparently produced any valid answers. The Russians employed mediums, possibly in the hope that some war-like advantage could be gained and the Americans also took more than a passing interest for identical reasons.

Science, opposed to any material circumstances which could not be explained by their criteria, decided that inexplicable events were the province of defective brains and did not exist.

To the Churches such claims as were made involving mediumship were anathema, poaching upon their prophet's preserves so to speak; and reiterations concerning pagan practices and the dangers of witchcraft were reiterated as Awful Warnings. It seemed that claims involving precognitive experiences etc automatically gave birth to the belief that evil was emerging.

A time of flux and it was during this era that the decision to write of my own varied experiences was made. I was given some advice by an erudite scholar:

'Write everything you can think of. Get as much in as possible' and at first I followed this advice. Some time had to pass before I realized that such mundane details were merely part of the fabric, that it was the astounding experiences that eventually coalesced into answers.

But we do not live our lives experiencing such mind blowing experiences on so narrow a basis, rather it is that our lives are composed of tiny intrusions which are taken for granted. Tiny bright incidents inspiring no investigation, no response apart from thinking, 'That's a bit odd ...'

There is déjà vu. An uncanny sense which causes one to think, 'I know this, I have been here before', in spite of the conscious mind declaring 'You've never set foot in the area in your life.'

Science of course, has produced some laborious and involved mechanisms which purport to show that we have had a kind of instant reversal of memory in that the brain has recognized the location prior to the conscious mind's ability to recognize the surroundings which then impress the conscious mind to assume it already knows the location. This somewhat neglects to show what sense in the brain is moving faster than the conscious mind.

Then there is dowsing, an emotive word, with different connotations; but serendipitous also. As it is usually associated with the finding of underground water I will describe this phenomenon, but not because I have ever taken up a hazel wand and sought water. But several of the experiences I described earlier took place when I was standing beside the kitchen sink with water in a bowl. It happened too often for 'coincidental' to be used, so although I knew at the time some connection was present I knew no explanations. Now I put the case that as the other mind is light and energy a parallel exists between the inexplicable, invisible phenomenon and the visible phenomenon of dowsing. As we well know it is dangerous to foolishly turn switches with wet hands, for electricity can and does arc even over distance and if water is present fatal connections can be made and a flash occurs, light in other words. The dowser uses a hazel twig, or whatever he feels to be appropriate. It is his other mind which is finding the water source for it emerges as light and energy, but to the conscious mind all the forces are invisible.

Some dowse with pendulums, seeking a location upon a map; as I have never attempted such an exercise I hold no views upon the subject. Predictably, a but ...

To find who and what you are, dowsing is necessary and it is surprising the amount which can be dredged from one's past. It is alarming at times to review one's life and wonder remorsefully how one could have been so blind as not to recognize the so obvious. Admittedly, we have compiled social ethics so involved and intermingled that to fight one's way through the distortions is not easy. To repudiate conventional beliefs is not easy but in my own case it was inevitable for I lived experiences that opposed the status quo in many fields.

Continuing to describe precognitive experiences of even the most trivial instances is unnecessary, for all such are too numerous to compile. All that is necessary is to omit all conscious and physical knowledge, all apparently logical constructions to explain the phenomenon of recognition of an event prior to its physical appearance, and then ask oneself how one knew of the event. To paraphrase Sir Arthur Conan Doyle, 'When all the obvious is eliminated, only the impossible must be the answer.' In some degree we are all mediums and we all must sleep.

As I wrote earlier I have by no means written of the number of small precognitive experiences that arose in my life as they were too numerous to mention and of no possible interest. Consequently it did not and does not fit into the flat surface curriculum, is an improvable subject and the object of much skeptical appraisal. Is spite of hostility, belief in Supernatural events is on the increase, as are the various Eastern beliefs which themselves are varied into differing sects. Overall, they combine into what has come to be called 'New Age' thinking and is itself a source of august disapproval and outright hostility. Much could be written on the latter topic: I shall write no comment as I own no labels beyond knowing myself to be a member of the human race and an insignificant one to boot. In short, I do not 'fit' into the recognized categories; therefore I leave the subject of proof to whomsoever reads these words. All that is necessary is to begin at the first chapter of this writing and to insert the hitherto missing factor, which is that another mind, invisible, proposed the precognitive events which are described; for that one answer clarifies the whole sequence. Clumsily, inappropriately, I had called it the 'Sixth Sense'. It was the miniscule trace of the other MIND, unhampered by time, space or matter.

If we can love, emit light, know joy, can create (be it simply a gentle ambience) we can know the absolute truth of ourselves. And it all depends on what we permit to coagulate our physical brains: the negatives or the positives: Good or evil.

Chapter 33 – The Supernatural is the Natural State

What can be deduced overall from a world in the throes of disorder? Is it possible to deduce anything of value given the fact that so many erstwhile values appear to be dissolving into apparent chaos? Nation fears nation, neighbours fear each other, barricades become ever more sophisticated but do not protect, exhortations are received with cynicism and platitudes are ignored. A smile amongst strangers can be construed as evidence of some unnatural motive.

Is there any concept which has remained constant throughout our turbulent history? Yes, there is. It runs like a threnody throughout: it is the belief that some superior force exists which, although it is invisible, is more powerful than our physical persons and that belief is indestructible. It was in the interpretations of that invisible Force that dissensions arose, for they became many and varied; some bizarre in execution; some acquiring such physical power they sought to obliterate other beliefs and still so attempt. As the more sophisticated our creations became, so, pro rata, did the weapons of oppression; but if the Australian aborigine believes his 'Dreamtime' to be sacred why should he be oppressed for his belief? In similar vein why ought not the Navajo believe in his 'Great White Spirit', or the Inuit believe that the seal he hopes to eat must be assured that he is only killing in order to feed his family. He respects the seal as a sentient being. Is the homage all pay to the 'Something Else' any the less valid?

Religious fervours insult the very concept of the mystery and the resultant slaying, apparently unending, is because of the names and a more futile reason would be difficult to conceive. Infantile, even amusing were it not so vile. For to name something irrespective of what it may be – is to define it in words, pin it to a card, so to speak, give it a validity it may not possess by the mere fact of bestowing upon it an image, an identity which may or not be its actual truth.

It is useless now to elaborate further and I leave the subject with Shakespeare's apposite remark:

'A rose by any other name would smell as sweet'.

Inexorably, the concept of Science is now the dominant hierarchy, superseding all others. Some of the aspects and findings are positive, some are negative. What Science cannot do is destroy the concept that 'something else' (so ill defined by many) is the dominant Force to those who have, often with justification, repudiated all formal religious beliefs. What has happened in recent years following the collapse of Communism? The ideology which was conceived to be the ultimate reply to discrimination between the obscenely rich and the obscenely poor was conceived by men with no understanding of human nature. With no regret I will borrow something which is reputed to have been said by Jesus:

'Man does not live by bread alone.'

Because there is 'something else' and it cannot be eradicated. So when the dismemberment of the communist regimes occurred, millions returned to their churches. What the communist czars could not accomplish was suppression of the 'something else and Science no matter how powerful, however inventive and dexterous, cannot eradicate it either. They might ignore it, disdain it, vilify it, but it will be present throughout, for this is life, living intelligent energy which does not die and which no theorist can kill, nor any fabricated ideology suppress.

Now to resurrect a topic I wrote of earlier which centred upon black holes. It is insufficient to accept the fact that we are born of the demise of massive stars which, having attained monolith size, erupt as supernova, thereby hurling forth newer substances from which living species can emerge. There is a pattern and inevitably so, for this is an intelligent Universe and not the chaos which would be the case if intelligent planning were absent. One need only apply the identical simple formula which governed the learning of time's nature: remove what one observes and then consider what would result if the concept one is observing were no longer present. In the case of the universe, if intelligence and planning were removed the result would be chaos, it is that simple.

For some time following the discovery of black holes it was supposed that as no light could be emitted from the unimaginable force existing within the hole and the horizon of which caused time itself to virtually cease to exist, that nothing whatsoever could emerge from this astounding facet of nature. A thinker appeared on the scene with a newer explanation: Stephen Hawking no less, and as he could perform virtually no physical acts, he thought and his thoughts led him to produce an unusual theory concerning the fate of black holes. He believed that they entered a kind of tunnel which led to a White

Universe.

This is a statement of some significance; and the question to which I have discovered no reply is not whether the statement is accurate, nor if it is feasible, nor even if it is logical; it is the descriptive value I find unusual. Why the definition White Universe?

The subject is described as a black hole, specifically so because no light can escape from it as the generated gravity is so immeasurable If it worm-like tunnels through space it must preserve this immeasurable gravity to home into a White Universe. Therefore, is it not reasonable to suppose this attractive Universe to possess an immeasurably larger gravity than the black hole? Be that as it may, there is no possible method by which black holes can be studied for whatever could be set to study them would be pulverized before results could be analyzed; therefore all that is known is the result of analytical processes, nor can proof be obtained from the computers as to the conditions within the black hole.

In lieu of direct proof (although it appears that black holes exist at the centres of galaxies) the remaining question is why, when reaching its destination is the Universe which gobbles it, described as White? The Universe as described appears to have undergone a reversal of identity in that the energy, hitherto black, is now White Light. A most mysterious transformation. Any logical conclusion would quite naturally conjecture that a black hole would succumb to the infinitely greater gravitational pull of a black hole of massive proportions and – as is the nature of black holes – emit no light, but the description is of a White Universe which is presumed to be all Light. I have my own opinions on this question but do not intend to write them, as they would involve long, turgid philosophical arguments.

Rather I concentrate upon the question of tunnelling for it proposes some analogies. When I learned that the only dimension of time in which we could exist is future time I found myself in a tunnel, which was itself Time. Only later did I learn the nature of the mind which moves unhindered through time and space and this was, of course the trace of the Infinite MIND itself permeating through my brain to show aspects which could not be deduced by what we believe to be logical methods. At the end of the tunnel was an Infinity of Light.

There is a curious parallel between our own demise and the theory that Stephen Hawkins proposes, for I saw the energy which had informed me of the deaths of my sons, it was imploded to a point of energy and it would have been physically undetectable yet it was not so imploded as to prevent my seeing. I looked through it and saw the truths.

By the courtesy of some television producers I learned of cases in which people suffering near-death situations all spoke of being in a tunnel and too many cases exist for this to be regarded as a series of coincidences.

More questions remain, one of which is why I selected Science in general for so much scrutiny which some might find unacceptable given that many lives (including my own) have been made easier by their findings? My reply is simple: if the pursuit of knowledge was for positive purposes and to afford positive results to other than themselves, then they have all my support. For to spend one's life in pursuit of positive knowledge cannot inspire anything but approbation from all sides. It is when the aim is destruction that Creation is defined, for this results in wholesale destruction which causes abysmal miseries and is entirely negative. There is another avenue and that is the satisfying of deep curiosity as to the structure of the Universe which is visible. The motives are understandable but the results are of mainly a semantic nature, costly as they undoubtedly are and unfruitful in many aspects. To propose constructing a smaller earth in space in order that the vastnesses of space can be explored begs the question 'Is the life on earth so unappealing that you wish to abandon it?' However, curiosity is a demanding mistress and never appeased.

Seeking the reasons for Science's hostile refusal to admit Supernatural events reveals that there are several contenders in the field. I seriously wonder if some of the antics of the more attention-seeking spiritualists themselves is one, for the thought of sitting in a so-called séance fills me with repugnance, as do stories of trumpet blowing and the like, so I well appreciate the reluctance of scientists to associate themselves with such activities. The criteria was that an event must be repeatable as was the case in material experiments, but naturally this criteria could not be maintained concerning precognitive events and was an incorrect premise in any case. Nor could it be said that there was any lack of evidence of precognition for thousands of accounts were to hand. Pursuing further reasons is unnecessary and unfruitful; rather it is I pose a question to which I expect no reply and it is: 'Why, having investigated matter to the nth degree in pursuit of the building blocks of matter did not the physicists ever consider the properties of energy as being the instigator of the natural patterns which were being revealed?' For all knew of Newton's Law which states (I paraphrase here) 'That all phenomena has equal and opposite reactions. Therefore was it not deemed possible that in energy answers would be found?'

Clearly, it was but too evident that when the atom was split, energy was released. The horrendous results were only too terrifying because energy is invisible until it impacts upon matter. But we are all aware of what occurs when energy finally leaves the body, for the matter which composes the body quickly deteriorates; no matter how splendid the brain it is useless when energy is removed. Patently, this simple answer was not discovered: I only knew of it because I saw it through the mind which was not my property; but then, I do not claim any status whatsoever, for the simple reason that I own none.

It may appear that as I switch from the two apparently unrelated topics of Science and Religion that this is an errant policy, but it is quite deliberate policy as I will show; for these two hierarchies are the dominant pair, more so than governments as the latter are elected by people and people's wills are governed by passions; except when they are foolish enough to permit some megalomaniac dictator to seize power.

Consequently I am about to dissect some more obscure truths concerning religious beliefs, specifically the Jewish, Christian and Islamic faiths. They were all based upon the premise that their god was Loving and indisputably male; although the Jewish interpretation also permitted merciless rejection as did the Christian combine. Their prophets were male, their writings were created by males and their temples erected by males. In physical stature they were larger and more powerful than the females, so the latter were in some cases excluded from worship of the loving god and at best allotted inferior entry. By such exclusion they exposed their own deficiencies, remembering that Love was the key factor.

It is an energy. It is invisible. It cannot be scrutinized by any mechanical device. Therefore, the only material through which it can be detected is by way of a living form. By extension, the only living forms which could be created by men, were women and men. It was inevitable, if the women did not love their husbands (many of whom were less than loveable) it could be relied upon that they would love their children. Even if the children were the kin of characters, only a mother could love.

Indeed, this invisible feeling flourished in abundance and it was so plentiful as to be regarded as a perfectly natural phenomenon; to find a diminution of this universal quality was unnatural, for it was expected to be constant, as much a part of being as air. It was because it was so constant, so plentiful that insufficient attention was paid to it and therein lay the problem, for it was not analyzed as being a quality in its own right, nor was the value of the quality. If one is deprived of air, one chokes and if one is deprived of love one can be crippled. Conversely, if one grows within an abundance of love one does not attempt to assess either its quality or its actual extent. Love is simply taken for granted. Being so immeasurable it is also elusive; it only becomes unnatural if a lack of it appears.

Predictably, when the religions were formulated into written constitutions the love for their god and the pleadings that god would love them in return were prominently displayed. Much ritual evolved which had to be scrupulously followed, but all through the pageantry the fact that they were surrounded by the evidence of Love passed unremarked; it was a natural state of being for women. Yet the latter, in defense of their children, could and did fight; could and did deprive themselves of food, of luxuries; sell their bodies if necessary in order to feed their children. Nevertheless, women were excluded from religious literal for it was assumed that they did not understand the male love for the male god. Women were unfit to decipher it.

A poet once wrote: 'Man's love is of man's life a thing apart, 'Tis woman's whole existence.' Not a truism but a truth. But changes occur.

So why were they excluded?

In recent years the Church of England, after much ponderous deliberation and by a very small majority, permitted women to be priests; causing thereby a number of their group to retire – with chagrin – from the Church itself. As I followed these proceedings I marvelled much, but it is unnecessary to elaborate on my conclusions; requiring neither their approval nor patronage.

What possible connection can the above have with Science? A very great deal… There exists on the flat surface level of what we believe to be reality the somewhat ill defined conception of the scientist. This individual has been popularly conceived to be a remote, chilly character engrossed in his field of research to the exclusion of the riotous, ill-judged and frequently disastrous activities of lesser breeds, lesser minds. To some extent he has earned this somewhat sweeping characterization. Scientists tend to closet themselves from the distractions of errant behaviour as practiced by the masses, preferring to conduct their investigations in conducive-to-thought environments, popularly known as 'ivory towers'.

Pure thought must be sought without the intrusion of passions in order to reach objective conclusions, for – or so it is supposed – only truths may be defined in isolation as human relationships blur and fray the outlines.

The greatest problem of all is that the individual, in order to conduct his researches into pure truths must deflect or delete his human characteristics. For they themselves are distractions howsoever he may attempt to rescind them. Let it be supposed that he has managed to eradicate those characteristics, leaving only the physical characteristics: he can now see, smell, taste, touch and hear. He cannot love, experience joy, emit light, does not create but still seeks pure truth. So what is he and what is pure truth? Will he ever discover it?

The simple reply is 'NO' he will not for he has repudiated the mechanisms which would have led him; choosing to retain all the physical mechanisms and disregarding all the invisible mechanisms. He may be fully conversant with the physical set, but if he repudiates the invisible set he is in trouble, for the bottom line is that the physical is matter, but it can only function if the energy is present. But he did not take the energy into his calculations for he supposed that they were an indivisible unit and they were not, they were twins.

The twins were matter and energy. And of the two the energy was the more important, for a person's body will die, but the energy will not.

Can it now be seen how the apparently opposing hierarchies, each in their own way, have caused such havoc? Each owned – and owns – considerable clout, but none could see the wood for the trees. Their labels stifled their perceptions, for they were very, very self-conscious where those labels were concerned, those labels defined their status which was and is power.

Dismantling egos is a risky venture but I have no regrets. These findings stem directly from the subjective, from the female half of the equation and have been unheard for five thousand years. It is by no coincidence that women have begun to unshackle themselves from male domination, but the real danger is that they will adopt male tactics in order to do so, telling themselves that in a man's world one must be cleverer, more adaptable, more devious and if necessary more brutal. But brutality solves nothing.

Predictably one returns to the inevitable questions 'Who and what am I?' What is my greatest wish and hope? Is it to be happy.

And there are thousands of replies: to be rich; to be powerful; to remain always young; to be beautiful; to avoid death and leaving the body; to paint; to compose; to sing; to dance; to never know pain or physical want… the lists are endless, few of which are attainable. How many replies appertain exclusively to the physical person? How many are selfish and how many are selfless? For there is the true reply, we have a choice; we can love other than ourselves or love another (perhaps many others) with equal concentration. We can concentrate all our attention upon obtaining for our physical persons all possible physical advantages, but if we do so we choose our destination when, as inevitably we must leave those bodies, our minds, our living energy, will depart further and further from Creation, from the MIND and know true deprivation, for the MIND is wholly positive and we can only reach it by repudiating the negative.

As I write these words it is as if I were again in space, gazing at the dark Immensity, wholly benign. I am nothing but awe; but behind me is our glorious glowing planet swirling in jewel-like colours and I feel sadness when I see the depredations we have committed upon it, committed upon ourselves simply by not knowing our true identities in spite of the fact that we believe ourselves to be the superior living forms. Will we ever know? Perhaps…

Hope remains. The curious ratio of sixty per cent of belief that the Supernatural exists, moving unhampered by the limitations imposed upon the material, is still greater than the lower percentage who have no belief. And the difference in numerical values amounts to an enormous number, for there are billions of us.

No finis can be written, for Life goes on. We may kill living forms of all manner of species including ourselves, but living intelligent energy cannot be killed; we did not create it, it was created within the MIND, the Timeless MIND.

What, with exactitude, do we mean when we speak of A Super nature? Of the Supernatural? Beyond; exceeding the laws of nature; the doctrine that revelation is the only means by which man acquires the knowledge of God. Having just this minute consulted my old Webster's Dictionary I am surprised to find these definitions. The definitions I was about to write are these:

That the word Supernatural should be divided into its component parts ie that nature, as we experience it by use of our physical faculties, is by the observance of the planet and all species, living and static which we find upon it. In short, the world as we know it whilst we are living bodies. So where does the 'Super' enter the frame? Beyond? Exceeding the laws of nature? Nature in a superlative form or appearance?

To consider nature in all its aspects we must use the physical senses together with any apparatus we have invented which will aid us in our scrutinies. If, however, we find delight, amazed joy and become overwhelmed by the beauties of nature what senses are we then employing? Not the physical ones, that is certain. So they must be un-physical, to coin a word. Rather super, in fact, to make us feel such awe at the beauties of nature. Elusive though; untrappable. They cannot be herded onto a computer screen because they are feelings and that is an emotive word; but what would we be if we owned none? So to describe these invisible yet so-powerful mysteries which make us feel, well, Super, did we ever suppose that the Super Natural played any part in our makeup? It is the power, the energy which propels us.

Many take drugs which heighten perception and the more powerful drugs can produce ecstasies. I have read a little describing such artificial forays when the mind soars into realms of bliss; but of course the body cannot follow and as such experiences are unnaturally induced the body is damaged, perhaps even killed by such experiments.

So, the Supernatural. Much speculation there has been as to why, in a mere few thousand years, we are the only living species to not only create that which had never before been created by Nature, but to attain a rate of learning which now moves at an incalculable velocity. Vast libraries on command at the touch of a key, but do we know the nature of and the power of that which makes us 'tick'?

The French coined a phrase 'Joi de Vivre'. It causes little children to dance and sing, to bubble over with sheer delight, to giggle uncontrollably at the smallest silliness, causing the adult world to wish they too could retrieve that inexpressible joy in life.

From whence did all that knowledge spring? For there had to be a source. All that knowledge did not spring from Nothingness, for it is not that the fabric of the Universe is an errant collection of atoms; it is orderly, can be investigated and understood; just as we have investigated the millions of other living species all of which yield evidence of intelligence, of the ability to communicate. To suppose that the languages we humans use to communicate with each other are the only forms of communication is a mistaken concept. Life communicates with other life, emanating awareness with astonishing speed as any who have watched an enormous school of fry, turn and wheel to escape their predators. This is a living earth and the ability to communicate at the speed of light is a characteristic of life, for it is Light.

Obvious too, that animals group themselves, as we have formed groups, then tribes, then nations, but in the groupings emerged names, identities and in so doing we eroded our natural knowledge of ourselves, became the name and forgot the person; became bemused by our own creations and forgot to investigate from whence the prompting arrived. Bestowed, as we were with bi-pedal facility, with an opposing finger and thumb we believed ourselves to be invincible, masters of the living earth, so fascinated by the living earth that we ignored the energy which supplied the intelligence, for it was invisible: Life Itself.

One need only consider the alternatives… The more we learn of the animal and plant kingdoms, the more astonishing does the realization arrive that here is planning, here is knowledge, here is intelligence, yet the only common factor is Life itself. Some research has been conducted upon a plant which was attracted by classical music and which twined itself lovingly about the radio from which the music emerged. Every gardener knows that plants respond to loving encouragement: one does not require a brain in order to receive and emit communications; Life communicates without any artificial mechanisms.

But there is a Source. No other explanation is applicable. To assume that all the millions of living species upon this planet evolved by the chance encounter of colliding atoms makes a nonsense of credulity; for one would have to posit more chance encounters of the existence of the whole Universe over mega trillions of years.

In order to find answers one need only to consider the alternatives. In order to find the Whole one need only comprehend the two halves of the Whole: visible and invisible; male and female, the former relying on the objective and the latter the subjective; Creation and Nothingness. Round and round the explanations flow, for it is impossible to write of the whole of life in its varying aspects; we have created a world of immense perplexities, immense variations, convoluted descriptions and images so many of which are built upon flawed premises.

There are many who, finding themselves unable to accept many of the premises available, reject the lot; yet many of such people are exceedingly kind, generous and humane, accepting such positive attributes as natural behaviour. They are sensitive without ever realizing the fact, but if it were to be pointed out that they were, in fact, mediums they would protest that they had never had a precognitive experience in their lives. But they sleep, as do we all and then the kindly mind escapes to dimensions unavailable to the conscious mind. The resulting dreams may not be remembered, but we all dream.

So I make no apology from this circular pattern of writing, for irrespective of any topic all are, in fact, combined: as great a swirling mass as a galaxy. Ever more clearly the reason emerges as to why our so-distant ancestors carved the circles into stone. It was the symbol of a tunnel, disappearing at its heart into a point of Infinity; a conception accepted by brains which were unclouded by the extravagances we believe to be reality. It was simple knowledge. What better knowledge, for the answers are simple concerning Super nature; but to reach them one must approach that point of Infinity shedding the extraneous at every step; know oneself as matter and energy, then ask 'What dies?' We know these answers, but if we are afraid to ask them we cling to matter, the matter which is our physical person, knowing always is finite. It is the energy which is infinite; but it also has another unusual property; it dilates when it leaves the body, but can expand into the appearance of the body it has vacated into a ghostly apparition which can and does, penetrate such as stone walls without effort. For this there is a simple explanation provided by Science, for the nucleus of the atom is surrounded by mainly empty space, occupied only by electrons; but as the electrons are composed of energy the living energy encounters no barrier. The result is energy passing through energy. Super nature is beautiful in its simplicity.

Like a minor thunderbolt another simplicity exploded in my head and it was not that I had been thinking of the atom, nor any other scientific discovery. Indeed, I was kitchen cleaning at the time then found myself looking at the inside of an atom's nucleus. I know, of course, of the several pairs of quarks which had been conjectured to exist within the nucleus and as each pair were proposed each were given a name: 'strange', 'charm' and the like. As I read I began to feel that this collection was becoming too numerous for comfort, too slick somehow and I began to feel it somehow resembled what the Americans call 'The numbers racket'. Admittedly, the world of quantum physics is an Alice in Wonderland affair, but somehow this naming of pairs rang with a hollow chime, for although a balance of forces is necessary to permit equilibrium I felt (and this was pure feeling) that the scenario was too complicated, too contrived in that these pairs were deemed to be of matter. Let it be clear that I had no real knowledge; no training in physics and it seemed an arrant impertinence to question (although only to myself) these proposals. Fascinated, I read avidly throughout those reading years, but in that one area I had no conviction.

When the thunderbolt struck and this was years later, a reversal took place: all the pairs were composed of the identical force, except the force had different functions. The simplest analogy I can find is to consider the human hand, for this one hand can and does, operate in many different ways, so that although the operations are extensive, the same hand causes the operations to be performed. It was not that the quantum pairs differed in any material sense; it was the energy that directed them to operate in different ways.

I am but too well aware of the implications of that which has just been written, but I saw it happen and will not retract. Nor does the theory stop there, for in learning of the huge quantity of procedures when the brain is the subject, the ordering of cells to produce differing amino acids in order to establish differing activities, it is just as effective when one proposes that it is the energy which is directing the traffic, so to speak. It is insufficient explanation to declare that the messenger RNA is delivering orders to certain groups of cells because a certain chemical is required, for the question then is 'From where is the RNA getting its orders?' And the only reply is Living energy, for if that is removed the whole machine is brought to an irreversible halt.

It is with some trepidation that I have written these explanations, but I have been aware of them for some time, so have decided to include them in spite of the fact that I could only write in laymen's language.

In total it all amounts to the fact that Super Nature is basically beautifully simple. New discoveries, fascinating as they are and only exposed by long and patient research are still inadequate unless the source can be identified and the source is the mind, independent of matter, living intelligent energy which is invisible, does not die yet moves unhampered in space and time.

So from whence does the living energy obtain its intelligence? The energy moves as the body sleeps and enters that curious catatonic state which has been called 'The little death' into realms and dimensions forbidden to matter, to the body. What drew us from the caves to move amongst the stars in but a very few millennia? We are the only living species which do not know our identity as all other of the millions of living species know theirs without doubt or even the ability to question.

So how can we find our true identities; isolate that curious quality which differentiates us from all other living species? The quality which impels us to only discern our identities by the naming of ourselves by virtue of our tribal and national languages; by virtue of adopting the particular name of the land on which we happen to be born. Such descriptions might serve with some adequacy regarding our physical persons, but we are more than our physical persons; we can create that which did not previously exist upon earth; seek to find who and what and where and why we are here upon the only planet in the solar system which can support life. This we do, very visibly and at times disastrously; but our creations do not surrender the secret of why we are different from all other living species; who exist according to their genetic instructions, yet the living energy which impels them, is identical to our own. Where then, the subtle difference? Because we can and do, recognize the force, the impetus, the MIND which directs the difference rather than simply being moved by the physical characteristics. This is not to imply that the animal kingdom cannot be impelled by love, for it most surely is, but we can seek the source besides experiencing the results.

However feebly, however erroneously, however arrogantly we seek to deny the subjective characteristics which emerge as that despised description: 'Feelings' how can it be supposed that we can omit them from our activities?

Would one rather know Joy or misery?
Would one rather live in Light rather than stygian darkness?
Would one rather create that which is Positive or that which is Negative?
Would one rather know Love or Hatred?
Would one rather know truth which is absolute, or exist amongst partial truths or absolute lies?

Of all the invisible and immeasurable characteristics there are thousands of degrees of intensity, millions of degrees which can be permutated amongst them all. Inexorably, it is for the individual to find within him or her self how few or how many of those characteristics emerge. Only one certainty remains: if we are to even attempt to discover who and what we are in order to exist upon this planet without killing it and irreparably destroying ourselves in the process, we are going to have to find just what characteristics are required in order to name ourselves as humane human beings as opposed to inhumane. And to even commence this search we have to define the subjective, the mysterious, the invisible, yet the pivot on which all descriptions of ourselves as human beings rest and on which to justify our much vaunted claim to be superior to all other living forms.

The element that made us superior, was the trace of the MIND within us, allied to being bipedal and being able to create by use of the opposing finger and thumb. Gorillas and chimpanzees are deemed to be our nearest relatives, so from whence did the two attributes come which changed us from them? There had to be a source and evolution is an inadequate answer, for to evolve there has to be intelligence as the motivating impeller and this was so from the outset, from the time of the first living organisms.

Unifying Life was and is the source of the intelligence. This is Super Nature which emerges as the Supernatural and is invisible, uninhibited by either time or space.

And life had a source, just as the Universe had a source. Much is now known relating to the fabric of the Universe and much is now known concerning the fabric of living species. The vast stars are finite as living species are finite and the ultimate collapse results in imploded energy for both; very naturally as living species are born of the stars. We, the last living species to appear can comprehend the fabric of the Universe and what emerges is intelligent construction vis-à-vis the atomic table. Therefore, this displays intelligent construction, for the alternative would be chaos. Consequently, the pattern cannot be ignored nor held to be coincidental; the one corresponds to the other. Following the demise of both, Energy remains, imploded intelligence and there was, there is, a source. A MIND. A MIND invisible to the physical that exists in a timeless dimension.

A Kind of Summary

Is it even necessary to attempt to summarize? Was it even necessary to write of my strange secondary life? Some individuals have questioned the motivation which lay behind all those years of struggling to write of that which is beyond description. Of what use are these findings? To that simple question I could write thousands of replies, but I will write just one: I now know the origin of that which showed me my own future. This answer could not be discovered other than by living the complete answers; for they lay in none of the hierarchical definitions; indeed, they refute many of the prevalent beliefs, but they also explain many of the mysteries which lie behind many of the beliefs. It may be that only I am satisfied to know, but other seekers are so engaged which is why there is such a growing interest in the ancient Eastern writings; why so many sit in meditation in the hope or expectation of receiving enlightenment.

Being no confident evangelist; being incompetent to advocate any course which might enlighten anyone for the simple reason that I do not know why such revelations occurred to me, I can but offer that the apparently simple sight of the open brain has proved that it was one of the most revealing of experiences. It revealed the physical (for the brain was undoubtedly very much a living organ) and the effect of the soul, spirit, essence – or whatever name is appropriate, upon living matter. It caused the cells to meld into exquisite light. But. As ever, a 'but'...

If the physical brain cells are clogged with negativities little of that light can emerge to illuminate the living body. Comparisons are available: one need only consider the kind of person who lights a room by the simple act of walking into it, for the very ambience is charged with a glow. It is unforced, quite spontaneous, yet all within the room can feel the charging influence.

At twenty years of age I was taken to see a certain lady of whom no description was given, nor any information beyond the fact that this was someone I should meet. To my surprise we entered a medium sized sitting room, in the far corner of which was a bed containing what I first thought was a small brown monkey. As we drew nearer I could see that this was a tiny shrivelled woman, so crippled that the immaculate white sheet had been carefully smoothed under what appeared to be two brown claws. Then I looked into a pair of large brown eyes and melted, for the love, joy and power of those eyes submerged me in wonder. I later learned that there was a continual stream of visitors to that house composed of people who had great problems and who visited in order to unload their problems upon one who could not move a limb. But the Life was there and it flowed and glowed from a helpless cripple. Needless to say, I have never forgotten her.

Disastrously, the converse can also be true; megalomaniacs of an evil disposition can also attract, but ... yes, always a qualification: they do not endure. Sooner or later they suffer desuetude, for even if they kill millions which many of them have done and some still do so, they cannot kill life; bodies, yes, but they cannot kill living energy for it flees the machine but does not die.

Condensed, all is dependent on what the brain cells are filled with: positive impulses or negative impulses and we have a choice, we have a free will. It is possible to change one's impulses, to stifle and kill the negativities at birth and the oftener one does so it becomes habit forming in a very short space of time. The seven deadly sins have all been identified and I see no reason to repeat them, or to elaborate.

Consequently, if anyone were to seek in this writing some esoteric formula on how to experience events of a revelatory nature, I fear that he or she will be rather disappointed because I do not know why they happened to me, so all I may usefully write that it is not so much as pouring in but rather a pouring out; a ridding oneself of unnecessary encumbrances. Emptying the pot, so to speak. Vacate the brain cells of petty (or major) negativities and there is space for absolute truths, for the characteristics of living energy to emerge.

Ridding oneself of the collected images which bureaucratic demands insist we provide is more difficult. If we must define ourselves in terms of nationhood, marital status, definitions as to what we own in the way of possessions etc, we begin to define ourselves in such terms. Then the true image of ourselves as human beings recedes to the rear of the carapace which is formed by the collection of images required by flat surface realities which only yield an appearance of truth and not the actual truths of human beings. Such a carapace may have its uses to define the physical person, but we are more than the appearance of the physical; we are animated by living energy and the latter has its own full complement of characteristics; so all the flat surface definitions are merely a formula for identification, they do not describe that which makes us 'tick'. Once the recognition between matter and energy is assimilated it is simple to see how the divisions flow through differing aspects; the visible and the invisible, life and death, the twin lobes of the brain ... Our first act in the world when we are able to focus our eyes upon objects is to smile and this spontaneous act is performed without any formal conception of identity. Similarly, at the moment of death all the facile images which we believe in and use to identify our bodies, disappear as irrelevancies. At the beginning and the end it is of no consequence as to what nationality one holds, what titles, however important or unimportant, what club or group or ideology or political affiliation one claims to support; or what sect or religious belief one owns; nor whether one's skin is white, red, black or yellow; all are human beings and the surface appearances are as chaff in the wind.

Being no evangelist I cannot and will not, nor even wish to exhort anyone to accept these writings; and repetitively the spectre remains as to why I should feel it to be of any importance to write at all of my strange secondary existence. Who could possibly be interested or believe a word of truths which are so at variance with statements concerning religious beliefs which were defined millennia ago and which are still accepted as being holy writs of one kind or another? Could I logically expect any acceptance of such deflections of accepted beliefs? Does it matter? Weirdly, in truth, it is of no consequence as to whether there is acceptance or not, for I have described those experiences as well as I am able, conscious always of my own ineptitude; alert always to the impossibility of truly finding words which even remotely describe the wondrous sights I have seen. So why have I spent so many years in writing? My ultimate reply was and is, 'I believed they should be shared and having once begun I could not stop'.

Finally, I write of the genders, male and female; not because I wish to promote any furtherance of the age-old battle for I do not; but one aspect requires no wise male and does not physically resemble a male being. As a definition gender began as arrogance and has been so perpetuated. To many males it appears inconceivable that a mind can exist which diminishes male minds to inconsequentiality, but such is the case and those who pontificate in the attempts to translate what their god is thinking have almost no conception as to the indescribable enormity of what they profess to understand.

No understanding is possible; I saw that Void which is the source of all we can physically observe and knew on my return that I would never be able to describe what I had seen for our miniscule minds, our brains, are incapable of assimilating such a vastness of Intelligence. Some, no doubt, will be infuriated by those statements, but I will neither retract nor apologize: I was there, neither drunk nor drugged and with all my skepticism intact before I went. Nor did I imagine any part for to imagine any of those experiences I would have had to be a genius and I am nothing. Repetitively, all we can know are the characteristics of the Living Energy which had its origins in the MIND: Joy, Light, Truth which combine into Creation. In their full glory none can be described, none are visible to the physical, but remove them from humankind and only chaos remains.

Therefore, it is not so much that I trespass upon the male preserves but rather that under no compulsion will I accept their definitions. Creation is exactly what the word implies and for its continuance both genders are required for all living species and each are equally necessary.

Turbulent it has been, this strange secondary existence, but at least I can reply, should the question ever appear again in letters of white fire:

'Who am I? I know you now, you are my one cell's worth of the Timeless MIND.'

One final summary remains. It is strange, but it is the final explanation of what has been called the 'Supernatural'. Having previously written of seeing, explosively, that which was and is visible, separated from the invisible and thereby seeing that Twin Universes existed, all the perplexities of my strange existence flowed with immaculate precision into true perspective as did all the inexplicable instances which so many of us experience. When I stood in the kitchen of Garner's house and saw the screaming skeleton which was to be my father, I knew that it was death which was holding him; that which we suppose to be 'living' is actually the opposite from true life. This which we live is actually the death and when we depart our bodies it is to Life we go. We have got it all the wrong way round, for this is a dark tunnel and we traverse it the best we may, employing the invisible characteristics as best we may. This is, I know, a most startling concept; but if any person who reads these words cares to consider the experiences I have described he or she will find that such experiences can only be comprehended by that one concept. Moreover, any apparently inexplicable incident which the individual in question has experienced, seeing a ghost for instance, shows clearly that Life is the enduring factor. The supposed ghosts I have seen and described were all brilliantly alive, especially that group of artists in that dusty old shop.

Frequently, I could not see the wood for the trees during my turbulent existence, yet the answers were there throughout: to say that the immensities of learning each took years to analyze, to combine into true conclusions only serves to illustrate my own ineptitude, but at least I have never made any attempt to conceal my lack of scholarly talents.

Sadly, the very notion of death terrifies many, but if one can love other than oneself; can feel joy at seeing – really seeing one blade of grass; can feel or project even the most obscure of light; can create even a gentle ambience about one's person, one can know absolute truth, for it is toward this truth we so painfully proceed; and when we do so it is to know that which is truly Eternal.

Thus the Supernatural events that have dominated my life are now explicable and the answers define the perplexities. It was by no patient exploration conducted by me that the answers clarified into truths. I would never have learned by my own efforts: quite simply, I lived them.

It was as if the living world about me dilated so I could see how these answers clarified hundreds (and possibly thousands) of Supernatural events and experiences that occurred to other people around the world. Such experiences have been written of since the advent of writing, regardless of race or colour.

No doubt it will be argued that my experiences were not those of others whose circumstances differed. Consequently to hold that the answers explain the Supernatural in other lives is a suspect and improvable statement. It is for the person who has experienced such phenomena to make her or his own decision and I am not about to amend my statement.

Certainly the laws defining nations are varied as are habits, beliefs, conditions etc, but it is not of any value to define them by colour or creed.

We are people of a living world and God, for me, is the MIND, the void which is Indescribable, therefore in spite of the segregations which have evolved, it is my belief that in the final analysis we are all governed by the Spiritual laws and those have emanated from the MIND.